THE LIFE OF THE BLESSED EMPEROR CONSTANTINE

EUSEBIUS PAMPHILUS

AETERNA PRESS

PUBLISHED BY AETERNA PRESS.
COVER DESIGN BY AETERNA PRESS.

IN FOUR BOOKS, FROM 306 TO 337 A D.

BY EUSEBIUS PAMPHILUS.

ΠΟΛΛΑΙ ΜΕΝ ΘΝΗΤΟΙΣ ΓΛΩΤΤΑΙ, ΜΙΑ Δ'ΑΘΑΝΑΤΟΙΣΙΝ.

LONDON: SAMUEL BAGSTER AND SONS; WAREHOUSE FOR BIBLES, NEW TESTAMENTS, PRAYER-BOOKS, LEXICONS, GRAMMARS, CONCORDANCES, AND PSALTERS, IN ANCIENT AND MODERN LANGUAGES; PATERNOSTER ROW. M.DCCC.XLV.

ISBN-13: 978-1-78516-073-8

AVAILABLE AS AN E-BOOK:
WWW.AETERNAPRESS.COM

CONTENTS

ADDRESS 1

THE LIFE OF THE BLESSED EMPEROR CONSTANTINE, BY EUSEBIUS PAMPHILUS 3

BOOK I.....4

CHAPTER I 5

PREFACE—OF THE DEATH OF CONSTANTINE

CHAPTER II.....5

THE PREFACE CONTINUED

CHAPTER III 6

HOW GOD HONOURS PIOUS PRINCES, BUT DESTROYS TYRANTS

CHAPTER IV 7

HOW GOD HONOURED CONSTANTINE

CHAPTER V.....7

HE REIGNED ABOVE THIRTY YEARS, AND LIVED ABOVE SIXTY

CHAPTER VI 8

HE WAS THE SERVANT OF GOD, AND THE CONQUEROR OF NATIONS

CHAPTER VII 8

HE IS COMPARED WITH CYRUS KING OF THE PERSIANS, AND WITH ALEXANDER OF MACEDON

CHAPTER VIII.....9

HE CONQUERED NEARLY THE WHOLE WORLD

CHAPTER IX 9

HE WAS THE SON OF A PIOUS EMPEROR, AND BEQUEATHED THE IMPERIAL POWER TO HIS OWN SONS

CHAPTER X.....10

OF THE NECESSITY FOR THIS HISTORY, AND ITS VALUE IN A MORAL POINT OF VIEW

CHAPTER XI 10

HIS PRESENT OBJECT IS TO RECORD ONLY THE PIOUS ACTIONS OF CONSTANTINE

CHAPTER XII 11

LIKE MOSES, HE WAS REARED IN THE PALACES OF ROYALTY

CHAPTER XIII 12

OF CONSTANTIUS HIS FATHER, WHO REFUSED TO IMITATE DIOCLETIAN, MAXIMIAN, AND MAXENTIUS, IN THEIR PERSECUTION OF THE CHRISTIANS

CHAPTER XIV 13

HOW CONSTANTIUS HIS FATHER, BEING REPROACHED WITH POVERTY BY DIOCLETIAN, FILLED HIS TREASURY, AND AFTERWARDS RESTORED THE MONEY TO THOSE BY WHOM IT HAD BEEN CONTRIBUTED

CHAPTER XV 14

OF THE PERSECUTION RAISED BY HIS COLLEAGUES

CHAPTER XVI 14

HOW CONSTANTIUS, FEIGNING IDOLATRY, EXPELLED THOSE WHO CONSENTED TO OFFER SACRIFICE, BUT RETAINED IN HIS PALACE ALL WHO WERE WILLING TO CONFESS CHRIST

CHAPTER XVII 15

OF HIS DEVOTION AND LOVE TO CHRIST

CHAPTER XVIII 16

AFTER THE ABDICATION OF DIOCLETIAN AND MAXIMIAN, CONSTANTIUS BECAME CHIEF AUGUSTUS, AND WAS BLESSED WITH A NUMEROUS OFFSPRING

CHAPTER XIX 16

OF HIS SON CONSTANTINE, WHO IN HIS YOUTH ACCOMPANIED DIOCLETIAN INTO PALESTINE

CHAPTER XX 17

CONSTANTINE RETURNS TO HIS FATHER, IN CONSEQUENCE OF THE TREACHEROUS INTENTIONS OF DIOCLETIAN

CHAPTER XXI 17

DEATH OF CONSTANTIUS, WHO LEAVES HIS SON CONSTANTINE EMPEROR

CHAPTER XXII 18

AFTER THE BURIAL OF CONSTANTIUS, CONSTANTINE IS PROCLAIMED AUGUSTUS BY THE ARMY

CHAPTER XXIII 18

A BRIEF NOTICE OF THE DESTRUCTION OF THE TYRANTS

CHAPTER XXIV 19

IT WAS BY THE WILL OF GOD THAT CONSTANTINE BECAME POSSESSED OF THE EMPIRE

CHAPTER XXV 19

VICTORIES OF CONSTANTINE OVER THE BARBARIANS AND THE BRITONS

CHAPTER XXVI 19

HE RESOLVES TO DELIVER ROME FROM THE TYRANNY OF MAXENTIUS

CHAPTER XXVII 20

AFTER REFLECTING ON THE DOWNFALL OF THOSE WHO HAD WORSHIPPED IDOLS, HE MADE CHOICE OF CHRISTIANITY

CHAPTER XXVIII 21

HOW, WHILE HE WAS PRAYING, GOD SENT HIM A VISION OF A CROSS OF LIGHT IN THE HEAVENS AT MID-DAY, WITH AN INSCRIPTION ADMONISHING HIM TO CONQUER BY THAT

CHAPTER XXIX 21

HOW THE CHRIST OF GOD APPEARED TO HIM IN HIS SLEEP, AND COMMANDED HIM TO USE IN HIS WARS A STANDARD MADE IN THE FORM OF A CROSS

CHAPTER XXX 22

THE MAKING OF THE STANDARD OF THE CROSS

CHAPTER XXXI 22

A DESCRIPTION OF THE STANDARD OF THE CROSS, WHICH THE ROMANS NOW CALL THE LABARUM

CHAPTER XXXII 23

CONSTANTINE RECEIVES INSTRUCTION, AND READS THE SACRED SCRIPTURES

CHAPTER XXXIII 23

OF THE ADULTEROUS CONDUCT OF MAXENTIUS AT ROME

CHAPTER XXXIV 24

HOW THE WIFE OF A PREFECT SLEW HERSELF TO PRESERVE HER CHASTITY

CHAPTER XXXV 24

MASSACRE OF THE ROMAN PEOPLE BY MAXENTIUS

CHAPTER XXXVI 25

MAGIC ARTS OF MAXENTIUS AGAINST CONSTANTINE: AND FAMINE AT ROME

CHAPTER XXXVII 25

DEFEAT OF MAXENTIUS'S ARMIES IN ITALY

CHAPTER XXXVIII 26

DEATH OF MAXENTIUS ON THE BRIDGE OF THE TIBER

CHAPTER XXXIX 27

CONSTANTINE'S ENTRY INTO ROME

CHAPTER XL 27

OF THE STATUE OF CONSTANTINE HOLDING A CROSS, AND ITS INSCRIPTION

CHAPTER XLI ... 28

REJOICINGS THROUGHOUT THE PROVINCES; AND CONSTANTINE'S ACTS OF GRACE

CHAPTER XLII ... 28

OF THE HONOURS CONFERRED UPON BISHOPS, AND THE BUILDING OF CHURCHES

CHAPTER XLIII ... 29

CONSTANTINE'S LIBERALITY TO THE POOR

CHAPTER XLIV ... 29

HOW HE WAS PRESENT AT THE SYNODS OF BISHOPS

CHAPTER XLV ... 30

HOW HE BORE WITH IRRATIONAL OPPONENTS

CHAPTER XLVI ... 30

VICTORIES OVER THE BARBARIANS

CHAPTER XLVII ... 31

DEATH OF MAXIMIN, WHO HAD ATTEMPTED A CONSPIRACY, AND OF OTHERS WHOM CONSTANTINE DETECTED BY DIVINE REVELATION

CHAPTER XLVIII ... 31

CELEBRATION OF CONSTANTINE'S DECENNALIA

CHAPTER XLIX ... 31

IN WHAT MANNER LICINIUS OPPRESSED THE EAST

CHAPTER L ... 32

LICINIUS ATTEMPTS A CONSPIRACY AGAINST CONSTANTINE

CHAPTER LI ... 33

TREACHEROUS ARTS OF LICINIUS AGAINST THE BISHOPS, AND HIS PROHIBITION OF SYNODS

CHAPTER LII ... 33

BANISHMENT OF THE CHRISTIANS, WITH CONFISCATION AND SALE OF THEIR PROPERTY

CHAPTER LIII ... 34

LICINIUS'S EDICT THAT WOMEN AND MEN SHOULD NOT BE PERMITTED TO FREQUENT THE CHURCHES IN COMPANY

CHAPTER LIV ... 34

HE DISMISSES THOSE WHO REFUSE TO SACRIFICE FROM MILITARY SERVICE, AND FORBIDS THE SUPPLY OF NECESSARY FOOD TO THOSE IN PRISON

CHAPTER LV ... 35

THE LAWLESS CONDUCT AND COVETOUSNESS OF LICINIUS

CHAPTER LVI 35

AT LENGTH HE UNDERTAKES TO RAISE A PERSECUTION AGAINST THE CHRISTIANS

CHAPTER LVII 36

MAXIMIAN, BROUGHT LOW BY A FISTULOUS ULCER WITH WORMS, ISSUES AN EDICT IN FAVOUR OF THE CHRISTIANS

CHAPTER LVIII 36

HOW MAXIMIN, WHO HAD PERSECUTED THE CHRISTIANS, WAS COMPELLED TO FLY, AND CONCEAL HIMSELF IN THE DISGUISE OF A SLAVE

CHAPTER LIX 37

MAXIMIN, BLINDED BY MEANS OF HIS DISEASE, ISSUES AN ORDINANCE IN FAVOUR OF THE CHRISTIANS

BOOK II 39

CHAPTER I 40

SECRET PERSECUTION BY LICINIUS, WHO CAUSES SOME BISHOPS TO BE PUT TO DEATH AT AMASIA OF PONTUS

CHAPTER II 40

DEMOLITION OF CHURCHES, AND CRUEL BUTCHERY OF THE BISHOPS

CHAPTER III 41

HOW CONSTANTINE WAS MOVED WITH PITY ON BEHALF OF THE CHRISTIANS THUS IN DANGER OF PERSECUTION

CHAPTER IV 42

CONSTANTINE PREPARES HIMSELF FOR THE WAR BY PRAYER: LICINIUS BY THE PRACTICE OF DIVINATION

CHAPTER V 42

LICINIUS, WHILE SACRIFICING IN A GROVE, UTTERS HIS SENTIMENTS CONCERNING IDOLS, AND CONCERNING CHRIST

CHAPTER VI 43

AN APPARITION SEEN IN THE CITIES SUBJECT TO LICINIUS, AS OF CONSTANTINE'S VICTORIOUS TROOPS PASSING THROUGH THEM

CHAPTER VII 44

VICTORY EVERY WHERE FOLLOWS THE PRESENCE OF THE STANDARD OF THE CROSS IN BATTLE

CHAPTER VIII 44

FIFTY MEN ARE SELECTED TO CARRY THE CROSS

CHAPTER IX 45

ONE OF THE CROSS-BEARERS, WHO FLED FROM HIS POST, IS SLAIN; WHILE ANOTHER, WHO FAITHFULLY STOOD HIS GROUND, IS PRESERVED

CHAPTER X 45

VARIOUS BATTLES, AND CONSTANTINE'S VICTORIES

CHAPTER XI 46

FLIGHT, AND MAGIC ARTS OF LICINIUS

CHAPTER XII 46

CONSTANTINE, AFTER PRAYING IN HIS TABERNACLE, OBTAINS THE VICTORY

CHAPTER XIII 47

HIS HUMANE TREATMENT OF PRISONERS

CHAPTER XIV 47

A FURTHER MENTION OF HIS PRAYERS IN THE TABERNACLE

CHAPTER XV 48

PRETENDED FRIENDSHIP, AND IDOLATROUS PRACTICES OF LICINIUS

CHAPTER XVI 48

LICINIUS CHARGES HIS SOLDIERS NOT TO ATTACK THE STANDARD OF THE CROSS

CHAPTER XVII 49

CONSTANTINE'S VICTORY

CHAPTER XVIII 49

DEATH OF LICINIUS, AND CONSEQUENT TRIUMPH

CHAPTER XIX 49

GENERAL REJOICINGS

CHAPTER XX 50

CONSTANTINE'S ENACTMENTS IN FAVOUR OF THE CONFESSORS

CHAPTER XXI 51

HIS LAWS IN FAVOUR OF MARTYRS, AND RESPECTING THE PROPERTY OF THE CHURCHES

CHAPTER XXII 51

HOW HE CHERISHED THE INTERESTS OF THE SEVERAL NATIONS OF HIS EMPIRE

CHAPTER XXIII 52

HOW HE DECLARED GOD TO BE THE AUTHOR OF HIS PROSPERITY: AND CONCERNING HIS WRITTEN LAWS

CHAPTER XXIV 52

LAW OF CONSTANTINE RESPECTING PIETY TOWARDS GOD, AND THE CHRISTIAN RELIGION

CHAPTER XXV 53

AN ILLUSTRATION OF THESE TRUTHS FROM ANCIENT TIMES

CHAPTER XXVI 53

OF THOSE WHO SUFFERED, AND THOSE WHO RAISED PERSECUTION

CHAPTER XXVII 54

HOW THE PERSECUTION BECAME THE OCCASION OF CALAMITY TO THE AGGRESSORS

CHAPTER XXVIII 54

THAT GOD CHOSE CONSTANTINE TO BE THE MINISTER OF BLESSING

CHAPTER XXIX 55

CONSTANTINE'S EXPRESSIONS OF PIETY TOWARDS GOD; AND PRAISE OF THE CONFESSORS

CHAPTER XXX..56

A LAW GRANTING RELEASE FROM EXILE, RELIEF FROM SERVICE IN THE COURTS, AND FROM THE CONFISCATION OF PROPERTY

CHAPTER XXXI 56

RELEASE LIKEWISE GRANTED TO EXILES IN THE ISLANDS

CHAPTER XXXII 57

AND TO THOSE WHO HAD BEEN IGNOMINIOUSLY EMPLOYED IN THE MINES AND PUBLIC WORKS

CHAPTER XXXIII 57

CONCERNING THOSE CONFESSORS WHO HAD BEEN ENGAGED IN MILITARY SERVICE

CHAPTER XXXIV 57

CONCERNING THE LIBERATION OF THOSE FREE PERSONS WHO HAD BEEN CONDEMNED TO LABOUR IN THE WOMEN'S APARTMENTS, OR TO ANY OTHER SERVITUDE

CHAPTER XXXV 58

OF THE INHERITANCE OF THE PROPERTY OF MARTYRS AND CONFESSORS, ALSO OF THOSE WHO HAD SUFFERED BANISHMENT OR CONFISCATION

CHAPTER XXXVI 59

THE CHURCH IS DECLARED HEIR OF THOSE WHO LEAVE NO KINDRED; AND THEIR BEQUESTS ARE INALIENABLE

CHAPTER XXXVII 59

THE OCCUPIERS OF LANDS WHICH HAD BELONGED TO CHRISTIANS, ALSO OF GARDENS OR HOUSES, ARE TO MAKE RESTITUTION, EXCEPT OF THE ACTUAL PRODUCE

CHAPTER XXXVIII 59

IN WHAT MANNER APPEALS SHOULD BE MADE ON BEHALF OF SUCH PERSONS

CHAPTER XXXIX 60

THE TREASURY MUST RESTORE LANDS, GARDENS, AND HOUSES TO THE CHURCHES

CHAPTER XL 60

THE TOMBS OF MARTYRS, AND THE CEMETERIES, ARE TO BE RESTORED TO THE CHURCHES

CHAPTER XLI 61

THOSE WHO HAVE PURCHASED PROPERTY BELONGING TO THE CHURCH, OR RECEIVED IT AS A GIFT, ARE TO RESTORE IT

CHAPTER XLII 61

AN EARNEST EXHORTATION TO WORSHIP GOD

CHAPTER XLIII 62

CONSTANTINE'S ENACTMENTS WERE CARRIED INTO EFFECT

CHAPTER XLIV 62

HE PROMOTES CHRISTIANS TO OFFICES OF GOVERNMENT, AND FORBIDS GENTILES IN SUCH STATIONS TO OFFER SACRIFICE

CHAPTER XLV 62

STATUTES WHICH FORBADE SACRIFICE, AND ENJOINED THE BUILDING OF CHURCHES

CHAPTER XLVI 63

CONSTANTINE'S LETTER TO EUSEBIUS AND THE OTHER BISHOPS, RESPECTING THE BUILDING OF CHURCHES, WITH INSTRUCTIONS TO REPAIR THE OLD, AND ERECT NEW ONES ON A LARGER SCALE, WITH THE AID OF THE PROVINCIAL GOVERNORS

CHAPTER XLVII 64

THE EMPEROR WROTE A LETTER ALSO IN CONDEMNATION OF IDOLATRY

CHAPTER XLVIII 64

CONSTANTINE'S EDICT TO THE PEOPLE OF THE PROVINCES CONCERNING THE ERROR OF POLYTHEISM, COMMENCING WITH SOME GENERAL REMARKS ON VIRTUE AND VICE

CHAPTER XLIX 65

CONCERNING CONSTANTINE'S PIOUS FATHER, AND THE PERSECUTORS DIOCLETIAN AND MAXIMIAN

CHAPTER L 65

HOW THE PERSECUTION ORIGINATED FROM THE SILENCE OF THE ORACLE OF APOLLO, WHICH WAS ATTRIBUTED TO THE INFLUENCE OF "THE RIGHTEOUS MEN"

CHAPTER LI 65

CONSTANTINE, WHEN A YOUTH, UNDERSTOOD FROM HIM WHO DIRECTED THE PERSECUTION, THAT "THE RIGHTEOUS MEN" WERE THE CHRISTIANS

CHAPTER LII 66

THE MANIFOLD FORMS OF TORTURE AND PUNISHMENT OPENLY PRACTISED AGAINST THE CHRISTIANS

CHAPTER LIII 66

HOW THE BARBARIANS KINDLY RECEIVED THE CHRISTIANS

CHAPTER LIV 67

HOW VENGEANCE OVERTOOK THOSE WHOM THE WORDS OF THE ORACLE HAD INDUCED TO RAISE THE PERSECUTION

CHAPTER LV 67

CONSTANTINE GIVES GLORY TO GOD, CONFESSES THE EFFICACY OF THE STANDARD OF THE CROSS, AND PRAYS FOR THE CHURCHES AND PEOPLE

CHAPTER LVI 68

HE PRAYS THAT ALL MAY BE CHRISTIANS, BUT COMPELS NONE

CHAPTER LVII 68

HE RENDERS PRAISE TO GOD, WHO HAS GIVEN LIGHT BY HIS SON TO THOSE WHO WERE IN ERROR

CHAPTER LVIII 68

HE STILL FURTHER PRAISES HIM FOR HIS GOVERNMENT OF THE MATERIAL WORLD

CHAPTER LIX 69

PRAISE TO GOD, AS THE CONSTANT TEACHER OF GOOD THINGS

CHAPTER LX 69

AN ADMONITION AT THE CLOSE OF THE EDICT, THAT NO ONE SHOULD DISTURB THE PEACE OF HIS NEIGHBOUR

CHAPTER LXI 70

HOW CONTROVERSIES ORIGINATED AT ALEXANDRIA IN CONNEXION WITH ARIUS

CHAPTER LXII 71

CONCERNING THE SAME ARIUS, AND THE MELITIANS

CHAPTER LXIII 71

THAT CONSTANTINE SENT A LETTER, WITH A VIEW TO THE RE-ESTABLISHMENT OF CONCORD

CHAPTER LXIV 72

CONSTANTINE'S LETTER TO ALEXANDER THE BISHOP, AND ARIUS THE PRESBYTER

CHAPTER LXV 72

HIS CONTINUAL ANXIETY FOR PEACE

CHAPTER LXVI 72

HOW HE ADJUSTED THE CONTROVERSIES WHICH HAD ARISEN IN AFRICA

CHAPTER LXVII 73

THAT CHRISTIANITY BEGAN IN THE EAST

CHAPTER LXVIII 73

BEING GRIEVED BY THE DISSENSIONS, HE RECOMMENDS A SPIRIT OF CONCORD

CHAPTER LXIX 74

ORIGIN OF THE DIFFERENCE BETWEEN ALEXANDER AND ARIUS—THESE QUESTIONS ARE NOT FIT SUBJECTS FOR CONTROVERSY

CHAPTER LXX 75

AN EXHORTATION TO UNANIMITY

CHAPTER LXXI 75

THERE SHOULD BE NO CONTENTION BECAUSE OF EXPRESSIONS IN THEMSELVES OF LITTLE MOMENT

CHAPTER LXXII 76

THE EXCESS OF HIS PIOUS CONCERN CAUSED HIM TO SHED TEARS; AND HIS INTENDED JOURNEY TO THE EAST WAS POSTPONED BECAUSE OF THESE DISSENSIONS

CHAPTER LXXIII 77

THE CONTROVERSY CONTINUES WITHOUT ABATEMENT, EVEN AFTER THE RECEIPT OF THIS LETTER

BOOK III 78

CHAPTER I 79

A COMPARISON OF CONSTANTINE'S PIETY WITH THE WICKEDNESS OF THE PERSECUTORS

CHAPTER II 80

FURTHER REMARKS ON CONSTANTINE'S PIETY, AND HIS OPEN PROFESSION OF THE CROSS

CHAPTER III 81

OF HIS PICTURE SURMOUNTED BY A CROSS, AND HAVING BENEATH IT A WOUNDED DRAGON

CHAPTER IV 81

A FURTHER NOTICE OF THE CONTROVERSIES RAISED IN EGYPT THROUGH THE INSTRUMENTALITY OF ARIUS

CHAPTER V 82

OF THE DISSENSIONS RESPECTING THE CELEBRATION OF EASTER

CHAPTER VI 83

HE ORDERS A COUNCIL TO ASSEMBLE AT NICÆA

CHAPTER VII 83

OF THE GENERAL COUNCIL, AT WHICH BISHOPS FROM ALL NATIONS WERE PRESENT

CHAPTER VIII....84

THE ASSEMBLY WAS COMPOSED, AS IN THE ACTS OF THE APOSTLES, OF INDIVIDUALS FROM VARIOUS NATIONS

CHAPTER IX....84

OF THE VIRTUE AND AGE OF THE TWO HUNDRED AND FIFTY BISHOPS

CHAPTER X....85

MEETING IN THE PALACE, AT WHICH CONSTANTINE APPEARED, AND TOOK HIS SEAT IN THE ASSEMBLY

CHAPTER XI....85

SILENCE OF THE COUNCIL, AFTER SOME WORDS SPOKEN BY THE BISHOP EUSEBIUS

CHAPTER XII....86

CONSTANTINE'S ADDRESS TO THE COUNCIL, IN PRAISE OF PEACE

CHAPTER XIII....87

IN WHAT MANNER HE LED THE DISSENTIENT BISHORS TO UNITE IN HARMONY OF SENTIMENT

CHAPTER XIV....87

UNANIMOUS DECLARATION OF THE COUNCIL CONCERNING FAITH, AND THE CELEBRATION OF EASTER

CHAPTER XV....88

CONSTANTINE ENTERTAINS THE BISHOPS ON THE OCCASION OF HIS VICENNALIA

CHAPTER XVI....88

PRESENTS TO THE BISHOPS, AND LETTERS ADDRESSED TO THE PEOPLE GENERALLY

CHAPTER XVII....88

CONSTANTINE'S LETTER TO THE CHURCHES RESPECTING THE COUNCIL AT NICÆA

CHAPTER XVIII....89

HE SPEAKS OF THEIR UNANIMITY RESPECTING THE FEAST OF EASTER, AND AGAINST THE PRACTICE OF THE JEWS

CHAPTER XIX....90

HE HOLDS OUT FOR THEIR IMITATION THE EXAMPLE OF THE GREATER PART OF THE WORLD

CHAPTER XX....91

HE RECOMMENDS OBEDIENCE TO THE DECREES OF THE COUNCIL

CHAPTER XXI....92

HE EXHORTS THE BISHOPS, ON THEIR DEPARTURE, TO PRESERVE A SPIRIT OF CONCORD

CHAPTER XXII 93

HAVING HONOURABLY DISMISSED SOME, HE WROTE LETTERS TO OTHERS, BESTOWING LIKEWISE PRESENTS IN MONEY

CHAPTER XXIII 93

HE WRITES TO THE EGYPTIANS, EXHORTING THEM TO PEACE

CHAPTER XXIV 93

HE WRITES FREQUENT LETTERS OF A RELIGIOUS CHARACTER TO THE BISHOPS AND PEOPLE

CHAPTER XXV 94

HE ORDERS THE ERECTION OF A CHURCH AT JERUSALEM, IN THE HOLY PLACE OF OUR SAVIOUR'S RESURRECTION

CHAPTER XXVI 94

HOW THE HOLY SEPULCHRE HAD BEEN COVERED WITH RUBBISH AND PROFANED WITH IDOLS BY THE UNGODLY

CHAPTER XXVII 95

CONSTANTINE COMMANDS THE MATERIALS OF THE IDOL-TEMPLE, AND THE SOIL ITSELF, TO BE REMOVED AND THROWN TO A DISTANCE

CHAPTER XXVIII 96

DISCOVERY OF THE MOST HOLY SEPULCHRE

CHAPTER XXIX 96

HE WRITES CONCERNING THE ERECTION OF A CHURCH, BOTH TO THE GOVERNORS OF THE PROVINCES, AND TO THE BISHOP MACARIUS

CHAPTER XXX 96

CONSTANTINE'S LETTER TO MACARIUS RESPECTING THE BUILDING OF A MEMORIAL OF OUR SAVIOUR'S DEATH

CHAPTER XXXI 97

HE DESIRED THAT THE BUILDING SHOULD SURPASS ALL THE CHURCHES IN THE WORLD IN THE BEAUTY OF ITS WALLS, ITS COLUMNS, AND MARBLES

CHAPTER XXXII 98

DIRECTIONS TO THE PRESIDENTS CONCERNING THE BEAUTIFYING OF THE ROOF; ALSO CONCERNING THE WORKMEN, AND MATERIALS

CHAPTER XXXIII 98

HOW THE CHURCH OF OUR SAVIOUR WAS BUILT, WHICH ANSWERED TO THE NEW JERUSALEM PROPHESIED OF IN SCRIPTURE

CHAPTER XXXIV 99

DESCRIPTION OF THE FABRIC OF THE HOLY SEPULCHRE

CHAPTER XXXV 99

DESCRIPTION OF THE ATRIUM AND PORTICOS

CHAPTER XXXVI 99

DESCRIPTION OF THE WALLS, ROOF, DECORATION, AND GILDING, OF THE BODY OF THE CHURCH

CHAPTER XXXVII 100

DESCRIPTION OF THE DOUBLE PORTICOS ON EITHER SIDE, AND OF THE THREE EASTERN GATES

CHAPTER XXXVIII 100

DESCRIPTION OF THE HEMISPHERE, THE TWELVE COLUMNS, AND THEIR BOWLS

CHAPTER XXXIX 100

DESCRIPTION OF THE ATRIUM, THE COURTS, AND PORCHES

CHAPTER XL 101

OF THE NUMBER OF HIS OFFERINGS

CHAPTER XLI 101

OF THE ERECTION OF CHURCHES IN BETHLEHEM, AND ON THE MOUNT OF OLIVES

CHAPTER XLII 101

THAT HELENA AUGUSTA, CONSTANTINE'S MOTHER, HAVING VISITED THIS LOCALITY FOR DEVOTIONAL PURPOSES, BUILT THESE CHURCHES

CHAPTER XLIII 102

A FURTHER NOTICE OF THE CHURCHES AT BETHLEHEM

CHAPTER XLIV 103

OF HELENA'S GENEROSITY, AND BENEFICENT ACTS

CHAPTER XLV 103

HER PIOUS CONDUCT IN THE CHURCHES

CHAPTER XLVI 103

SHE MAKES HER WILL, AND DIES AT THE AGE OF EIGHTY YEARS

CHAPTER XLVII 104

HOW CONSTANTINE BURIED HIS MOTHER, AND HOW HE HONOURED HER DURING HER LIFE

CHAPTER XLVIII 104

HE BUILDS CHURCHES IN HONOUR OF MARTYRS, AND ABOLISHES IDOLATRY AT CONSTANTINOPLE

CHAPTER XLIX 105

REPRESENTATION OF THE CROSS IN THE PALACE, AND OF DANIEL AT THE PUBLIC FOUNTAINS

CHAPTER L 105

HE ERECTS CHURCHES IN NICOMEDIA, AND IN OTHER CITIES

CHAPTER LI ... 106

HE ORDERS A CHURCH TO BE BUILT AT MAMBRE

CHAPTER LII ... 106

CONSTANTINE'S LETTER TO EUSEBIUS CONCERNING MAMBRE

CHAPTER LIII ... 107

THAT OUR SAVIOUR APPEARED IN THIS PLACE TO ABRAHAM

CHAPTER LIV ... 108

THE IDOL TEMPLES AND IMAGES EVERY WHERE DESTROYED

CHAPTER LV ... 109

OVERTHROW OF AN IDOL TEMPLE, AND ABOLITION OF LICENTIOUS PRACTICES, AT APHACA IN PHŒNICIA

CHAPTER LVI ... 110

DESTRUCTION OF THE TEMPLE OF ÆSCULAPIUS AT ÆGÆ

CHAPTER LVII ... 110

HOW THE GENTILES ABANDONED IDOL WORSHIP, AND TURNED TO THE KNOWLEDGE OF GOD

CHAPTER LVIII ... 111

CONSTANTINE DESTROYS THE TEMPLE OF VENUS AT HELIOPOLTS, AND BUILDS THE FIRST CHURCH IN THAT CITY

CHAPTER LIX ... 112

OF THE DISTURBANCES RAISED AT ANTIOCH ON ACCOUNT OF EUSTATHIUS

CHAPTER LX ... 113

CONSTANTINE'S LETTER TO THE ANTIOCHIANS, DIRECTING THEM NOT TO WITHDRAW EUSEBIUS FROM CÆSAREA, BUT TO SEEK FOR ANOTHER BISHOP

CHAPTER LXI ... 115

THE EMPEROR'S LETTER TO EUSEBIUS, ON THE OCCASION OF HIS REFUSING THE BISHOPRIC OF ANTIOCH

CHAPTER LXII ... 116

CONSTANTINE'S LETTER TO THE COUNCIL, DEPRECATING THE REMOVAL OF EUSEBIUS FROM CÆSAREA

CHAPTER LXIII ... 116

HOW HE DISPLAYED HIS ZEAL FOR THE EXTIRPATION OF HERESIES

CHAPTER LXIV ... 117

CONSTANTINE'S EDICT AGAINST THE HERETICS

CHAPTER LXV ... 118

THE HERETICS ARE DEPRIVED OF THEIR PLACES OF ASSEMBLY, AND THEIR MEETINGS SUPPRESSED

CHAPTER LXVI 119

ON THE DISCOVERY OF PROHIBITED BOOKS AMONG THE HERETICS, MANY OF THEM RETURN TO THE CATHOLIC CHURCH

BOOK IV 120

CHAPTER I 121

CONSTANTINE CONFERS NUMEROUS HONOURS IN THE WAY OF PRESENTS AND PROMOTIONS

CHAPTER II 121

REMISSION OF A FOURTH PART OF THE TRIBUTES

CHAPTER III 122

EQUALISATION OF THE MORE OPPRESSIVE TAXES

CHAPTER IV 122

HIS LIBERALITY, FROM HIS PRIVATE RESOURCES, TO THE LOSERS IN SUITS OF A PECUNIARY NATURE

CHAPTER V 122

DEFEAT AND CONQUEST OF THE SCYTHIANS THROUGH THE STANDARD OF THE SAVIOUR'S CROSS

CHAPTER VI 123

CONQUEST OF THE SARMATIANS, CONSEQUENT ON THE REBELLION OF THEIR SLAVES

CHAPTER VII 123

AMBASSADORS FROM DIFFERENT BARBAROUS NATIONS RECEIVE PRESENTS FROM THE EMPEROR

CHAPTER VIII 124

HE WRITES TO THE KING OF PERSIA, WHO HAD SENT HIM AN EMBASSY, ON BEHALF OF THE CHRISTIANS IN HIS REALM

CHAPTER IX 124

LETTER OF CONSTANTINE AUGUSTUS TO SAPOR KING OF THE PERSIANS, CONTAINING A TRULY PIOUS CONFESSION OF GOD AND CHRIST

CHAPTER X 125

THE WRITER DENOUNCES IDOLS, AND PRAISES GOD

CHAPTER XI 125

REMARKS CONDEMNATORY OF THE TYRANTS AND PERSECUTORS; AND ON THE CAPTIVITY OF VALERIAN

CHAPTER XII 126

HE DECLARES THAT, HAVING WITNESSED THE FALL OF THE PERSECUTORS, HE NOW REJOICES AT THE PEACE ENJOYED BY THE CHRISTIANS

CHAPTER XIII 126

HE BESPEAKS HIS AFFECTIONATE INTEREST FOR THE CHRISTIANS IN HIS COUNTRY

CHAPTER XIV 127

HOW THE ZEALOUS PRAYERS OF CONSTANTINE PROCURED PEACE TO THE CHRISTIANS

CHAPTER XV 127

HE CAUSES HIMSELF TO BE REPRESENTED ON HIS COINS, AND IN HIS PORTRAITS, IN THE ATTITUDE OF PRAYER

CHAPTER XVI 127

HE FORBIDS BY LAW THE PLACING HIS LIKENESS IN IDOL TEMPLES

CHAPTER XVII 128

OF HIS PRAYERS IN THE PALACE, AND HIS READING THE HOLY SCRIPTURES

CHAPTER XVIII 128

HE ENJOINS THE GENERAL OBSERVANCE OF THE LORD'S DAY, AND THE DAY BEFORE THE SABBATH

CHAPTER XIX 129

HE DIRECTED EVEN HIS PAGAN SOLDIERS TO PRAY ON THE LORD'S DAY

CHAPTER XX 129

THE FORM OF PRAYER GIVEN BY CONSTANTINE TO HIS SOLDIERS

CHAPTER XXI 129

HE ORDERS THE SIGN OF THE CROSS TO BE ENGRAVEN ON HIS SOLDIERS' SHIELDS

CHAPTER XXII 130

OF HIS ZEAL IN PRAYER, AND THE HONOUR HE PAID TO THE FEAST OF EASTER

CHAPTER XXIII 130

HE FORBIDS IDOLATROUS WORSHIP, BUT HONOURS MARTYRS AND THEIR FESTIVALS

CHAPTER XXIV 131

HE DESCRIBES HIMSELF AS A BISHOP, IN CHARGE OF AFFAIRS EXTERNAL TO THE CHURCH

CHAPTER XXV 131

PROHIBITION OF SACRIFICES, OF PROFANE MYSTERIES, AND COMBATS OF GLADIATORS: ALSO SUPPRESSION OF THE IMPIOUS PRIESTHOOD OF THE NILE

CHAPTER XXVI 132

AMENDMENT OF THE LAW IN FORCE RESPECTING CHILDLESS PERSONS, AND OF THE LAW OF WILLS

CHAPTER XXVII 133

AMONG OTHER ENACTMENTS, HE FORBIDS THE JEWS TO POSSESS CHRISTIAN SLAVES, AND AFFIRMS THE VALIDITY OF THE DECISIONS OF COUNCILS

CHAPTER XXVIII 133

HIS OFFERINGS TO THE CHURCHES, AND DISTRIBUTIONS OF MONEY TO THE VIRGINS, AND TO THE POOR

CHAPTER XXIX 134

OF CONSTANTINE'S DISCOURSES AND DECLAMATIONS

CHAPTER XXX 135

HE ATTEMPTS TO SHAME A COVETOUS PERSON, BY MARKING OUT BEFORE HIM THE MEASURE OF A GRAVE

CHAPTER XXXI 135

HE IS DERIDED BECAUSE OF HIS EXCESSIVE CLEMENCY

CHAPTER XXXII 135

OF CONSTANTINE'S ORATION WHICH HE WROTE TO THE ASSEMBLY OF THE SAINTS

CHAPTER XXXIII 136

HE LISTENED IN A STANDING POSTURE TO EUSEBIUS'S DECLAMATION IN HONOUR OF OUR SAVIOUR'S SEPULCHRE

CHAPTER XXXIV 136

HE WRITES TO EUSEBIUS RESPECTING EASTER, AND THE SACRED BOOKS OF SCRIPTURE

CHAPTER XXXV 137

CONSTANTINE'S LETTER TO EUSEBIUS, IN PRAISE OF HIS DISCOURSE CONCERNING EASTER

CHAPTER XXXVI 137

CONSTANTINE'S LETTER TO EUSEBIUS ON THE PREPARATION OF COPIES OF THE SCRIPTURES

CHAPTER XXXVII 138

HOW THE COPIES WERE PROVIDED

CHAPTER XXXVIII 138

THE PORT OF GAZA IS MADE A CITY FOR ITS PROFESSION OF CHRISTIANITY, AND RECEIVES THE NAME OF CONSTANTIA

CHAPTER XXXIX 139

A PLACE IN PHŒNICIA ALSO IS MADE A CITY, AND IN OTHER CITIES IDOLATRY IS ABOLISHED, AND CHURCHES BUILT

CHAPTER XL 139

HAVING CONFERRED THE DIGNITY OF CÆSARS ON HIS THREE SONS AT THE THREE DECENNIAL PERIODS OF HIS REIGN, HE DEDICATED THE CHURCH AT JERUSALEM

CHAPTER XLI 140

IN THE MEANTIME HE ORDERS A COUNCIL TO BE CONVENED AT TYRE, BECAUSE OF CONTROVERSIES RAISED IN EGYPT

CHAPTER XLII 140

CONSTANTINE'S LETTER TO THE COUNCIL AT TYRE

CHAPTER XLIII 141

BISHOPS FROM EVERY PROVINCE ATTENDED THE DEDICATION OF THE CHURCH AT JERUSALEM

CHAPTER XLIV 142

OF THEIR RECEPTION BY THE NOTARY MACARIUS; THE DISTRIBUTION OF MONEY TO THE POOR; AND OFFERINGS TO THE CHRUCH

CHAPTER XLV 142

VARIOUS DISCOURSES BY THE ASSEMBLED BISHOPS; ALSO BY EUSEBIUS THE WRITER OF THIS HISTORY

CHAPTER XLVI 143

EUSEBIUS AFTERWARDS REPEATED HIS DESCRIPTION OF THE CHURCH, AND HIS ORATION ON THE TRICENNALIA, BEFORE CONSTANTINE HIMSELF

CHAPTER XLVII 144

THE COUNCIL AT NICÆA WAS HELD IN THE TWENTIETH, THE DEDICATION OF THE CHURCH AT JERUSALEM IN THE THIRTIETH YEAR OF CONSTANTINE'S REIGN

CHAPTER XLVIII 144

CONSTANTINE TESTIFIES HIS AVERSION TO EXCESSIVE PRAISE

CHAPTER XLIX 144

MARRIAGE OF HIS SON CONSTANTIUS CÆSAR

CHAPTER L 145

AN EMBASSY ARRIVES, WITH PRESENTS, FROM THE INDIANS

CHAPTER LI 145

CONSTANTINE DIVIDES THE EMPIRE BETWEEN HIS THREE SONS, WHOM HE HAD INSTRUCTED IN THE ARTS OF GOVERNMENT AND THE DUTIES OF RELIGION

CHAPTER LII 146

HIS PIOUS INSTRUCTIONS AFTER THEY HAD REACHED MATURITY

CHAPTER LIII 146

HAVING REIGNED ABOUT THIRTY TWO YEARS, AND LIVED ABOVE SIXTY, HE STILL ENJOYED SOUND BODILY HEALTH

CHAPTER LIV 147

HIS EXTREME BENEVOLENCE WAS ABUSED BY SOME AS AN ENCOURAGEMENT TO AVARICE AND HYPOCRISY

CHAPTER LV 147

CONSTANTINE EMPLOYED HIMSELF IN COMPOSITION OF VARIOUS KINDS TO THE CLOSE OF HIS LIFE

CHAPTER LVI 148

HE IS ATTENDED BY BISHOPS ON AN EXPEDITION AGAINST THE PERSIANS, AND TAKES WITH HIM A TENT IN THE FORM OF A CHURCH

CHAPTER LVII 149

HIS FAVOURABLE RECEPTION OF AN EMBASSY FROM THE PERSIANS. HE KEEPS THE NIGHT VIGIL WITH OTHERS AT THE FEAST OF EASTER

CHAPTER LVIII 149

BUILDING OF A CHURCH IN HONOUR OF THE APOSTLES AT CONSTANTINOPLE

CHAPTER LIX 149

FURTHER DESCRIPTION OF THE SAME CHURCH

CHAPTER LX 150

HE ALSO ERECTED HIS OWN SEPULCHRAL MONUMENT IN THIS CHURCH

CHAPTER LXI 150

HIS SICKNESS AT HELENOPOLIS, AND PRAYERS RESPECTING HIS BAPTISM

CHAPTER LXII 151

CONSTANTINE'S APPEAL TO THE BISHOPS, REQUESTING THEM TO CONFER UPON HIM THE RITE OF BAPTISM

CHAPTER LXIII 151

AFTER HIS BAPTISM HE RENDERS THANKS TO GOD

CHAPTER LXIV 152

CONSTANTINE'S DEATH AT NOON ON THE FEAST OF PENTECOST

CHAPTER LXV 152

LAMENTATIONS OF THE SOLDIERY AND THEIR OFFICERS

CHAPTER LXVI 153

REMOVAL OF THE BODY FROM NICOMEDIA TO THE PALACE AT CONSTANTINOPLE

CHAPTER LXVII 153

HE RECEIVED THE SAME HONOURS FROM THE COUNTS AND OTHER OFFICERS AS BEFORE HIS DEATH

CHAPTER LXVIII 154

RESOLUTION OF THE ARMY TO CONFER THENCE-FORWARD THE TITLE OF AUGUSTUS ON HIS SONS

CHAPTER LXIX 154

MOURNING ROR CONSTANTINE AT ROME; AND PAINTINGS IN MEMORY OF HIS DEATH

CHAPTER LXX 155

HIS BURIAL BY HIS SON CONSTANTIUS AT CONSTANTINOPLE

CHAPTER LXXI 155

SACRED SERVICE IN THE CHURCH OF THE APOSTLES ON THE OCCASION OF CONSTANTINE'S FUNERAL

CHAPTER LXXII 156

AN ALLUSION TO THE PHŒNIX

CHAPTER LXXIII 156

CONSTANTINE IS REPRESENTED ON COINS IN THE ACT OF ASCENDING TO HEAVEN

CHAPTER LXXIV 157

THE GOD WHOM HE HAD HONOURED DESERVEDLY HONOURED HIM IN RETURN

CHAPTER LXXV 157

HE SURPASSED ALL PRECEDING EMPERORS IN DEVOTION TO GOD

THE ORATION OF THE EMPEROR CONSTANTINE, WHICH HE ADDRESSED "TO THE ASSEMBLY OF THE SAINTS" 158

CHAPTER I 159

PRELIMINARY REMARKS ON THE FEAST OF EASTER: AND HOW THE WORD OF GOD, HAVING CONFERRED MANIFOLD BENEFITS ON MANKIND, RECEIVED A BASE AND TREACHEROUS RETURN

CHAPTER II 160

AN APPEAL TO THE CHURCH AND HIS AUDIENCE GENERALLY, TO PARDON AND CORRECT THE ERRORS OF HIS SPEECH

CHAPTER III 161

THAT GOD IS THE FATHER OF THE WORD, AND THE CREATOR OF ALL THINGS: AND THAT MATERIAL OBJECTS COULD NOT CONTINUE TO EXIST, WERE THEIR CAUSES DIFFERENT

CHAPTER IV 162

ON THE ERROR OF IDOLATROUS WORSHIP

CHAPTER V 163

THAT CHRIST, THE SON OF GOD, CREATED ALL THINGS, AND HAS APPOINTED TO EVERY THING THE TERM OF ITS EXISTENCE

CHAPTER VI 164

THE FALSITY OF THE GENERAL OPINION RESPECTING FATE IS PROVED BY THE CONSIDERATION OF HUMAN LAWS, AND BY THE WORKS OF CREATION, THE COURSE OF WHICH IS NOT FORTUITOUS, BUT ACCORDING TO A DEFINITE ARRANGEMENT WHICH EVINCES THE DESIGN OF THE CREATOR

CHAPTER VII 166

IN REGARD TO THINGS ABOVE OUR COMPREHENSION, WE SHOULD GLORIFY THE CREATOR'S WISDOM, AND ATTRIBUTE THEIR CAUSES TO HIM ALONE, AND NOT TO CHANCE

CHAPTER VIII 166

THAT GOD BESTOWS AN ABUNDANT SUPPLY OF WHATEVER IS SUITED TO THE WANTS OF MAN, AND MINISTERS BUT SPARINGLY TO HIS PLEASURES; IN BOTH CASES WITH A VIEW TO HIS ADVANTAGE

CHAPTER IX 167

OF THE PHILOSOPHERS, WHO WERE LED INTO ERRORS OF JUDGMENT, AND SOME OF THEM INTO DANGER, BY THEIR DESIRE OF UNIVERSAL KNOWLEDGE—ALSO OF THE DOCTRINES OF PLATO

CHAPTER X 169

OF THOSE WHO REJECT THE DOCTRINES OF PHILOSOPHERS, AS WELL AS THOSE OF SCRIPTURE: AND THAT WE OUGHT TO YIELD OUR ASSENT TO THE POETS IN ALL THINGS, OR NOT AT ALL

CHAPTER XI 170

ON THE COMING OF OUR LORD IN THE FLESH; ITS NATURE, AND CAUSE

CHAPTER XII 174

OF THOSE WHO ARE IGNORANT OF THIS MYSTERY; AND THAT THEIR LGNORANCE IS VOLUNTARY. THE BLESSINGS WHICH AWAIT THOSE WHO KNOW IT, ESPECIALLY SUCH AS DIE IN THE CONFESSION OF THE FAITH

CHAPTER XIII 175

THAT THERE IS A NECESSARY DIFFERENCE BETWEEN CREATED THINGS. THAT THE PROPENSITY TO GOOD AND EVIL DEPENDS ON THE WILL OF MAN: AND THAT, CONSEQUENTLY, JUDGMENT IS A NECESSARY AND REASONABLE THING

CHAPTER XIV 175

THAT CREATED NATURE DIFFERS INFINITELY FROM UNCREATED BEING; TO WHICH MAN MAKES THE NEAREST APPROACH BY A LIFE OF VIRTUE

CHAPTER XV 176

OF THE SAVIOUR'S DOCTRINES AND MIRACLES; AND THE BENEFITS HE CONFERS ON THOSE WHO OWN SUBJECTION TO HIM

CHAPTER XVI 178

THE COMING OF CHRIST WAS PREDICTED BY THE PROPHETS; AND WAS ORDAINED TO BE THE OVERTHROW OF IDOLS AND IDOLATROUS CITIES

CHAPTER XVII 179

OF THE WISDOM OF MOSES, WHICH WAS AN OBJECT OF IMITATION TO THE WISE AMONG HEATHEN NATIONS. ALSO CONCERNING DANIEL, AND THE THREE CHILDREN

CHAPTER XVIII 180

OF THE ERYTHRÆAN SIBYL, WHO POINTED IN A PROPHETIC ACROSTIC AT OUR LORD AND HIS PASSION. THE ACROSTIC IS "JESUS CHRIST, SON OF GOD, SAVIOUR, CROSS"

CHAPTER XIX 182

THAT THIS PROPHECY RESPECTING OUR SAVIOUR WAS NOT THE FICTION OF ANY MEMBER OF THE CHRISTIAN CHURCH, BUT THE TESTIMONY OF THE ERYTHRÆAN SIBYL, WHOSE BOOKS WERE TRANSLATED INTO LATIN BY CICERO BEFORE THE COMING OF CHRIST. ALSO THAT VIRGIL MAKES MENTION OF THE SAME, AND OF THE BIRTH OF THE VIRGIN'S CHILD: THOUGH HE SPOKE OBSCURELY, FROM FEAR OF THE RULING POWERS

CHAPTER XX 183

A FURTHER QUOTATION FROM VIRGIL RESPECTING CHRIST, WITH ITS INTERPRETATION, SHEWING THAT THE MYSTERY WAS INDICATED THEREIN DARKLY, AS MIGHT BE EXPECTED FROM A POET

CHAPTER XXI 186

THAT THESE THINGS CANNOT HAVE BEEN SPOKEN OF A MERE MAN: AND THAT UNBELIEVERS, OWING TO THEIR IGNORANCE OF RELIGION, KNOW NOT EVEN THE ORIGIN OF THEIR OWN EXISTENCE

CHAPTER XXII 187

THE EMPEROR THANKFULLY ASCRIBES HIS VICTORIES AND ALL OTHER BLESSINGS TO CHRIST; AND CONDEMNS THE CONDUCT OF THE TYRANT MAXIMIN, THE VIOLENCE OF WHOSE PERSECUTION HAD ENHANCED THE GLORY OF THE CHRISTIAN RELIGION

CHAPTER XXIII 188

OF CHRISTIAN CONDUCT. THAT GOD IS PLEASED WITH THOSE WHO LEAD A LIFE OF VIRTUE: AND THAT WE MUST EXTECT A JUDGMENT AND FUTURE RETRIBUTION

CHAPTER XXIV 189

OF DECIUS, VALERIAN, AND AURELIAN, WHO EXPERIENCED A MISERABLE END IN CONSEQUENCE OF THEIR PERSECUTION OF THE CHURCH

CHAPTER XXV 190

OF DIOCLETIAN, WHO IGNOBLY ABDICATED THE IMPERIAL THRONE, AND WAS TERRIFIED BY THE DREAD OF LIGHTNING FOR HIS PERSECUTION OF THE CHURCH

CHAPTER XXVI 191

THE EMPEROR ASCRIBES HIS PERSONAL PIETY TO GOD; AND SHEWS THAT WE ARE BOUND TO SEEK SUCCESS FROM GOD, AND ATTRIBUTE IT TO HIM; BUT TO CONSIDER FAILURE AS THE RESULT OF OUR OWN NEGLIGENCE

THE ORATION OF EUSEBIUS PAMPHILUS, IN PRAISE OF THE EMPEROR CONSTANTINE, PRONOUNCED ON THE THIRTIETH ANNIVERSARY OF HIS REIGN 192

PROLOGUE TO THE ORATION 193

CHAPTER I 195

THE ORATION

CHAPTER II 197

CHAPTER III 198

CHAPTER IV 200

CHAPTER V 201

CHAPTER VI 203

CHAPTER VII 208

CHAPTER VIII 211

CHAPTER IX 213

CHAPTER X 216

CHAPTER XI 218

CHAPTER XII 222

CHAPTER XIII 227

CHAPTER XIV 231

CHAPTER XV 233

CHAPTER XVI 236

CHAPTER XVII 239

CHAPTER XVIII 243

ADDRESS

THE Translator desires to present the following pages to the English reader, as, in many respects, an interesting memorial of that eventful period in the world's history to which they mainly refer.

At the same time he would earnestly disclaim any intention of hereby sanctioning the thought, too commonly entertained, that the general external profession of Christianity by the nations of the Roman empire at this period is to be regarded as a distinct blessing from the hand of God.

If it be contended that the vision of the Cross (which stands forth as the emperor's warrant for the authoritative promulgation of Christianity as the religion of the world) is to be received as a true miracle, because no evidence can be adduced to prove the contrary, we need not fear to concede the point. We must, however, be permitted seriously to question whether this miracle, the ostensible object of which was the compulsory establishment, by the sword of war wherever necessary, of the religion of the Prince of Peace, can be received as of heavenly origin; though doubtless permitted by Him who is able to cause the worst manifestations of human or Satanic evil to subserve the purposes of His own all-wise and sovereign will.

Regard for historic truth will surely rather lead us to revert to the public assumption by Constantine of the title of a Christian emperor, as the point of time from which the comparatively dormant principles of worldly greatness, pride, and superstition, which afterwards pervaded and corrupted Gentile Christianity, started as it were into life, and attained a fearfully rapid maturity.

Viewed as a sketch of the circumstances which conspired to usher in this most momentous era in the history of visible Christianity, the "Life of Constantine" stands invested with a peculiar and a solemn interest:—from any more delusive estimate of those circumstances, it is hoped that the instructed and humble Christian will mercifully be preserved.

Of the two orations subjoined to the work, that of Constantine, replete as it is with arguments tending to the exaltation of Christianity and the overthrow of idol worship, yet betrays the credulity of the imperial champion, or that of his age, in the prophetic inspiration therein ascribed to the fictitious Sibylline acrostic, and the verses of a heathen poet.

The elaborate oration of Eusebius, in praise of Constantine, will not be without its value, as a fair and favourable specimen of the learned Author's style and eloquence.

THE LIFE OF THE BLESSED EMPEROR CONSTANTINE, BY EUSEBIUS PAMPHILUS

BOOK I

CHAPTER I

PREFACE—OF THE DEATH OF CONSTANTINE

ALREADY have all mankind united in celebrating with joyous festivities the completion of the second and third decennial periods of this great Emperor's reign: already, on the occasion of the first of these periods, have we ourselves received him as a triumphant conqueror in the assembly of God's ministers, and greeted him with the due meed of praise: and still more recently we have woven as it were garlands of eulogistic words, wherewith we encircled his sacred head in his own palace on the thirtieth anniversary of his reign.

But now, while I much desire to give utterance to some of the sentiments I have been accustomed to entertain, I stand perplexed and doubtful which way to turn, being wholly lost in wonder at the extraordinary spectacle before me. For to whatever quarter I direct my view, whether to the east, or to the west, or over the whole world, or toward heaven itself, I see the blessed emperor everywhere present. On earth I behold his sons, like some new reflectors of his brightness, diffusing every where the lustre of their father's character; and I see him still living and powerful, and governing the general interests of mankind more completely than ever before, being multiplied as it were by the succession of his children to the Imperial power. They had indeed previously shared the dignity of Cæsars; but now, being invested with their father's entire authority, and graced by his accomplishments, for the excellence of their piety they are proclaimed by the titles of Sovereign, Augustus, Worshipful, and Emperor.

CHAPTER II

THE PREFACE CONTINUED

AND I am indeed amazed when I consider that he who was but lately visible and present with us in his mortal body, is still, even after death, when the natural thought disclaims all superfluous distinctions as unsuitable, most marvellously endowed with the same imperial dwellings, and honours, and praises as heretofore. But further, when I raise my thoughts even to the arch of heaven, and there contemplate his thrice blessed soul in communion with God

Himself, freed from every mortal and earthly vesture, and shining in a refulgent robe of light; and when I perceive that it is no more connected with the fleeting periods and occupations of mortal life, but honoured with an ever-blooming crown, and an immortality of endless and blessed existence; I stand as it were entranced and deprived of all power of utterance: and so, while I condemn my own weakness, and impose silence on myself, I resign the task of speaking his praises worthily to one who is better able, even to Him who alone has power (being the immortal God—the Word), to confirm the truth of His own sayings.

CHAPTER III

HOW GOD HONOURS PIOUS PRINCES, BUT DESTROYS TYRANTS

AND whereas He has given assurance that those who glorify and honour Him will meet with an ample recompense at His hands, while those who set themselves against Him as enemies and adversaries will compass the ruin of their own souls; already has He established the truth of these His own declarations. He has shown that the lives of those tyrants who denied and opposed Him have had a fearful end, and at the same time has made it manifest that even the death of His servant, as well as his life, is worthy of admiration and praise, and justly claims the memorial, not merely of perishable, but of immortal records.

Mankind have indeed devised some consolation for the frail and precarious duration of human life, and have thought by the erection of monuments to secure immortal honours to the memory of their ancestors. Some have employed the vivid delineations and colours of painting; some have carved statues from lifeless blocks of wood; while others, by engraving their inscriptions deep on tablets and monuments of wood and stone, have sought to keep the virtues of those whom they honoured in perpetual remembrance. All these indeed are perishable, and consumed by the lapse of time, being representations of the corruptible body, and incapable of expressing the image of the immortal soul. And yet these seemed sufficient to those who had no well-grounded hope of happiness after the termination of this mortal life. But God, that God, I say, who is the Preserver of the universe, has treasured up with Himself, for those who love godliness, greater blessings than human thought has conceived; and, by giving the earnest and first-fruits of future rewards even here, assures, in some sort, immortal hopes to mortal eyes. The ancient oracles of the prophets, delivered to us in the Scripture, declare this; the lives of pious men, who shone in old time with every virtue, attest the same; and our own days prove it to be true, wherein CONSTANTINE, who alone of all that ever wielded the Roman power was the friend of God the Sovereign of all, has appeared to all mankind so bright an example of a godly life.

CHAPTER IV

HOW GOD HONOURED CONSTANTINE

AND God Himself, whom Constantine worshipped, has confirmed this truth by the clearest manifestations of His will, being present to aid him at the commencement, during the course, and at the end of his reign, and holding him up to the human race as an exemplary pattern of godliness. Accordingly He has distinguished him alone of all the sovereigns of whom we have ever heard (by the manifold blessings He has conferred on him), as at once a mighty luminary and most distinct and powerful herald of genuine piety.

CHAPTER V

HE REIGNED ABOVE THIRTY YEARS, AND LIVED ABOVE SIXTY

WITH respect to the duration of his reign, God honoured him with three complete periods of ten years, and rather more, and limited the whole term of his mortal life to twice this number of years. And being pleased to make him a representative of His own sovereign power, He displayed him as the conqueror of the whole race of tyrants, and the destroyer of those godless great ones of the earth who had ventured with desperate audacity to raise their impious arms against Him, the supreme King of the universe. They appeared indeed but for a very little space, and were destroyed together: while the one and only true God, when He had enabled His servant, clad in heavenly panoply, to stand singly against many foes, and by his means had relieved mankind from the multitude of the ungodly, constituted him a teacher of His worship to all nations, to testify with a loud voice in the hearing of all, that he acknowledged the true God, and turned with abhorrence from the error of them that are no gods.

CHAPTER VI

HE WAS THE SERVANT OF GOD, AND THE CONQUEROR OF NATIONS

THUS, like a faithful and good servant, did he act and testify, openly declaring and owning himself the obedient minister of the supreme King. And God forthwith rewarded him, by making him ruler and sovereign, and victorious to such a degree that he alone of all the emperors pursued a continual course of conquest, unsubdued and invincible, and holding imperial power greater than tradition records to have been possessed by any before. So dear was he to God, and so blessed; so pious and so fortunate in all that he undertook, that with the greatest facility he compelled the submission of more nations than any who had preceded him, and yet retained his power, undisturbed, to the very close of his life.

CHAPTER VII

HE IS COMPARED WITH CYRUS KING OF THE PERSIANS, AND WITH ALEXANDER OF MACEDON

ANCIENT history describes Cyrus as by far the most illustrious of all the Persian kings. And yet if we regard the end of his days, we find it but little corresponded with his past prosperity, since he met with an inglorious and dishonourable death at the hands of a woman.

Again, the Greeks celebrate Alexander the Macedonian as the conqueror of very many and diverse nations; yet we find that he was removed by an early death, before he had reached the full vigour of manhood, being carried off by the effects of revelry and drunkenness. His whole life embraced but the space of thirty-two years, and his reign extended to no more than a third part of that period. Unsparing as the thunderbolt, he pursued his career of slaughter, and reduced entire nations and cities with all their inhabitants to slavery. But when he had scarcely arrived at the maturity of life, and was lamenting the loss of youthful pleasures, death fell upon him with terrible stroke, and (lest he should make still further havoc of the human race) cut him off in a foreign and hostile land, leaving no children to inherit his fame, and without a home to call his own. His kingdom too was instantly dismembered, each of his officers at once tearing away and seizing on a portion for himself. And yet this man is extolled for such deeds as these!

CHAPTER VIII

HE CONQUERED NEARLY THE WHOLE WORLD

BUT our emperor began his reign at the time of life at which the Macedonian died, and lived as long again, and trebled the length of that prince's reign. And when he had confirmed his soldiers in the mild and sober precepts of godliness, he carried his arms as far as the Britons, and the nations that dwell in the very bosom of the Western ocean. He subdued likewise all Scythia, though situated in the remotest North, and divided into numberless diverse and barbarous tribes. He even pushed his conquests to the Blemmyans and Ethiopians, on the very confines of the South; nor did he think the acquisition of the Eastern nations unworthy his care. In short, diffusing the effulgence of his holy light to the ends of the whole world, even to the most distant Indians and other nations dwelling within the compass of the inhabited earth, he received the submission of all the rulers, governors, and satraps of barbarous nations, who cheerfully welcomed and saluted him, sending embassies and presents, and setting the highest value on his acquaintance and friendship; insomuch that they honoured him with pictures and statues in their respective countries, and Constantine alone of all emperors was acknowledged and celebrated by all. Notwithstanding, even among these distant nations, he proclaimed the name of his God in his royal edicts with all boldness.

CHAPTER IX

HE WAS THE SON OF A PIOUS EMPEROR, AND BEQUEATHED THE IMPERIAL POWER TO HIS OWN SONS

NOR did he give this testimony in words merely, while exhibiting failure in his own practice, but pursued every path of virtue, and was rich in the varied fruits of godliness. He ensured the affection of his friends by magnificent proofs of liberality; and inasmuch as he governed on principles of humanity, he caused his rule to be but lightly felt and acceptable to all classes of his subjects: until at last, after a long course of years, and when he was wearied by his divine labours, the God whom he honoured crowned him with an immortal reward, and translated him from a transitory kingdom to that endless life which He has laid up in store for the souls of His saints, after He had raised him up three sons to succeed him in his power. As then the imperial throne had descended to him from his father, so, by the law of nature, was it reserved for his children and their descendants, and perpetuated (like some paternal inheritance) to endless generations. And indeed God Himself, who distinguished this blessed prince with divine honours while yet present with us, and who has adorned his death with choice blessings from His own hand, should be the writer of his actions; since He has recorded his labours and their successful results on tablets of heavenly memorial.

CHAPTER X

OF THE NECESSITY FOR THIS HISTORY, AND ITS VALUE IN A MORAL POINT OF VIEW

HOWEVER, hard as it is to speak worthily of this blessed character, and though silence were the safer and less perilous course, nevertheless it is incumbent on me, if I would escape the charge of negligence and sloth, to trace as it were a verbal portraiture, by way of memorial of the pious prince, in imitation of the delineations of human art. For I should be ashamed of myself were I not to employ my best efforts (feeble though they be and of little value), in praise of one who honoured God with such surpassing devotion. I think too that my work will be on other grounds both instructive and necessary, since it will contain a description of those royal and noble actions of which God, the universal Sovereign, is pleased to approve. For surely it would be disgraceful that the memory of Nero, and other wicked and impious tyrants far worse than he, should meet with diligent writers to embellish the relation of their worthless deeds with elegant language, and record them in voluminous histories, and that I should be silent, to whom God Himself has vouchsafed such an emperor as all history records not, and has permitted me to come into his presence, and enjoy his acquaintance and familiar intimacy.

CHAPTER XI

HIS PRESENT OBJECT IS TO RECORD ONLY THE PIOUS ACTIONS OF CONSTANTINE

WHEREFORE, if it is the duty of any one, it certainly is mine, to make an ample proclamation of his virtues to all in whom the example of noble actions is capable of inspiring the love of God. For some, who have written the lives of worthless characters, and the history of actions but little tending to the improvement of morals, from private motives either of gratitude or enmity, and possibly in some cases with no better object than the display of their own learning, have given an undue importance to their description of actions intrinsically base, by a refinement and elegance of diction. And thus they have communicated to others, who by the Divine favour had been kept apart from evil, the knowledge of conduct not only vile in itself, but deserving rather to be silenced in darkness and oblivion. But the course of my narrative, however unequal to the greatness of the deeds it has to describe, will yet derive lustre even from the bare relation of noble actions. And surely the record of conduct that has been pleasing to God will afford a far from unprofitable, indeed a most instructive occupation, to persons of well-ordered minds.

It is my intention, however, to pass over very many of the royal deeds of this thrice blessed prince; as, for example, his conflicts and engagements in the field, his personal valour, his victories and successes against the enemy, and the many triumphs he obtained: likewise his provisions for the interests of individuals, his legislative enactments for the social advantage of his subjects, and a multitude of other imperial labours which are fresh in the memory of all.

The design of my present undertaking leads me to speak and write of those circumstances only which have reference to his religious character: and, since these are themselves of almost infinite variety, I shall select from the facts which have come to my knowledge such as are most suitable, and worthy of lasting record, and endeavour to narrate them as briefly as possible. Henceforward indeed there is a full and free opportunity for celebrating in every way the praises of this most blessed prince, which hitherto we have been unable to do, on the ground that we are forbidden to judge any one blessed before his death, because of the uncertain vicissitudes of life. Let me implore then the help of God, and may the inspiring aid of the heavenly Word be with me, while I commence my history from the very earliest period of his life.

CHAPTER XII

LIKE MOSES, HE WAS REARED IN THE PALACES OF ROYALTY

ANCIENT history relates that a cruel race of tyrants oppressed the Hebrew nation; and that God, who graciously regarded them in their affliction, provided that the prophet Moses, who was then an infant, should be brought up in the very palaces and bosoms of the oppressors, and instructed in all the wisdom they possessed. And when he had arrived at the age of manhood, and the time was come for Divine justice to avenge the wrongs of the afflicted people, then the prophet of God, in obedience to the will of a more powerful Lord, forsook the royal household, and, estranging himself in word and deed from those by whom he had been brought up, openly preferred the society of his true brethren and kinsfolk. And in due time God exalted him to be the leader of the whole nation; and, after delivering the Hebrews from the bondage of their enemies, inflicted Divine vengeance through his means on the tyrant race. This ancient story, though regarded by too many as fabulous, has reached the ears of all. But now the same God has given to us to be eye-witnesses of miracles more wonderful than fables, and, from their recent appearance, more authentic than any report. For the tyrants of our day have ventured to war against the Supreme God, and have sorely afflicted His Church. And in the midst of these, Constantine, who was shortly to become their destroyer, but at that time of tender age, and blooming with the down of early youth, dwelt, as God's servant Moses had done, in the very home of the tyrants. Young, however, as he was, he shared not in the pursuits of the impious: for from that early period his noble nature (under the leading of the Divine Spirit), inclined him to a life of piety and acceptable service to God. A desire moreover to emulate the example of his father had its influence in stimulating the son to a virtuous course of conduct. The name of his father was Constantius (and we ought to revive his memory at this time), the most illustrious emperor of our age; of whose life it is necessary briefly to relate a few particulars, which tell to the honour of his son.

CHAPTER XIII

OF CONSTANTIUS HIS FATHER, WHO REFUSED TO IMITATE DIOCLETIAN, MAXIMIAN, AND MAXENTIUS, IN THEIR PERSECUTION OF THE CHRISTIANS

AT a time when four princes shared the administration of the Roman empire, Constantius alone adopted a course of conduct different from that pursued by his colleagues, and avowed himself the friend of the Supreme God.

For while they besieged and wasted the churches of God, levelling them to the ground, and obliterating the very foundations of the houses of prayer, he kept his hands pure from their abominable impiety, and never in any respect resembled them. They polluted their provinces by the indiscriminate slaughter of holy men and women; but he preserved himself free from the stain of this fearful crime: they, involved in the mazes of impious idolatry, enthralled first themselves, and then all under their authority, in bondage to the errors of evil demons; while he at the same time originated the profoundest peace throughout his dominions, and secured to his subjects the privilege of celebrating without hindrance the worship of God. In short, while his colleagues oppressed all men by the most grievous exactions, and rendered their lives intolerable, and even worse than death, Constantius alone governed his people with a mild and tranquil sway, and exhibited towards them a truly parental and fostering care.

Numberless indeed are the excellences of his character, which are the theme of praise to all; of these I will record one or two instances, as specimens of the quality of those which I must pass by in silence, and then I will proceed to the proposed course of my narrative.

CHAPTER XIV

HOW CONSTANTIUS HIS FATHER, BEING REPROACHED WITH POVERTY BY DIOCLETIAN, FILLED HIS TREASURY, AND AFTERWARDS RESTORED THE MONEY TO THOSE BY WHOM IT HAD BEEN CONTRIBUTED

IN consequence of the many reports in circulation respecting this prince, describing his kindness and gentleness of character, and the extraordinary elevation of his piety, alleging too, that by reason of his extreme indulgence to his subjects, he had not even a supply of money laid up in his treasury; the emperor who at that time occupied the place of supreme power sent to reprehend his neglect of the public weal, at the same time reproaching him with poverty, and alleging in proof of the charge the empty state of his treasury. On this he desired the messengers of the emperor to remain with him awhile, and, calling together the wealthiest of his subjects of all nations under his dominion, he informed them that he was in want of money, and that this was the time for them all to give a voluntary proof of their affection for their prince.

As soon as they heard this (as though they had long been desirous of an opportunity for shewing the sincerity of their good will), with zealous alacrity they filled the treasury with gold and silver and other wealth; each eager to surpass the rest in the amount of his contribution: and this they did with cheerful and joyous countenances. And now Constantius desired the messengers of the supreme emperor personally to inspect his treasures, and directed them to give a faithful report of what they had seen; adding, that on the present occasion he had taken this money into his own hands, but that it had long been kept for his use in the custody of the owners, as securely as if under the charge of faithful treasurers. The ambassadors were overwhelmed with astonishment at what they had witnessed: and on their departure it is said that the truly generous prince sent for the owners of the property, and, after commending them severally for their obedience and true loyalty, restored it all, and bade them return to their homes.

This one circumstance, then, conveys a proof of the generosity of him whose character we are attempting to illustrate: another will bear the clearest testimony to his piety.

CHAPTER XV

OF THE PERSECUTION RAISED BY HIS COLLEAGUES

BY command of the supreme authorities of the empire, the governors of the several provinces had set on foot a general persecution of those who professed the worship of God. Indeed, it was from the imperial courts themselves that the very first of the pious martyrs proceeded, who passed through those conflicts which were the test of their faith, and most readily endured both fire and sword, and the depths of the sea; in short, every form of death: so that in a short time all the royal palaces were bereft of godly men. The result was, that the authors of this wickedness were entirely deprived of the protecting care of God, since by their persecution of His worshippers they at the same time silenced the prayers that were wont to be made on their own behalf.

CHAPTER XVI

HOW CONSTANTIUS, FEIGNING IDOLATRY, EXPELLED THOSE WHO CONSENTED TO OFFER SACRIFICE, BUT RETAINED IN HIS PALACE ALL WHO WERE WILLING TO CONFESS CHRIST

ON the other hand, Constantius conceived an expedient full of sagacity, and carried it into effect, strange as it seems even to mention, but most of all remarkable in its execution.

He made a proposal to all the officers of his court, including even those in the highest stations of authority, offering them the following alternative: either that they should offer sacrifice to demons, and thus be permitted to remain with him, and enjoy their usual honours; or, in case of refusal, that they should be shut out from all access to his person, and entirely disqualified from acquaintance and association with him. Accordingly, when they had individually made their selection, and the choice of each had been ascertained, then this admirable prince disclosed the secret meaning of his expedient, and condemned the cowardice and selfishness of the one party, while he highly commended the other for their conscientious devotion to God. He declared too, that those who had been false to their God must be unworthy of the confidence of their prince; for how was it possible that they should preserve their fidelity to him, who had proved themselves faithless to a higher power? He determined, therefore, that such persons should be removed altogether from the imperial court.

On the other hand, he intrusted with the guardianship of his person and empire those men whom the evidence of truth had proved to be worthy servants of God, declaring that they would manifest the same fidelity to their king, and that he was bound to treat such persons with special regard as his nearest and most valued friends, and to esteem them far more highly than the richest treasures.

CHAPTER XVII

OF HIS DEVOTION AND LOVE TO CHRIST

THE father of Constantine, then, is said to have possessed such a character as we have briefly described. And what kind of death was vouchsafed to him in consequence of such devotion to God, and how far He whom he honoured made his lot to differ from that of his colleagues in the empire, may be known to any one who will give his attention to the circumstances of the case. For after he had for a long time given many proofs of royal nobility of soul, in acknowledging the Supreme God alone, and condemning the polytheism of the impious, and had fortified his household by the prayers of holy men, he is said to have passed the remainder of his life in repose and tranquillity, in the enjoyment of that happiness which consists in neither molesting others nor being molested ourselves.

Accordingly, during the whole course of his quiet and peaceful reign, he dedicated his entire household, his children, his wife, and domestic attendants, to the One Supreme God: so that the company assembled within the walls of his palace differed in no respect from a Church of God; wherein were also to be found His ministers, who offered continual supplications on behalf of their prince, and this at a time when, generally speaking, it was not allowable to make any allusion, even by name, to the worshippers of God.

CHAPTER XVIII

AFTER THE ABDICATION OF DIOCLETIAN AND MAXIMIAN, CONSTANTIUS BECAME CHIEF AUGUSTUS, AND WAS BLESSED WITH A NUMEROUS OFF-SPRING

THE immediate consequence of this conduct was a recompense from the hand of God, insomuch that he came into the supreme authority of the empire. For those princes who were his superiors in respect of age, for some unknown reason, resigned their power; and this sudden change took place in the first year which followed their persecution of the churches.

From that time Constantius alone received the honours of chief Augustus, having been previously indeed distinguished by the diadem of the imperial Cæsars, among whom he held the first rank; but after his worth had been proved in this capacity, he was invested with the highest dignity of the Roman empire, being named chief Augustus of the four who were afterwards elected to that honour. Moreover he surpassed most of the emperors in regard to the number of his family, having gathered around him a very large circle of male and female children. And, lastly, when he had attained to a happy old age, and was about to pay the common debt of nature, and exchange this life for another, God once more manifested His power in a special manner on his behalf, by providing that his eldest son Constantine should be present during his last moments, and ready to receive the imperial power from his hands.

CHAPTER XIX

OF HIS SON CONSTANTINE, WHO IN HIS YOUTH ACCOMPANIED DIOCLETIAN INTO PALESTINE

FOR Constantine had been already accustomed to the society of his father's imperial colleagues, and had passed his time among them (like God's ancient prophet Moses), as we have said. And even in the very earliest period of his youth he was judged by them to be worthy of the highest honour. An instance of this we have ourselves seen, when he passed through Palestine with the senior emperor, at whose right hand he stood, and commanded the admiration of all who beheld him by the indications he gave even then of royal greatness. For no one was comparable to him for grace and beauty of person, or height of stature; and he so far surpassed his compeers in personal strength as to be a terror to them. He was, however, even more conspicuous for the excellence of his mental qualities than for his superior personal endowments; being gifted in the first place with a sound and temperate judgment, and having also reaped the advantages of a liberal education. He was also distinguished in no ordinary degree both by natural intelligence and divinely imparted wisdom.

CHAPTER XX

CONSTANTINE RETURNS TO HIS FATHER, IN CONSEQUENCE OF THE TREACHEROUS INTENTIONS OF DIOCLETIAN

A YOUTH thus proudly conspicuous soon attracted the notice of the emperors then in power, who observed his manly and vigorous figure and superior mind with feelings of jealousy and fear, and thenceforward carefully watched for an opportunity of inflicting some brand of disgrace on his character. But he, being aware of their designs (the details of which, through the providence of God, were more than once laid open to his view), sought safety in flight; and in this respect his conduct still affords a parallel to that of the great prophet Moses. Indeed, in every sense God was his helper; and He had before ordained that he should be present in readiness to succeed his father.

CHAPTER XXI

DEATH OF CONSTANTIUS, WHO LEAVES HIS SON CONSTANTINE EMPEROR

IMMEDIATELY therefore on his escape from the plots which had been thus insidiously laid for him, he made his way with all haste to his father, and arrived at length at the very time that he was lying at the point of death. As soon as Constantius saw his son thus unexpectedly in his presence, he leaped from his couch, embraced him tenderly, and, declaring that the only anxiety which had troubled him in the prospect of death, namely that caused by the absence of his son, was now removed, he rendered thanks to God, and said that he now thought death better than the longest life. He next completed the arrangement of his private affairs, and took a final leave of the circle of sons and daughters by whom he was surrounded; and then, in his own palace, and on the imperial couch, he committed the administration of the empire, according to the law of nature, to his eldest son, and breathed his last.

CHAPTER XXII

AFTER THE BURIAL OF CONSTANTIUS, CONSTANTINE IS PROCLAIMED AUGUSTUS BY THE ARMY

NOR did the imperial throne remain long unoccupied: for Constantine invested himself with his father's purple, and proceeded from the palace, presenting to all a renewal, as it were, in his own person, of his father's life and reign. He then conducted the funeral procession in company with his father's friends, some preceding, others following the train, and performed the last offices for the pious deceased with an extraordinary degree of magnificence.

Meantime all united in honouring this thrice blessed prince with acclamations and praises, and while with one common feeling they regarded the rule of the son as the restoration of the departed parent to life, they hastened at once to hail their new sovereign by the titles of Imperial and Worshipful Augustus, with joyful shouts. Thus the memory of the deceased emperor received honour from the praises bestowed upon his son, while the latter was pronounced blessed in being the successor of such a father. All the nations also under his dominion were filled with inexpressible joy and gladness at not being even for a moment deprived of the benefits of imperial government.

In the instance of the emperor Constantius, God has made manifest to our generation what the end of those is who in their lives have honoured and loved Him.

CHAPTER XXIII

A BRIEF NOTICE OF THE DESTRUCTION OF THE TYRANTS

WITH respect to the other princes, who persecuted and wasted the churches of God, I have not thought it fit to give any distinct account of their downfall, nor to stain the memory of the good by mentioning them in connexion with those of an opposite character. The knowledge of the facts themselves will of itself suffice for the wholesome admonition of those who have witnessed or heard of the evils which severally befell them.

CHAPTER XXIV

IT WAS BY THE WILL OF GOD THAT CONSTANTINE BECAME POSSESSED OF THE EMPIRE

THUS then the God of all, the Supreme Governor of the world, by His own will appointed Constantine, the descendant of so renowned a parent, to be prince and sovereign: so that, while others have been raised to this distinction by the election of their fellow-men, he is the only one to whose elevation no mortal may boast of having contributed.

CHAPTER XXV

VICTORIES OF CONSTANTINE OVER THE BARBARIANS AND THE BRITONS

AS soon then as he was established on the throne, he began to care for the interests of his paternal inheritance, and visited with much considerate kindness all those provinces which had previously been under his father's government. Some tribes of the barbarians who dwelt on the banks of the Rhine, and the shores of the Western ocean, having ventured to revolt, he reduced them all to obedience, and brought them from their savage state to one of gentleness and submission. He contented himself with checking the inroads of others, and drove from his dominions, like untamed and savage beasts, those whom he perceived to be altogether incapable of the settled order of civilized life. Having disposed of these affairs to his satisfaction, he directed his attention to other quarters of the world, and first passed over to the British nations, which lie in the very bosom of the ocean. These he reduced to submission, and then proceeded to consider the state of the remaining portions of the empire, that he might be ready to tender his aid wherever circumstances might require it.

CHAPTER XXVI

HE RESOLVES TO DELIVER ROME FROM THE TYRANNY OF MAXENTIUS

WHILE therefore he regarded the entire world as one immense body, and perceived that the head of it all, the royal city of the Roman empire, was bowed down by the weight of a tyrannous oppression; at first he had left the task of liberation to those who governed the other divisions of the empire, as being his superiors in point of age. But when none of these proved able to afford relief, and those who had attempted it had experienced a disastrous termination of their enterprise, he said that life was without enjoyment to him as long as he saw the imperial city thus afflicted, and prepared himself for the effectual suppression of the tyranny.

CHAPTER XXVII

AFTER REFLECTING ON THE DOWNFALL OF THOSE WHO HAD WORSHIPPED IDOLS, HE MADE CHOICE OF CHRISTIANITY

BEING convinced, however, that he needed some more powerful aid than his military forces could afford him, on account of the wicked and magical enchantments which were so diligently practised by the tyrant, he began to seek for Divine assistance; deeming the possession of arms and a numerous soldiery of secondary importance, but trusting that the co-operation of a Deity would be his security against defeat or misfortune. He considered, therefore, on what God he might rely for protection and assistance. While engaged in this inquiry, the thought occurred to him, that, of the many emperors who had preceded him, those who had rested their hopes in a multitude of gods, and served them with sacrifices and offerings, had in the first place been deceived by flattering predictions, and oracles which promised them all prosperity, and at last had met with an unhappy end, while not one of their gods had stood by to warn them of the impending wrath of Heaven. On the other hand he recollected that his father, who had pursued an entirely opposite course, who had condemned their error, and honoured the one Supreme God during his whole life, had found Him to be the Saviour and Protector of his empire, and the Giver of every good thing. Reflecting on this, and well weighing the fact that they who had trusted in many gods had also fallen by manifold forms of death, without leaving behind them either family or offspring, stock, name, or memorial among men: and considering further that those who had already taken arms against the tyrant, and had marched to the battle field under the protection of a multitude of gods, had met with a dishonourable end (for one of them had shamefully retreated from the contest without a blow, and the other, being slain in the midst of his own troops, had become as it were the mere sport of death); reviewing, I say, all these considerations, he judged it to be folly indeed to join in the idle worship of those who were no gods, and, after such convincing evidence, to wander from the truth; and therefore felt it incumbent on him to honour no other than the God of his father.

CHAPTER XXVIII

HOW, WHILE HE WAS PRAYING, GOD SENT HIM A VISION OF A CROSS OF LIGHT IN THE HEAVENS AT MID-DAY, WITH AN INSCRIPTION ADMONISHING HIM TO CONQUER BY THAT

ACCORDINGLY he called on Him with earnest prayer and supplications that He would reveal to him who he was, and stretch forth His right hand to help him in his present difficulties. And while he was thus praying with fervent entreaty, a most marvellous sign appeared to him from heaven, the account of which it might have been difficult to receive with credit, had it been related by any other person. But since the victorious emperor himself long afterwards declared it to the writer of this history, when he was honoured with his acquaintance and society, and confirmed his statement by an oath, who could hesitate to accredit the relation, especially since the testimony of after-time has established its truth? He said that about mid-day, when the sun was beginning to decline, he saw with his own eyes the trophy of a cross of light in the heavens, above the sun, and bearing the inscription, CONQUER BY THIS. At this sight he himself was struck with amazement, and his whole army also, which happened to be following him on some expedition, and witnessed the miracle.

CHAPTER XXIX

HOW THE CHRIST OF GOD APPEARED TO HIM IN HIS SLEEP, AND COMMANDED HIM TO USE IN HIS WARS A STANDARD MADE IN THE FORM OF A CROSS

HE said, moreover, that he doubted within himself what the import of this apparition could be. And while he continued to ponder and reason on its meaning, night imperceptibly drew on; and in his sleep the Christ of God appeared to him with the same sign which he had seen in the heavens, and commanded him to procure a standard made in the likeness of that sign, and to use it as a safeguard in all engagements with his enemies.

CHAPTER XXX

THE MAKING OF THE STANDARD OF THE CROSS

AT dawn of day he arose, and communicated the secret to his friends: and then, calling together the workers in gold and precious stones, he sat in the midst of them, and described to them the figure of the sign he had seen, bidding them represent it in gold and precious stones. And this representation I myself have had an opportunity of seeing.

CHAPTER XXXI

A DESCRIPTION OF THE STANDARD OF THE CROSS, WHICH THE ROMANS NOW CALL THE LABARUM

NOW it was made in the following manner. A long spear, overlaid with gold, formed the figure of the cross by means of a piece transversely laid over it. On the top of the whole was fixed a crown, formed by the intertexture of gold and precious stones; and on this, two letters indicating the name of Christ, symbolized the Saviour's title by means of its first characters, the letter P being intersected by X exactly in its centre: and these letters the emperor was in the habit of wearing on his helmet at a later period. From the transverse piece which crossed the spear was suspended a kind of streamer of purple cloth, covered with a profuse embroidery of most brilliant precious stones; and which, being also richly interlaced with gold, presented an indescribable degree of beauty to the beholder. This banner was of a square form, and the upright staff, which in its full extent was of great length, bore a golden half-length portrait of the pious emperor and his children on its upper part, beneath the trophy of the cross, and immediately above the embroidered streamer.

The emperor constantly made use of this salutary sign as a safeguard against every adverse and hostile power, and commanded that others similar to it should be carried at the head of all his armies.

CHAPTER XXXII

CONSTANTINE RECEIVES INSTRUCTION, AND READS THE SACRED SCRIPTURES

THESE things were done shortly afterwards. But at the time above specified, being struck with amazement at the extraordinary vision, and resolving to worship no other God save Him who had appeared to him, he sent for those who were acquainted with the mysteries of His doctrines, and inquired who that God was, and what was intended by the sign of the vision he had seen.

They affirmed that He was God, the only begotten Son of the one and only God: that the sign which had appeared was the symbol of immortality, and the trophy of that victory over death which He had gained in time past when sojourning on earth. They taught him also the causes of His advent, and explained to him the true account of His incarnation. Thus he sought instruction in these matters, but was still impressed with wonder at the divine manifestation which had been presented to his sight. Comparing, therefore, the heavenly vision with the interpretation given, he found his judgment confirmed; and, in the persuasion that the knowledge of these things had been imparted to him by Divine teaching, he determined thenceforth to devote himself to the perusal of the Inspired writings.

Moreover, he made the priests of God his counsellors, and deemed it incumbent on him to honour the God who had appeared to him with all devotion. And after this, being fortified by well-grounded hopes in Him, he undertook to quench the fury of the fire of tyranny.

CHAPTER XXXIII

OF THE ADULTEROUS CONDUCT OF MAXENTIUS AT ROME

FOR he who had tyrannically possessed himself of the imperial city, had proceeded to great lengths in impiety and wickedness, so as to venture without hesitation on every vile and impure action.

For example: he would part lawfully-married women from their husbands, and after most grievously dishonouring them, send them back to their husbands; and these insults he offered not to men of mean or obscure condition, but to those who held the first places in the Roman senate. Moreover, though he shamefully dishonoured almost numberless free women, he was unable to satisfy his ungoverned and intemperate desires. But when he essayed to corrupt

Christian women also, he could no longer secure success to his designs, since they chose rather to expose their lives to death than yield their persons to be defiled by him.

CHAPTER XXXIV

HOW THE WIFE OF A PREFECT SLEW HERSELF TO PRESERVE HER CHASTITY

Now a certain woman, wife of one of the senators who held the authority of Prefect in the city, when she understood that those who ministered to the tyrant's lusts were standing before her house (she was a Christian), and knew that her husband through fear had bidden them take her and lead her away, begged a short space of time for arraying herself in her usual dress, and entered her chamber. There, being left alone, she sheathed a sword in her own breast, and immediately expired, leaving indeed her dead body to her conductors, but declaring to all mankind, both to present and future generations, by an act which spoke louder than any words, that the chastity for which Christians are famed is alone invincible and not to be destroyed. Such was the conduct displayed by this woman.

CHAPTER XXXV

MASSACRE OF THE ROMAN PEOPLE BY MAXENTIUS

ALL men, therefore, both people and magistrates, whether of high or low degree, trembled through fear of him whose daring wickedness was such as I have described, and were oppressed by his grievous tyranny. Nay, though they submitted quietly, and endured this bitter servitude, still there was no escape from the tyrant's sanguinary cruelty. For at one time, on some trifling pretence, he exposed the populace to be slaughtered by his own body-guard; and countless multitudes of the Roman people were slain in the very midst of the city by the lances and weapons, not of Scythians or barbarians, but of their own fellow-citizens. And besides this, it is impossible to calculate the number of senators whose blood was shed with a view to the seizure of their respective estates, since at different times and on various fictitious charges, multitudes of them suffered death.

CHAPTER XXXVI

MAGIC ARTS OF MAXENTIUS AGAINST CONSTANTINE: AND FAMINE AT ROME

BUT the crowning point of the tyrant's wickedness was his having recourse to sorcery: sometimes for magic purposes opening women with child, at other times searching into the bowels of new-born infants. He slew lions also, and practised certain horrid arts for evoking demons, and averting the approaching war, hoping by these means to make himself secure of victory. In short, it is impossible to describe the manifold acts of oppression by which this tyrant of Rome enslaved his subjects: so that by this time they were reduced to the most extreme penury and want of necessary food, a scarcity such as our contemporaries do not remember ever before to have existed at Rome.

CHAPTER XXXVII

DEFEAT OF MAXENTIUS'S ARMIES IN ITALY

CONSTANTINE, however, filled with compassion on account of all these miseries, began to arm himself with all warlike preparation against the tyranny. Assuming therefore the Supreme God as his patron, and invoking His Christ to be his preserver and aid, and setting the victorious trophy, the salutary symbol, in front of his soldiers and body-guard, he marched with his whole forces, eager to reinstate the Romans in the freedom they had inherited from their ancestors.

And whereas, Maxentius, trusting more in his magic arts than in the affection of his subjects, dared not even advance outside the city gates, but had guarded every place and district and city subject to his tyranny, with large bodies of soldiers and numberless ambuscades; the emperor, confiding in the help of God, advanced against the first and second and third divisions of the tyrant's forces, defeated them all with ease at the first assault, and made his way into the very interior of Italy.

CHAPTER XXXVIII

DEATH OF MAXENTIUS ON THE BRIDGE OF THE TIBER

AND already he was approaching very near Rome itself, when, to save him from the necessity of fighting with all the Romans for the tyrant's sake, God Himself drew the tyrant, as it were by secret cords, a long way outside the gates.

And now those miracles recorded in Holy Writ, which God of old wrought against the ungodly (discredited by most as fables, yet believed by the faithful), did He in very deed confirm to all alike, believers and unbelievers, who were eye-witnesses of the wonders I am about to relate. For as once in the days of Moses and the Hebrew nation, who were worshippers of God, He cast Pharaoh's chariots and his host into the waves, and drowned his chosen chariot-captains in the Red Sea,—so at this time did Maxentius, and the soldiers and guards with him, sink to the bottom as a stone, when, in his flight before the divinely-aided forces of Constantine, he essayed to cross the river which lay in his way, over which he had made a strong bridge of boats, and had framed an engine of destruction, really against himself, but in the hope of ensnaring thereby him who was beloved by God. For his God stood by the one to protect him, while the other, destitute of His aid, proved to be the miserable contriver of these secret devices to his own ruin. So that one might well say, "He made a pit, and digged it, and shall fall into the ditch which he made. His mischief shall return upon his own head, and his iniquity shall come down upon his own pate." Thus, in the present instance, under divine direction, the machine erected on the bridge, with the ambuscade concealed therein, giving way unexpectedly before the appointed time, the passage began to sink down, and the boats with the men in them went bodily to the bottom. And first the wretch himself, then his armed attendants and guards, even as the sacred oracles had before described, "sank as lead in the mighty waters." So that they who thus obtained victory from God might well, if not in the same words, yet in fact in the same spirit as the people of His great servant Moses, sing and speak as they did concerning the impious tyrant of old: "Let us sing unto the Lord, for He has been glorified exceedingly: the horse and his rider has He thrown into the sea. He is become my helper and my shield unto salvation." And again, "Who is like to Thee, O Lord, among the gods? who is like Thee, glorious in holiness, marvellous in praises, doing wonders?"

CHAPTER XXXIX

CONSTANTINE'S ENTRY INTO ROME

HAVING then at this time sung these and such-like praises to God, the Ruler of all and the Author of victory, after the example of His great servant Moses, Constantine entered the imperial city in triumph. And here the whole body of the senate, and others of rank and distinction in the city, freed as it were from the restraint of a prison, along with the whole Roman populace, their countenances expressive of the gladness of their hearts, received him with acclamations and excess of joy; men, women and children, with countless multitudes of servants, greeting him as deliverer, preserver, and benefactor, with incessant shouts. But he, being possessed of inward piety toward God, was neither rendered arrogant by these plaudits, nor uplifted by the praises he heard: but, being sensible that he had received help from God, he immediately rendered a thanksgiving to Him as the Author of his victory.

CHAPTER XL

OF THE STATUE OF CONSTANTINE HOLDING A CROSS, AND ITS INSCRIPTION

MOREOVER, by many writings and monumental inscriptions he made known to all men the salutary symbol, setting up this great trophy of victory over his enemies in the midst of the imperial city, and expressly causing it to be engraven in indelible characters, that the salutary sign was the preservative of the Roman government and of the entire empire. Accordingly, he immediately ordered a lofty spear in the figure of a cross to be placed beneath the hand of a statue representing himself, in the most frequented part of Rome, and the following inscription to be engraved on it in the Latin language:—BY VIRTUE OF THIS SALUTARY SIGN, WHICH IS THE TRUE SYMBOL OF VALOUR, I HAVE PRESERVED AND LIBERATED YOUR CITY FROM THE YOKE OF TYRANNY. I HAVE ALSO SET AT LIBERTY THE ROMAN SENATE AND PEOPLE, AND RESTORED THEM TO THEIR ANCIENT GREATNESS AND SPLENDOUR

CHAPTER XLI

REJOICINGS THROUGHOUT THE PROVINCES; AND CONSTANTINE'S ACTS OF GRACE

THUS the pious emperor, glorying in the confession of the victorious cross, proclaimed the Son of God to the Romans with great boldness of testimony. And all the inhabitants of the city with one consent, both senate and people, reviving as it were from the pressure of a bitter and tyrannical domination, seemed to enjoy the rays of a purer light, and to experience the renovating power of a fresh and new existence. All the nations too, as far as the limit of the western ocean, being set free from the calamities which had heretofore distressed them, and gladdened by joyous festivals, ceased not to praise him as the victorious, the pious, the common benefactor: all indeed, with one voice and one mouth, declared that Constantine had appeared through the special favour of God as a general blessing to mankind. The imperial edict also was every where published, whereby those who had been wrongfully deprived of their estates were permitted again to enjoy their own, while those who had unjustly suffered exile were recalled to their homes. Moreover, he freed from imprisonment, and from every kind of danger and fear, those who by reason of the tyrant's cruelty had been subject to these sufferings.

CHAPTER XLII

OF THE HONOURS CONFERRED UPON BISHOPS, AND THE BUILDING OF CHURCHES

THE emperor was also accustomed personally to invite the society of God's ministers, whom he distinguished with the highest possible respect and honour, treating them in every sense as persons consecrated to the service of his God. Accordingly, they were admitted to his table, though mean in their attire and outward appearance; yet not so in his estimation, since he judged not of their exterior as seen by the vulgar eye, but thought he discerned in them somewhat of the character of God Himself. He made them also his companions in travel, believing that He whose servants they were would thus be more favourably inclined to himself. Besides this, he gave from his own private resources costly benefactions to the Churches of God, both enlarging and heightening the sacred edifices, and embellishing the august sanctuaries of the Church with abundant offerings.

CHAPTER XLIII

CONSTANTINE'S LIBERALITY TO THE POOR

HE likewise distributed money largely to those who were in need. And not only so, but his kindness and beneficence extended even to the heathen who had no claim on him; and he provided not money only, or necessary food, but also decent clothing for the poor outcasts who begged alms in the forum. But in the case of those who had once been prosperous, and had experienced a reverse of circumstances, his aid was still more lavishly bestowed. On such persons, in a truly royal spirit, he conferred magnificent benefactions; giving grants of land to some, and honouring others with various offices of trust. To unfortunate orphans he sustained the relation of a careful father, while he relieved the forlorn condition of widows, and cherished them with special care. Nay, he even gave virgins, left unprotected by their parents' death, in marriage to wealthy men with whom he was personally acquainted. But this he did after first bestowing on the brides such portions as it was fitting they should bring to their future husbands. In short, as the sun, when he rises upon the earth, liberally imparts his rays of light to all, so did Constantine, proceeding at early dawn from the imperial palace, and rising as it were with the heavenly luminary, impart the rays of his own beneficence to all who approached his person. It was scarcely possible to be near him without receiving some benefit, nor did it ever happen that any who had expected to obtain his assistance were disappointed in their hope.

CHAPTER XLIV

HOW HE WAS PRESENT AT THE SYNODS OF BISHOPS

SUCH, then, was his general conduct towards all. But he exercised a peculiar care over the Church of God: and whereas, in the several provinces there were some who differed from each other in judgment, he assumed as it were the functions of a general bishop constituted by God, and convened synods of His ministers. Nor did he disdain to be present and sit with them in their assembly, but bore a share in their deliberations, endeavouring to minister to them all what pertained to the peace of God. He took his seat too in the midst of them, as an individual amongst many, dismissing his guards and soldiers, and all whose duty it was to defend his person; feeling himself sufficiently protected by the fear of God, and secure in the affection of his most faithful Christian friends. Those whom he saw inclined to a sound judgment, and exhibiting a calm and conciliatory temper, received his high approbation, for he evidently delighted in a general harmony of sentiment; while he regarded the refractory and obstinate with aversion.

CHAPTER XLV

HOW HE BORE WITH IRRATIONAL OPPONENTS

MOREOVER he endured with patience some who were exasperated against himself, directing them in mild and gentle terms to conduct themselves with temper, and not excite seditious tumults. And some of these respected his admonitions, and desisted; but as to those who proved incapable of sound judgment, he left them entirely at the disposal of God, and never himself resolved on severe measures against any one. Hence it naturally happened that the disaffected in Africa advanced so far in a course of licentiousness as even to venture on overt acts of audacity; some evil spirit, as it seems probable, being jealous of the present great prosperity, and impelling these men to atrocious deeds, that he might excite the emperor's anger against them. He gained nothing, however, by this malicious conduct; for the emperor treated these proceedings with contempt, and declared that he recognised their origin to be from the evil one; inasmuch as these were not the actions of sober persons, but of those who were either utterly devoid of reason, or else possessed by some evil spirit; and that such should be pitied rather than punished; since, though justice might check the fury of madmen, refined humanity had rather sympathise with their condition.

CHAPTER XLVI

VICTORIES OVER THE BARBARIANS

THUS the emperor in all his actions honoured God the Controller of all things, and exercised an unwearied oversight over His churches. And God requited him, by subduing all barbarous nations under his feet, so that he was able every where to raise trophies over his enemies: and He proclaimed his name as conqueror to all mankind, and made him a terror to his adversaries: not indeed that this was his natural character, since he was rather the meekest, and gentlest, and most benevolent of men.

CHAPTER XLVII

DEATH OF MAXIMIN, WHO HAD ATTEMPTED A CONSPIRACY, AND OF OTHERS WHOM CONSTANTINE DETECTED BY DIVINE REVELATION

WHILE he was thus engaged, the second of those who had resigned the throne being detected in a treasonable conspiracy, suffered a most ignominious death. He was the first whose pictures, statues, and all similar marks of honour and distinction were every where destroyed, on the ground of his crimes and impiety. After him others also of the same family were discovered in the act of framing secret machinations against the emperor; all their intentions being miraculously revealed by God through visions to His servant.

For He frequently vouchsafed to him manifestations of Himself, the Divine presence appearing to him in a most marvellous manner, and according to him manifold intimations of future events. Indeed it is impossible to describe in words the inexpressible wonders of divine grace which God was pleased to vouchsafe to His servant. Surrounded by these, he passed the residue of his life in security, rejoicing in the true affection of his subjects, rejoicing too because he saw all beneath his government leading contented and peaceful lives; but above all delighted at the flourishing condition of the churches of God.

CHAPTER XLVIII

CELEBRATION OF CONSTANTINE'S DECENNALIA

WHILE he was thus circumstanced, he completed the tenth year of his reign. On this occasion he ordered the celebration of general festivals, and offered thanksgivings to God the Supreme King, as pure sacrifices free from flame and smoke. And from this employment he derived much pleasure: not so from the tidings he received of the ravages committed in the Eastern provinces.

CHAPTER XLIX

IN WHAT MANNER LICINIUS OPPRESSED THE EAST

FOR he was informed that in that quarter a certain savage beast was besetting both the Church of God and the other inhabitants of the provinces, owing, as it were, to the efforts of the evil spirit to produce effects quite contrary to the deeds of the pious emperor: so that the Roman empire, divided into two parts, seemed to all men to resemble night and day; since darkness overspread the provinces of the East, while the brightest day illumined the inhabitants of the opposite portion. And whereas the latter were receiving manifold blessings at the hand of God, the sight of these blessings proved intolerable to that envy which hates all good, as well as to the tyrant who afflicted the other division of the empire; and who, notwithstanding that his government was prospering, and he had been honoured by affinity with so great an emperor as Constantine, yet cared not to follow the steps of that pious prince, but strove rather to imitate the evil purposes and practice of impious men; choosing to adopt their counsels, of whose ignominious end he had himself been an eyewitness, rather than to maintain amicable relations with him who was his superior.

CHAPTER L

LICINIUS ATTEMPTS A CONSPIRACY AGAINST CONSTANTINE

ACCORDINGLY he engaged in an irreconcileable war against his benefactor, altogether regardless of the laws of friendship, the obligation of oaths, the ties of kindred, and already existing treaties. For the most benignant emperor had given him a proof of sincere affection in bestowing on him the hand of his sister, thus granting him the privilege of a place in family relationship and his own ancient imperial descent, and investing him also with the rank and dignity of his colleague in the empire. But the other, in a spirit the very opposite to this, employed himself in machinations against his superior, and devised various means for ungratefully invading his benefactor's tranquillity. At first, under the specious mask of friendship, he conducted all his plots with art and treachery, expecting thus to succeed in concealing his designs; but God enabled His servant to detect the schemes thus darkly devised. Licinius, however, being discovered in his first attempts, had recourse to fresh frauds; at one time pretending friendship, at another claiming confidence on the ground of solemn treaties; then at once violating every engagement, and again beseeching pardon by embassies, yet after all foully falsifying his word: till at last he declared open war, and with desperate infatuation resolved thenceforward to carry arms against God Himself, whose worshipper he knew the emperor to be.

CHAPTER LI

TREACHEROUS ARTS OF LICINIUS AGAINST THE BISHOPS, AND HIS PROHIBITION OF SYNODS

AND at first he made secret inquiry respecting the ministers of God subject to his dominion (and who had never in any respect offended against his government), and with industrious malice sought occasions of accusation against them. And when he found himself at a loss to substantiate any charge, or find a real ground of objection against them, he next enacted a law, to the effect that the bishops should never on any account hold communication with each other, nor should any one of them be permitted to absent himself on a visit to a neighbouring church; nor, lastly, should the holding of synods, or councils for the consideration of affairs of common interest, be further sanctioned. Now this was clearly a pretext for displaying his malice against us. For we were compelled either to violate the law, and thus be amenable to punishment, or else, by compliance with its injunctions, to nullify the statutes of the Church: inasmuch as it is impossible to bring important questions to a satisfactory adjustment, except by means of synods. In other cases also this enemy of God, being determined to act in opposition to our pious prince, gave his directions accordingly. For whereas the one encouraged the social intercourse of the priests of God, desiring thus to honour Him whom they served, and with a view to peace and unity of judgment; the other, whose object it was to destroy every thing that was good, used all his endeavours to bring discord into the general harmony.

CHAPTER LII

BANISHMENT OF THE CHRISTIANS, WITH CONFISCATION AND SALE OF THEIR PROPERTY

AND whereas Constantine, the friend of God, had granted to His worshippers freedom of access to the imperial palaces; His enemy, in a spirit the very reverse of this, expelled thence all Christians subject to his authority. He banished those who had proved themselves his most faithful and devoted servants, and compelled others, on whom he had himself conferred honour and distinction as a reward for their former eminent services, to the performance of menial offices as slaves to others: and at length, being bent on seizing the property of all as his prey, he even threatened with death those who professed the Saviour's name. Moreover, being himself of a nature hopelessly debased by sensuality, and degraded by the continual practice of adultery and other shameless vices, he assumed his own worthless character as a specimen of human nature generally, and denied that the virtue of chastity and continence existed among men.

CHAPTER LIII

LICINIUS'S EDICT THAT WOMEN AND MEN SHOULD NOT BE PERMITTED TO FREQUENT THE CHURCHES IN COMPANY

ACCORDINGLY he passed a second law, which enjoined that men should not appear in company with women in the houses of prayer, and forbade women to attend the sacred schools of virtue, or to receive instruction from the bishops, directing the appointment of women to be teachers of their own sex. These regulations being received with general ridicule, he devised other means for effecting the ruin of the churches. He ordered that the usual congregations of the people should be held in the open country outside the gates; alleging that the open air without the city was far more suitable for a multitude than the houses of prayer within the walls.

CHAPTER LIV

HE DISMISSES THOSE WHO REFUSE TO SACRIFICE FROM MILITARY SERVICE, AND FORBIDS THE SUPPLY OF NECESSARY FOOD TO THOSE IN PRISON

FAILING, however, to obtain obedience in this respect also, at length he threw off the mask, and gave orders that those who held military commissions in the several cities of the empire should be deprived of their respective commands, in case of their refusal to offer sacrifices to the demons. Accordingly the forces of the authorities in every province suffered the loss of those who worshipped God: and he too who had decreed this order suffered loss, in that he thus deprived himself of the prayers of pious men. And why should I still further mention how he directed that no one should obey the dictates of common humanity by distributing food to those who were pining in prisons, or should even pity the captives who perished with hunger: in short, that no one should perform a virtuous action, and that those whose natural feelings impelled them to sympathise with their fellow-creatures, should be prohibited from doing them a single kindness? Truly this was the most utterly shameless and scandalous of all laws, and one which surpassed the worst depravity of human nature: a law which inflicted on those who shewed mercy the same penalties as on those who were the objects of their compassion, and visited the exercise of mere humanity with the severest punishments.

CHAPTER LV

THE LAWLESS CONDUCT AND COVETOUSNESS OF LICINIUS

SUCH were the ordinances of Licinius. But why should I enumerate his innovations respecting marriage, or those which had in view the property of the dying, whereby he presumed to abrogate the ancient and wisely established laws of the Romans, and to introduce certain barbarous and cruel institutions in their stead, inventing a thousand pretences for oppressing his subjects? Hence it was that he devised a new method of measuring land, by which he reckoned the smallest portion at more than its actual dimensions, from an insatiable desire of unjust exaction. Hence too he registered the names of country residents who were now no more, and had long been numbered with the dead, procuring to himself by this expedient a sordid and unlawful gain. For his meanness was as unlimited as his rapacity was insatiable. So that when he had filled all his treasuries with gold, and silver, and boundless wealth, he bitterly bewailed his poverty, and suffered as it were the torments of Tantalus. But why should I mention how many innocent persons he punished with exile; how much property he confiscated; how many men of noble birth and unblemished character he imprisoned, whose wives he handed over to be basely insulted by his profligate slaves; in short, to how many married women and virgins he himself offered violence, though already feeling the infirmities of age? I need not enlarge on these subjects, since the enormity of his last actions causes the former to appear trifling and of little moment.

CHAPTER LVI

AT LENGTH HE UNDERTAKES TO RAISE A PERSECUTION AGAINST THE CHRISTIANS

FOR the final efforts of his fury appeared in his open hostility to the churches. And he directed his attacks against the bishops themselves, whom he regarded as his worst adversaries, bearing special enmity to a class of men whom the great and pious emperor treated as his friends. Accordingly he spent on us the utmost of his fury, and, being transported beyond the bounds of reason, he paused not to reflect on the example of those who had persecuted the Christians before him, nor of those whom he himself had been raised up to punish and destroy for their impious deeds: nor did he heed the facts of which he had been himself a witness, though he had seen with his own eyes the chief originator of these our calamities (whoever he was), smitten by the stroke of Divine vengeance.

CHAPTER LVII

MAXIMIAN, BROUGHT LOW BY A FISTULOUS ULCER WITH WORMS, ISSUES AN EDICT IN FAVOUR OF THE CHRISTIANS

FOR whereas this man had commenced the attack on the churches, and had been the first to pollute his soul with the blood of just and godly men, a judgment from God overtook him, which at first affected his body, but eventually extended itself to his soul. For suddenly an abscess appeared in the secret parts of his person, followed by a deeply seated fistulous ulcer; and these diseases fastened with incurable virulence on the intestines, which swarmed with a vast multitude of worms, and emitted a pestilential odour. Besides, his entire person had become loaded, through gluttonous excess, with an enormous quantity of fat, and this, being now in a putrescent state, is said to have presented to all who approached him an intolerable and dreadful spectacle. Having, therefore, to struggle against such sufferings, at length, though late, he became conscience-stricken on account of his past crimes against the Church; and, confessing his sins before God, he put a stop to the persecution of the Christians, and hastened to issue imperial edicts and rescripts for the rebuilding of their churches, at the same time enjoining them to perform their customary worship, and to offer up prayers on his behalf.

CHAPTER LVIII

HOW MAXIMIN, WHO HAD PERSECUTED THE CHRISTIANS, WAS COMPELLED TO FLY, AND CONCEAL HIMSELF IN THE DISGUISE OF A SLAVE

SUCH was the punishment which he underwent who had commenced the persecution. Licinius, however, of whom we were just now speaking, who had been a witness of these things, and known them by his own actual experience, banished the remembrance of them altogether from his mind, and reflected neither on the punishment of the first, nor the divine judgment which had been executed on the second persecutor. The latter had indeed endeavoured to outstrip his predecessor in the career of crime, and prided himself on the invention of new tortures for us. Not content with tormenting his victims by fire and sword, piercing them with nails, or destroying them by the fangs of wild beasts or in the depths of the sea; in addition to all these, he discovered a new and strange mode of punishment, and issued an edict directing that they should be partially bereft of sight. So that numbers, not of men only, but of women and children, after being deprived of the sight of their eyes, and the use of the joints of their feet, by mutilation or cautery, were consigned in this condition to the painful labour of the mines. Hence it was that this tyrant also was overtaken not long after by the righteous judgment of God, at a time when, confiding in the aid of the demons whom he worshipped as his gods, and relying on the countless multitudes of his troops, he had ventured to engage in battle. For, feeling himself on that occasion destitute of all hope in God, he threw from him the imperial dress which so ill became him, hid himself with unmanly timidity in the crowd around him, and sought safety in flight.

He afterwards lurked about the fields and villages in the habit of a slave, hoping he should thus be effectually concealed. He had not, however, eluded the mighty and all-searching gaze of God: for even while he was expecting to pass the residue of his days in security, he fell prostrate, smitten by God's fiery dart, and his whole body withered by the stroke of Divine vengeance; so that all trace of the original lineaments of his person was lost, and nothing remained to him but dry and parched bones, presenting the appearance of a lifeless image.

CHAPTER LIX

MAXIMIN, BLINDED BY MEANS OF HIS DISEASE, ISSUES AN ORDINANCE IN FAVOUR OF THE CHRISTIANS

AND still the stroke of God continued heavy upon him, so that his eyes protruded and fell from their sockets, leaving him quite blind: and thus he suffered, by a most righteous retribution, the very same punishment which he had been the first to devise for the martyrs of God. At length, however (for he survived even these sufferings), he too implored pardon of the God of the Christians, and confessed his impious opposition of the will of heaven: he too recanted, as the former persecutor had done; and by laws and ordinances explicitly acknowledged his error in worshipping those whom he had accounted gods, declaring that he now knew, by positive experience, that the God of the Christians was the only true God. These were facts which Licinius had not merely received on the testimony of others, but of which he had himself had personal knowledge: and yet, as though his understanding had been obscured by some dark cloud of error, he resolved to persist in the same evil course.

BOOK II

CHAPTER I

SECRET PERSECUTION BY LICINIUS, WHO CAUSES SOME BISHOPS TO BE PUT TO DEATH AT AMASIA OF PONTUS

IN this manner, he of whom we have spoken, continued to rush headlong towards that destruction which awaits the enemies of God; and once more, with a fatal emulation of their example whose ruin he had himself witnessed as the consequence of their impious conduct, he re-kindled the persecution of the Christians, like a long extinguished fire, and fanned the unhallowed flame to a fiercer height than any who had gone before him.

At first, indeed, though breathing fury and threatenings against God, like some savage beast of prey, or some closely coiled and crafty serpent, he dared not, from fear of Constantine, openly level his attacks against the Churches of God subject to his dominion; but dissembled the virulence of his malice, and endeavoured by secret measures, limited in the sphere of their operation, to compass the death of the bishops, the most eminent of whom he found means to remove, through charges laid against them by the governors of the several provinces. And the manner in which they suffered had in it something strange, and hitherto unheard of. At all events, the barbarities perpetrated at Amasia of Pontus, surpassed every known excess of cruelty.

CHAPTER II

DEMOLITION OF CHURCHES, AND CRUEL BUTCHERY OF THE BISHOPS

FOR in that city some of the churches were levelled with the ground (for the second time since the commencement of the persecutions), and others were closed by the governors of the several districts, in order to prevent any who frequented them from assembling together, or rendering clue worship to God. For he by whose orders these outrages were committed was too conscious of his own crimes to expect that these services were performed with any view to his benefit, and was convinced that all we did, and all our endeavours to obtain the favour of God, were on Constantine's behalf. These servile governors then, feeling assured that such a course would be pleasing to the impious tyrant, subjected the most distinguished prelates of the churches to capital punishment. Accordingly, men who had been guilty of no crime were led away, without any reason assigned, to undergo the penalties due to murderers: and some suffered a new kind of death, having their bodies cut piecemeal into many portions; and, after this horribly cruel and more than tragic punishment, being cast, as a prey to fishes, into the depths of the sea. The result of these horrors was once more (as on a former occasion), the flight of pious men, and again the fields and deserts afforded a refuge to the worshippers of God. But further, the tyrant having thus far succeeded in his object, began to consider how he might raise a general persecution of the Christians: and he would have gratified his wishes, nor could any thing have hindered him from carrying his resolution into effect, had not He who defends His own anticipated the coming evil, and by His special guidance conducted His servant Constantinc to this part of the empire, causing him to shine forth as a brilliant light in the midst of the dark and gloomy shades of night.

CHAPTER III

HOW CONSTANTINE WAS MOVED WITH PITY ON BEHALF OF THE CHRISTIANS THUS IN DANGER OF PERSECUTION

HE was not long in perceiving the intolerable nature of the evils of which he had heard; and, forming at once a stedfast resolution, he tempered the natural clemency of his character with a certain measure of severity and sternness, and hastened to succour those who were thus grievously oppressed. For he judged that it would rightly be deemed a pious and holy task to secure, by the removal of an individual, the safety of the greater part of the human race. He judged too, that if he listened to the dictates of clemency only, and bestowed his pity on one utterly unworthy of it, this would, on the one hand, confer no real benefit on a man whom nothing would induce to abandon his evil practices, and whose fury against his subjects would only be likely to increase; while, on the other hand, those who suffered from his oppression would thus be for ever deprived of all hope of deliverance.

Influenced by these reflections, the emperor resolved without further delay to extend a protecting hand to those who had fallen into such an extremity of distress. He accordingly made the usual warlike preparations, and assembled his whole forces, both of horse and foot. But before them all was carried the standard which I have before described, as the symbol of his full confidence in God.

CHAPTER IV

CONSTANTINE PREPARES HIMSELF FOR THE WAR BY PRAYER: LICINIUS BY THE PRACTICE OF DIVINATION

HE took with him also the priests of God, feeling well assured that now, if ever, he stood in need of the efficacy of prayer, and thinking it right that they should constantly be near and about his person, as most trusty guardians of the soul.

Now, as soon as the tyrant understood that Constantine's victories over his enemies were secured to him by no other means than the co-operation of God, and that the persons above alluded to were continually with him and about his person; and besides this, that the symbol of the salutary passion preceded both the emperor himself and his whole army; he regarded these precautions with ridicule (as might be expected), at the same time mocking and reviling the emperor with opprobrious terms.

On the other hand, he gathered round himself Egyptian diviners and soothsayers, with sorcerers and enchanters, and the priests of those whom he imagined to be gods. He then, after offering the sacrifices which he thought the occasion demanded, inquired how far he might reckon on a successful termination of the war. They replied with one voice, that he would unquestionably be victorious and triumphant in the war: and the oracles every where held out to him the same prospect in copious and elegant verses. The soothsayers certified him of favourable omens from the flight of birds; the priests declared the same to be indicated by the motion of the entrails of their victims. Elevated, therefore, by these fallacious assurances, he boldly advanced at the head of his army, and prepared for battle.

CHAPTER V

LICINIUS, WHILE SACRIFICING IN A GROVE, UTTERS HIS SENTIMENTS CONCERNING IDOLS, AND CONCERNING CHRIST

AND when he was now ready to engage, he desired the most approved of his body-guard and his most valued friends, to meet him in one of the places which they consider sacred. It was a well watered and shady grove, and in it were several marble statues of those whom he accounted to be gods. After lighting tapers and performing the usual sacrifices in honour of these, he is said to have delivered the following speech:—

"Friends and fellow-soldiers! These are our country's gods, and these we honour with a worship derived from our remotest ancestors. But he who leads the army now opposed to us has proved false to the religion of his forefathers, and adopted the sentiments of those who deny the existence of the gods. And yet he is so infatuated as to honour some strange and unheard-of Deity, with whose despicable standard he now disgraces his army, and confiding in whose aid he has taken up arms, and is now advancing, not so much against us as against those very gods whom he has despised. However, the present occasion shall prove which of us is mistaken in his judgment, and shall decide between our gods and those whom our adversaries profess to honour. For either it will declare the victory to be ours, and so most justly evince that our gods are the true saviours and assistants; or else, if this God of Constantine's, who comes we know not whence, shall prove superior to our many deities (for at least ours have the advantage in point of numbers), let no one henceforth doubt which god he ought to worship, but attach himself at once to the superior power, and ascribe to him the honours of the victory. Suppose then this strange God, whom we now regard with contempt, should really prove victorious; then indeed we must acknowledge and give him honour, and so bid a long farewell to those for whom we light our tapers in vain. But if our own gods triumph (and of this there can be no real doubt), then, as soon as we have secured the present victory, let us prosecute the war without delay against these despisers of the gods."

Such were the words he addressed to those then present, as reported not long after to the writer of this history by some who heard them spoken. And as soon as he had concluded his speech, he gave orders to his forces to commence the attack.

CHAPTER VI

AN APPARITION SEEN IN THE CITIES SUBJECT TO LICINIUS, AS OF CONSTANTINE'S VICTORIOUS TROOPS PASSING THROUGH THEM

ABOUT this time a supernatural appearance is said to have been observed in the cities subject to the tyrant's rule. Different detachments of Constantine's army seemed to present themselves to the view, marching at noonday through these cities, as though they had obtained the victory. In reality, not a single soldier was any where present at the time, and yet this appearance was seen through the agency of a divine and superior power: and it was a vision which foreshadowed what was shortly coming to pass. For as soon as the armies were ready to engage, he who had broken through the ties of friendly alliance was the first to commence the battle; on which Constantine, calling on the name of "God the Supreme Saviour," and giving this as the watchword to his soldiers, overcame him in this first conflict: and not long after in a second battle he gained a still more important and decisive victory; for on this occasion the salutary trophy preceded the ranks of his army.

CHAPTER VII

VICTORY EVERY WHERE FOLLOWS THE PRESENCE OF THE STANDARD OF THE CROSS IN BATTLE

INDEED, wherever this appeared, the enemy soon fled before his victorious troops. And the emperor perceiving this, whenever he saw any part of his forces hard pressed, gave orders that the salutary trophy should be moved in that direction, like some triumphant and effectual remedy against disasters: the combatants were divinely inspired, as it were, with fresh strength and courage, and immediate victory was the result.

CHAPTER VIII

FIFTY MEN ARE SELECTED TO CARRY THE CROSS

ACCORDINGLY, he selected those of his body-guard who were most distinguished for personal strength, valour, and piety, and intrusted them with the sole care and defence of the standard. They were in number not less than fifty; and their only duty was to surround and vigilantly defend the standard, which they carried each in turn on their shoulders. These circumstances were related to the writer of this narrative by the emperor himself in his leisure moments, long after the occurrence of the events: and he added another incident well worthy of being recorded.

CHAPTER IX

ONE OF THE CROSS-BEARERS, WHO FLED FROM HIS POST, IS SLAIN; WHILE ANOTHER, WHO FAITHFULLY STOOD HIS GROUND, IS PRESERVED

FOR he said that once, during the very heat of an engagement, a sudden tumult and panic attacked his army, which threw the soldier who then bore the standard into an agony of fear, so that he handed it over to another, in order to secure his own escape from the battle. As soon, however, as his comrade had received it, and he had withdrawn, and resigned all charge of the standard, he was struck in the belly by a dart, and lost his life. Thus he paid the penalty of his cowardice and unfaithfulness, and lay dead on the spot: but the other who had taken his place as the bearer of the salutary standard, found it to be the safeguard of his life. For though he was assailed by a continual shower of darts, the bearer remained unhurt, the staff of the standard receiving every weapon. It was indeed a truly marvellous circumstance, that the enemies' darts all fell within and remained in the slender circumference of this spear, and thus saved the standard-bearer from death; so that none of those engaged in this service ever received a wound.

This story is none of mine, but for this too I am indebted to the emperor's own authority, who related it in my hearing along with other matters. And now, having thus through the power of God secured these first victories, he put his forces in motion and continued his onward march.

CHAPTER X

VARIOUS BATTLES, AND CONSTANTINE'S VICTORIES

THE van, however, of the enemy, unable to resist the emperor's first assault, threw down their arms, and prostrated themselves at his feet. All these experienced his clemency, and he joyfully embraced the opportunity of sparing human life. But there were others who still continued in arms, and prepared to hazard the event of a battle. Against these the emperor, after vainly endeavouring to conciliate them by friendly overtures, ordered his army to commence the attack. On this they immediately turned and betook themselves to flight; and some were overtaken and slain according to the laws of war, while others fell on each other in the confusion of their flight, and perished by the swords of their comrades.

CHAPTER XI

FLIGHT, AND MAGIC ARTS OF LICINIUS

IN these circumstances their commander, finding himself bereft of the aid of his followers, having lost his lately numerous array, both of regular and allied forces, having proved too, by experience, how vain his confidence had been in false gods, was fain to submit to the disgrace of an ignominious flight, by which he effected his escape, and secured his personal safety. For the pious emperor had forbidden his soldiers to follow him too closely, and thus allowed him an opportunity for escape. And this he did in the hope that he might hereafter, on conviction of the desperate state of his affairs, be induced to abandon his insane and presumptuous ambition, and assume a more reasonable tone of temper and conduct. Such were the thoughts which Constantine's extreme humanity prompted, and such his willingness patiently to bear past injuries, and extend his forgiveness to one who so ill deserved it. Licinius, however, far from renouncing his evil practices, still added crime to crime, and ventured on more daring atrocities than ever. Nay, he once more attempted to raise his courage by tampering with the detestable arts of magic: so that it might well be said of him, as it was of the Egyptian tyrant of old, that God had hardened his heart.

CHAPTER XII

CONSTANTINE, AFTER PRAYING IN HIS TABERNACLE, OBTAINS THE VICTORY

IN this manner Licinius gave himself up to these impieties, and rushed blindly towards the gulf of destruction. But as soon as the emperor was aware that he must meet his enemies in a second battle, he applied himself with earnestness to the worship of his Saviour. He pitched the tabernacle of the cross outside and at a distance from his camp, and there passed his time in pure and holy seclusion, and in offering up prayers to God; following thus the example of His ancient prophet, of whom the sacred oracles testify, that he pitched the tabernacle without the camp. He was attended only by a few, of whose faith and piety, as well as affection to his person, he was well assured. And this custom he continued to observe whenever he meditated an engagement with the enemy. For he was deliberate in his measures, the better to insure safety, and desired in every thing to be directed by divine counsel. And since his prayers ascended with fervour and earnestness to God, he was always honoured with a manifestation of His presence. And then, as if moved by a divine impulse, he would rush from the tabernacle, and suddenly give orders to his army to move at once without delay, and on the instant to draw their swords. On this they would immediately commence the attack, with great and general slaughter, so as with incredible celerity to secure the victory, and raise trophies in token of the overthrow of their enemies.

CHAPTER XIII

HIS HUMANE TREATMENT OF PRISONERS

TO such exercises as these the emperor had long accustomed both himself and his army, whenever there was a prospect of an engagement; for his God was ever present to his thoughts, and he desired to do every thing according to His will. He had also a pious abhorrence of any wanton sacrifice of human life, which induced him to be anxious for the preservation not only of his own subjects, but even of his enemies. Accordingly he directed his victorious troops to spare the lives of their prisoners, admonishing them, as human beings, not to forget the claims of their common nature. And whenever he saw the passions of his soldiery excited beyond the limits of self-control, he repressed their fury by a largess of money, rewarding every man who saved the life of an enemy with a certain weight of gold. Constantine's own sagacity led him to discover this inducement to spare human life; and great numbers even of the barbarians were thus saved, and owed their lives to the emperor's gold.

CHAPTER XIV

A FURTHER MENTION OF HIS PRAYERS IN THE TABERNACLE

NOW these, and a thousand such acts as these, were familiarly and habitually practised by the emperor: but on the present occasion he retired (as his custom was before battle) to the privacy of his tabernacle, and there employed himself in earnest prayer to God. Meanwhile he strictly abstained from any thing like levity of spirit, or luxurious living, and disciplined himself by fasting and bodily mortification, imploring the favour of God by supplication and prayer, that he might obtain His concurrence and aid, and be ready to execute whatever He might be pleased to suggest to his thoughts. In short, he exercised an unceasing care and watchfulness over all alike, and interceded with God as much for the safety of his enemies as for that of his own subjects.

CHAPTER XV

PRETENDED FRIENDSHIP, AND IDOLATROUS PRACTICES OF LICINIUS

AND inasmuch as he who had lately fled before him now dissembled his real sentiments, and again petitioned for a renewal of friendship and alliance, the emperor thought fit, on certain conditions, to grant his request, in the hope that such a measure might be expedient, and generally advantageous to the community. Licinius, however, while he pretended a ready submission to the terms prescribed, and attested his sincerity by oaths, at this very time was secretly engaged in collecting a military force, and again meditated war and strife, inviting even the barbarians to join his standard. He began also to look about him for other gods, having been deceived by those in whom he had hitherto trusted: and, without bestowing a thought on what he had himself publicly spoken on the subject of false deities, or choosing to acknowledge that God who had fought on the side of Constantine, he made himself ridiculous by seeking for a multitude of new gods.

CHAPTER XVI

LICINIUS CHARGES HIS SOLDIERS NOT TO ATTACK THE STANDARD OF THE CROSS

HAVING by this time had full proof of the Divine and mysterious power which resided in the salutary trophy, by means of which Constantine's army had become habituated to victory, he admonished his soldiers never to direct their attack against this standard, nor even incautiously to allow their eyes to rest upon it; assuring them that it possessed a terrible power, and was especially hostile to him; so that they would do well carefully to avoid any collision with it. And now, having given these directions, he prepared for a decisive conflict with him whose humanity prompted him still to hesitate, and to postpone the fate which he foresaw awaited his adversary. The enemy, however, confident in the aid of a multitude of gods, advanced to the attack with a powerful array of military force, preceded by certain images of the dead, and lifeless statues, as their defence. On the other side, the emperor, secure in the armour of godliness, opposed to the numbers of the enemy the salutary and life-giving sign, as at once a terror to the foe, and a protection from every harm. And for a while he paused, and preserved at first the attitude of forbearance, from respect to the treaty of peace to which he had given his sanction, that he might not be the first to commence the contest.

CHAPTER XVII

CONSTANTINE'S VICTORY

BUT as soon as he perceived that his adversaries persisted in their resolution, and were already drawing their swords, he gave free scope to his indignation, and by a single charge overthrew in a moment the entire body of the enemy, thus triumphing at once over them and the evil spirits whom they served.

CHAPTER XVIII

DEATH OF LICINIUS, AND CONSEQUENT TRIUMPH

HE then proceeded to deal with this adversary of God and his followers according to the laws of war, and consign them to the fate which their crimes deserved. Accordingly the tyrant himself, and they whose counsels had supported him in his impiety, were together subjected to the just punishment of death. After this, those who had so lately been deceived by their vain confidence in false deities, acknowledged with unfeigned sincerity the God of Constantine, and openly professed their belief in Him as the true and only God.

CHAPTER XIX

GENERAL REJOICINGS

AND now, the impious being thus removed, the sun once more shone brightly after the gloomy cloud of tyrannic power. Each separate portion of the Roman dominion became blended with the rest; the Eastern nations united with those of the West, and the whole body of the Roman empire was graced as it were by its head in the person of a single and supreme ruler, whose authority pervaded the whole. Now too the bright rays of the light of godliness gladdened the days of those who had heretofore been sitting in darkness and the shadow of death.

Past sorrows were no more remembered, for all united in celebrating the praises of the victorious prince, and avowed their recognition of his preserver as the only true God. Thus our emperor, whose character shone with all the graces of religion, with the title of VICTOR (for he had himself adopted this name as a most fitting appellation to express the victory which God had granted him over all who hated or opposed him), assumed the dominion of the East, and thus singly governed the Roman empire, re-united, as in former times, under one head. Thus, as he was the first to proclaim to all the sole sovereignty of God, so he himself, as monarch of the Roman world, extended his authority over the whole human race. Every apprehension of those evils under the pressure of which all had suffered was now removed: men whose heads had drooped in sorrow now regarded each other with smiling countenances, and looks expressive of their inward joy. And first of all, with processions and hymns of praise they ascribed the supreme sovereignty to God, as in truth the King of kings; and then with continued acclamations rendered honour to the victorious emperor, and the Cæsars, his most discreet and pious sons. The former afflictions were forgotten, and all past impieties forgiven; while with the enjoyment of present happiness was mingled the expectation of still future blessings.

CHAPTER XX

CONSTANTINE'S ENACTMENTS IN FAVOUR OF THE CONFESSORS

MOREOVER, the emperor's humane and benignant edicts were published among us also, as they had been among the inhabitants of the western division of the empire; and his laws, which breathed a spirit of piety toward God, gave promise of manifold blessings, since they secured many advantages to his provincial subjects in every nation, and at the same time prescribed measures suited to the exigencies of the churches of God. For first of all they recalled those who, in consequence of their refusal to join in idol worship, had been driven to exile, or ejected from their homes by the governors of their respective provinces. In the next place, they relieved from their burdens those who for the same reason had been adjudged to serve in the civil courts, and ordained restitution to be made to any who had been deprived of property. They too, who in the time of trial had signalised themselves by fortitude of soul in the cause of God, and had therefore been condemned to the dreadful labour of the mines, or consigned to the solitude of islands, or compelled to toil in the public works, all received an absolute release from these burdens; while others, whose religious constancy had cost them the forfeiture of their military rank, were vindicated by the emperor's generosity from this dishonour: for he granted them the alternative either of resuming their rank, and enjoying their former privileges, or (in the event of their preferring a more settled life), of perpetual exemption from all service. Lastly, all who had been compelled by way of disgrace and insult to serve in the employments of women, obtained an equal emancipation with the rest.

CHAPTER XXI

HIS LAWS IN FAVOUR OF MARTYRS, AND RESPECTING THE PROPERTY OF THE CHURCHES

SUCH were the benefits secured by the emperor's written mandates to the persons of those who had thus suffered for the faith; and his laws made ample provision for their property also.

With regard to those holy martyrs of God who had laid down their lives in the confession of His name, he directed that their estates should be enjoyed by their nearest kindred; and, in default of any of these, that the right of inheritance should be vested in the churches. Further, whatever property had been consigned to other parties from the treasury, whether in the way of sale or gift, together with that retained in the treasury itself, the generous mandate of the emperor directed should be restored to the original owners. Such benefits did his bounty, thus widely diffused, confer on the Church of God.

CHAPTER XXII

HOW HE CHERISHED THE INTERESTS OF THE SEVERAL NATIONS OF HIS EMPIRE

BUT his munificence bestowed still further and more numerous favours on the heathen tribes and other nations of his empire. So that the inhabitants of our Eastern regions (who had heard of the privileges experienced in the opposite portion of the empire, and had blessed the fortunate recipients of them, and longed for the enjoyment of a similar lot for themselves), now with one consent proclaimed their own happiness, when they saw themselves in possession of all these blessings; and confessed that the appearance of such a monarch to the human race was indeed a marvellous event, and such as the world's history had never yet recorded. Such were the sentiments which animated their breasts.

CHAPTER XXIII

HOW HE DECLARED GOD TO BE THE AUTHOR OF HIS PROSPERITY: AND CONCERNING HIS WRITTEN LAWS

AND now that (through the powerful aid of God his Saviour), all nations owned their subjection to the emperor's authority, he openly proclaimed to all the name of Him to whose bounty he owed all his blessings, and declared that He, and not himself, was the author of his past victories. This declaration, written both in the Latin and Greek languages, he caused to be transmitted through every province of the empire. Now the excellence of his style of expression may be known from a perusal of his letters themselves, which were two in number; one addressed to the churches of God; the other to the heathen population in the several cities of the empire. The latter of these I think it well to insert here, as connected with my present subject, in order on the one hand that a copy of this document may be recorded as matter of history, and thus preserved to posterity, and on the other that it may serve to confirm the truth of my present narrative. It is taken from an authentic copy of the imperial statute in my own possession; and the signature in the emperor's own handwriting attaches as it were the impress of truth to the statement I have made.

CHAPTER XXIV

LAW OF CONSTANTINE RESPECTING PIETY TOWARDS GOD, AND THE CHRISTIAN RELIGION

"VICTOR CONSTANTINUS, MAXIMUS AUGUSTUS, to the inhabitants of the province of Palestine.

"To all who entertain just and wise sentiments respecting the character of the Supreme Being, it has long been most clearly evident, and beyond the possibility of doubt, how vast a difference there has ever been between those who maintain a careful observance of the hallowed duties of the Christian religion, and those who treat this religion with hostility or contempt. But at this present time, we may see by still more manifest proofs, and still more decisive instances, both how unreasonable it were to question this truth, and how mighty is the power of the Supreme God: since it appears that they who faithfully observe His holy laws, and shrink from the transgression of His commandments, are rewarded with abundant blessings, and are endued with well-grounded hope as well as ample power for the accomplishment of their undertakings. On the other hand, they who have cherished impious sentiments have experienced results corresponding to their evil choice. For how is it to be expected that any blessing would be obtained by one who neither desired to acknowledge nor duly to worship that God who is the source of all blessing? Indeed, facts themselves are a confirmation of what I say.

CHAPTER XXV

AN ILLUSTRATION OF THESE TRUTHS FROM ANCIENT TIMES

"BUT besides this, whoever will mentally retrace the course of events from the earliest period down to the present time, and allow himself to reflect on what has occurred in past ages, will find that all who have made justice and probity the basis of their conduct, have not only carried their undertakings to a successful issue, but have gathered as it were a store of sweet fruit as the produce of this pleasant root. Again, whoever observes the career of those who have been bold in the practice of oppression or injustice; who have either directed their senseless fury against God Himself, or have conceived no kindly feelings towards their fellow-men, but have dared to afflict them with exile, disgrace, confiscation, massacre, or other miseries of the like kind (and all this without any sense of compunction, or wish to direct their thoughts to a better course), will find that such men have received a recompense proportioned to their crimes. And these are results which might naturally and reasonably be expected to ensue.

CHAPTER XXVI

OF THOSE WHO SUFFERED, AND THOSE WHO RAISED PERSECUTION

"FOR whoever have addressed themselves with integrity of purpose to any course of action, keeping the fear of God continually before their thoughts, and holding fast an unwavering faith in Him, without allowing present fears or dangers to outweigh their hope of future blessings—such persons, though for a season they may have experienced painful trials, have borne their afflictions lightly, being supported by the belief of greater rewards in store for them; and their character has acquired a brighter lustre in proportion to the severity of their past sufferings. With regard, on the other hand, to those who have either foully slighted the principles of justice, or refused to acknowledge the Supreme God themselves, and yet have dared to subject others who have faithfully maintained His worship to the most cruel insults and punishments; who have failed equally to recognise their own vileness in oppressing others on such grounds, and the happiness and blessing of those who preserved their devotion to God even in the midst of such sufferings: with regard, I say, to such men, many a time have their armies been slaughtered, many a time have they been put to flight; and their warlike preparations have ended in total ruin and defeat.

CHAPTER XXVII

HOW THE PERSECUTION BECAME THE OCCASION OF CALAMITY TO THE AGGRESSORS

"FROM the causes I have described, grievous wars arose, and destructive devastations. Hence followed a scarcity of the common necessaries of life, and a crowd of consequent miseries: hence, too, the authors of these impieties have either terminated the extremity of suffering by a disastrous death, or have dragged out an ignominious existence, and confessed it to be worse than death itself, thus receiving as it were a measure of punishment proportioned to the heinousness of their crimes. For each experienced a degree of calamity according to the blind fury with which he had been led to combat, and (as he thought) defeat the Divine will: so that they not only felt the pressure of the ills which could reach them in this present life, but were tormented also by a most lively apprehension of punishment in a future world.

CHAPTER XXVIII

THAT GOD CHOSE CONSTANTINE TO BE THE MINISTER OF BLESSING

"AND now, with such a mass of impiety pervading the human race, and the commonwealth in danger of being utterly destroyed, as if by the agency of some pestilential disease, and therefore needing powerful and effectual aid; what was the relief, and what the remedy which God devised for these evils? (I need not say that we are to understand Him who is alone and truly God, the possessor of almighty and eternal power: and surely it cannot be deemed arrogance in one who has received benefits from God, to acknowledge them in the loftiest terms of praise). I myself, then, was the instrument whose services He chose, and esteemed suited for the accomplishment of His will. Accordingly, beginning at the remote Britannic ocean, and the regions where the sun sinks beneath the horizon in obedience to the law of nature, through the aid of divine power I banished and utterly removed every form of evil which prevailed, in the hope that the human race, enlightened through my instrumentality, might be recalled to a due observance of the holy laws of God, and at the same time our most blessed faith might prosper under the guidance of His almighty hand.

CHAPTER XXIX

CONSTANTINE'S EXPRESSIONS OF PIETY TOWARDS GOD; AND PRAISE OF THE CONFESSORS

"I SAID, under the guidance of His hand; for I would desire never to be forgetful of the gratitude due to His grace. Believing, therefore, that this most excellent service had been confided to me as a special gift, I proceeded as far as the regions of the East, which, being under the pressure of severer calamities, seemed to demand still more effectual remedies at my hands. At the same time I am most certainly persuaded that I myself owe my life, my every breath, in short, my very inmost and secret thoughts, entirely to the favour of the Supreme God. Now I am well aware that they who are sincere in the pursuit of the heavenly hope, and have fixed this hope in heaven itself as the peculiar and predominant principle of their lives, have no need to depend on human friendship, but rather have enjoyed a higher degree of dignity in proportion as they have separated themselves from the vices and evils of this earthly existence. Nevertheless I deem it incumbent on me to remove at once and most completely from all such persons the hard necessities laid upon them for a season, and the cruel and unjust inflictions under which they have suffered, though free from any stain of guilt. For it would be strange indeed, that the fortitude and constancy of soul displayed by such men should be fully apparent during the reign of those whose first object it was to persecute them on account of their devotion to God, and yet that the glory of their character should receive no accession of lustre, and be viewed in no more exalted light, under the administration of a prince who is His servant.

CHAPTER XXX

A LAW GRANTING RELEASE FROM EXILE, RELIEF FROM SERVICE IN THE COURTS, AND FROM THE CONFISCATION OF PROPERTY

"LET all therefore who have exchanged their country for a foreign land, because they dared not abandon that reverence and faith toward God to which they had devoted themselves with their whole hearts, and have in consequence at different times been subject to the cruel sentence of the judge; together with any who have been enrolled in the registers of the public courts, though in time past exempt from such office; let these, I say, now render thanks to God the Liberator of all, in that they are restored to their hereditary property, and the tranquillity they once enjoyed. Let those also who have been despoiled of their goods, and have hitherto passed a wretched existence, mourning under the loss of all that they possessed, once more return to their former homes, their families, and estates, and receive with joy these proofs of the bountiful kindness of God.

CHAPTER XXXI

RELEASE LIKEWISE GRANTED TO EXILES IN THE ISLANDS

"FURTHERMORE, it is our command that all those who have been detained in the islands against their will should receive the benefit of this present provision; in order that they who till now have been surrounded by impassable mountains and the encircling barrier of the ocean, being now set free from that frightful and dreary solitude, may fulfil the fondest wishes of their hearts by revisiting their dearest friends. Those, too, who have prolonged a miserable life in the midst of abject and loathsome wretchedness, welcoming their restoration as an unlooked-for gain, and discarding henceforth all anxious thoughts, may pass their lives with us in freedom from all fear. For that any one could live in a state of fear under our government, whose glory it is to feel confident that we are the servant of God, would surely be a thing most absurd even to hear of, far more to believe as true; since the natural desire of our heart would be completely to rectify the errors of our predecessors in this respect.

CHAPTER XXXII

AND TO THOSE WHO HAD BEEN IGNOMINIOUSLY EMPLOYED IN THE MINES AND PUBLIC WORKS

"AGAIN, with regard to those who have been condemned either to the grievous labour of the mines, or to service in the public works, let them enjoy the sweets of leisure in place of these long continued toils, and henceforth lead a far easier life, and more accordant with the wishes of their hearts, exchanging the incessant hardships of their tasks for a pleasing and quiet rest. And if any have forfeited the common privilege of liberty, or have unhappily fallen under any mark of infamy; let them hasten back every one to the country of his nativity, and resume with becoming joy their former positions in society, from which they have been as it were estranged by long absence in a foreign land.

CHAPTER XXXIII

CONCERNING THOSE CONFESSORS WHO HAD BEEN ENGAGED IN MILITARY SERVICE

"ONCE more, with respect to those who had previously been preferred to any military distinction, of which they were afterwards deprived, for the cruel and unjust reason that they chose rather to acknowledge their allegiance to God than to retain the rank they held; we leave them perfect liberty of choice, either to occupy their former stations, should they be content again to engage in military service, or to live in undisturbed tranquillity, with an honourable discharge from all duty. For it is fair and reasonable that men who have displayed such magnanimity and fortitude in meeting the perils to which they have been exposed, should be allowed the choice either of enjoying peaceful leisure, or resuming their former rank.

CHAPTER XXXIV

CONCERNING THE LIBERATION OF THOSE FREE PERSONS WHO HAD BEEN CONDEMNED TO LABOUR IN THE WOMEN'S APARTMENTS, OR TO ANY OTHER SERVITUDE

"LASTLY, if any have wrongfully been deprived of the privileges of noble lineage, and subjected to a judicial sentence which has consigned them to the women's apartments for weaving or spinning, there to undergo a cruel and miserable labour, or reduced them to servitude for the benefit of the public treasury, without any exemption on the ground of superior birth; let such persons, resuming the honours they had previously enjoyed, and their proper dignities, henceforward exult in the blessings of liberty, and lead a life of happiness and joy. Let the free man, too, whom the unjust and inhuman fury of his persecutors has made a slave, who has felt the sudden and mournful transition from liberty to bondage, and ofttimes bewailed his unwonted labours, return to his family once more a free man in virtue of this our ordinance, and seek those employments which befit a state of freedom: and let him dismiss from his remembrance those services which he found so oppressive, and which so ill became his condition.

CHAPTER XXXV

OF THE INHERITANCE OF THE PROPERTY OF MARTYRS AND CONFESSORS, ALSO OF THOSE WHO HAD SUFFERED BANISHMENT OR CONFISCATION

"NOR must we omit to notice those estates of which individuals have been deprived on various pretences. For if any of those who have engaged with dauntless resolution in the noble and divine conflict of martyrdom, have also been stripped of their fortunes; or if the same has been the lot of the confessors, who have won for themselves the hope of eternal treasures; or if the loss of property has befallen those who were driven from their native land because they could not yield that obedience to the will of their persecutors which involved a betrayal of their faith: lastly, if any who have escaped the sentence of death have yet been despoiled of their worldly goods; we ordain that the inheritances of all such persons be transferred to their nearest kindred. And whereas the laws expressly assign this right to those most nearly related, it will be easy to ascertain to whom these inheritances severally belong. And it is evidently reasonable that the succession in these cases should belong to those who would have stood in the place of nearest affinity, had the deceased experienced a natural death.

CHAPTER XXXVI

THE CHURCH IS DECLARED HEIR OF THOSE WHO LEAVE NO KINDRED; AND THEIR BEQUESTS ARE INALIENABLE

"BUT should there be no surviving relation to succeed in due course to the property of those above-mentioned, I mean the martyrs, or confessors, or those whom a similar devotion has driven from their native soil; in such cases we ordain that the church locally nearest in each instance shall succeed to the inheritance. And surely it will be no wrong to the departed that that church should be their heir, for whose sake they have endured every extremity of suffering. We think it necessary to add this also, that in case any of the above-mentioned persons have chosen to bequeath any part of their property in the way of free gift, possession of such property shall be assured (as is reasonable) to those who have thus received it.

CHAPTER XXXVII

THE OCCUPIERS OF LANDS WHICH HAD BELONGED TO CHRISTIANS, ALSO OF GARDENS OR HOUSES, ARE TO MAKE RESTITUTION, EXCEPT OF THE ACTUAL PRODUCE

"AND that there may be no apparent obscurity in this our ordinance, but every one may readily apprehend its requirements, let all men hereby know that if they are now maintaining themselves in possession of a piece of land, or a house, or garden, or any thing else which had appertained to those persons of whom we have before spoken, it will be good and advantageous for them to acknowledge the fact, and make restitution with the least possible delay. On the other hand, although it should appear that some individuals have reaped abundant profits from this unjust possession, we do not consider that justice absolutely demands the restitution of such profits.

CHAPTER XXXVIII

IN WHAT MANNER APPEALS SHOULD BE MADE ON BEHALF OF SUCH PERSONS

"THEY must, however, declare explicitly what amount of benefit they have thus derived, and from what sources, and intreat our pardon for this offence; in order that their past covetousness may in some measure be atoned for, and that the Supreme Being may accept this compensation as a token of contrition, and be pleased graciously to pardon the sin. But it is possible that those who have become masters of such property (if it be right or possible to allow them such a title), will assure us by way of apology for their conduct, that it was not in their power to abstain from this appropriation at a time when a spectacle of misery in all its forms every where met the view; when men were cruelly driven from their homes, slaughtered without mercy, thrust forth without remorse: when the proscription of innocent persons was a common thing; when the fury of persecution was insatiable, and property seized and openly exposed for sale. If any defend their conduct by such reasons as these, and still persist in their avaricious temper, they shall be made sensible that such a course will bring punishment on themselves, and the rather so, because this correction of evil is the very characteristic of our service to the Supreme God. So that it will henceforth be dangerous to retain what dire necessity may in time past have compelled men to take; especially because it is in any case incumbent on us to discourage covetous desires, both by persuasion, and by making examples of the guilty.

CHAPTER XXXIX

THE TREASURY MUST RESTORE LANDS, GARDENS, AND HOUSES TO THE CHURCHES

"NOR shall the treasury itself, should it claim a right to any of the things we have spoken of, be permitted to maintain that right; but, without venturing as it were to raise its voice against the holy churches, it shall justly relinquish in their favour what it has long unjustly retained. We ordain, therefore, that all things whatsoever which shall appear really to belong to the churches (whether the property consist of houses, or fields and gardens, or whatever the nature of it may be), shall be restored in their full value and integrity, and with undiminished right of possession.

CHAPTER XL

THE TOMBS OF MARTYRS, AND THE CEMETERIES, ARE TO BE RESTORED TO THE CHURCHES

"AGAIN, with respect to those places which are honoured in being the depositories of the remains of martyrs, and continue to be memorials of their glorious departure; how can we doubt that they rightly belong to the churches, or refrain from issuing our injunction to that effect? For surely there can be no better liberality, no labour more pleasing or profitable, than to be thus employed under the guidance of the Divine Spirit, in order that those rights which have been appropriated on false pretences by unjust and wicked men, may be restored, as justice demands, and once more secured to the holy churches.

CHAPTER XLI

THOSE WHO HAVE PURCHASED PROPERTY BELONGING TO THE CHURCH, OR RECEIVED IT AS A GIFT, ARE TO RESTORE IT

"AND since it would be wrong in a provision intended to include all cases, to pass over those who have either procured any such property by right of purchase from the treasury, or have retained it when conveyed to them in the form of a gift; let all who have thus rashly indulged their insatiable thirst of gain be assured that, although by daring to make such purchases they have done all in their power to alienate our clemency from themselves, they shall nevertheless not fail of obtaining it, so far as is possible and consistent with propriety in each case.

CHAPTER XLII

AN EARNEST EXHORTATION TO WORSHIP GOD

"AND now, since it appears by the clearest and most convincing evidence, that the miseries which erewhile oppressed the entire human race are now banished from every part of the world, partly by the power of Almighty God, and partly by means of the counsel and aid which He is pleased on many occasions to administer through our agency; it remains for all, both individually and unitedly, to observe and seriously consider how great this power and how efficacious this grace are, which have annihilated and utterly destroyed this generation (as I may call them) of most wicked and evil men; have restored joy to the good, and diffused it over all countries; and now guarantee the fullest liberty both to honour the Divine law as it should be honoured, with all reverence, and to pay due observance to those who have dedicated themselves to the service of that law, and who will now lift up their heads as it were after a period of profound darkness, and, with an enlightened knowledge of the present course of events, will henceforward render to its precepts that becoming reverence and honour which are consistent with their pious character.

"Let this ordinance be published in our Eastern provinces."

CHAPTER XLIII

CONSTANTINE'S ENACTMENTS WERE CARRIED INTO EFFECT

SUCH were the injunctions contained in the first letter which the emperor addressed to us. And the provisions of this enactment were speedily carried into effect, every thing being conducted in a manner quite different from the atrocities which had but lately been daringly perpetrated during the cruel ascendancy of the tyrants. Those persons also who were legally entitled to it, received the benefit of the emperor's liberality.

CHAPTER XLIV

HE PROMOTES CHRISTIANS TO OFFICES OF GOVERNMENT, AND FORBIDS GENTILES IN SUCH STATIONS TO OFFER SACRIFICE

AFTER this the emperor continued to address himself to matters of high importance, and first he sent governors to the several provinces, mostly such as were devoted to the saving faith; and if any appeared inclined to adhere to Gentile worship, he forbade them to offer sacrifice. This law applied also to those who surpassed the provincial governors in rank and dignity, and even to those who occupied the highest station, and held the authority of the Prætorian Præfecture. If they were Christians, they were free to act consistently with their profession: if otherwise, the law required them to abstain from idolatrous sacrifices.

CHAPTER XLV

STATUTES WHICH FORBADE SACRIFICE, AND ENJOINED THE BUILDING OF CHURCHES

SOON after this, two laws were promulgated about the same time; one of which was intended to restrain the idolatrous abominations which in time past had been practised in every city and country; and it provided that no one should erect images, or practise divination and other false and foolish arts, or offer sacrifice in any way. The other statute commanded the erection of oratories on a loftier scale, and the enlargement of the churches of God; as though the hope were entertained that, now the madness of polytheism was wholly removed, almost all mankind would henceforth attach themselves to the service of God. His own personal piety induced the emperor to devise and address these instructions to the governors of the several provinces: and the law further admonished them not to spare the expenditure of money, but to draw supplies from the imperial treasury itself. Similar instructions were written also to the bishops of the several churches; and the emperor was pleased to transmit the same to myself, being the first letter which he personally addressed to me.

CHAPTER XLVI

CONSTANTINE'S LETTER TO EUSEBIUS AND THE OTHER BISHOPS, RESPECTING THE BUILDING OF CHURCHES, WITH INSTRUCTIONS TO REPAIR THE OLD, AND ERECT NEW ONES ON A LARGER SCALE, WITH THE AID OF THE PROVINCIAL GOVERNORS

"VICTOR, CONSTANTINUS, MAXIMUS AUGUSTUS, to Eusebius.

"Forasmuch as the unholy and wilful rule of tyranny has persecuted the servants of our Saviour until this present time, I believe and am fully persuaded, best beloved brother, that the buildings belonging to all the churches have either become ruinous through actual neglect, or have received inadequate attention from the dread of the violent spirit of the times.

"But now, that liberty is restored, and that serpent driven from the administration of public affairs by the providence of the Supreme God, and our instrumentality, we trust that all can see the efficacy of the Divine power, and that they who through fear of persecution or through unbelief have fallen into any errors, will now acknowledge the true God, and adopt in future that course of life which is according to truth and rectitude. With respect, therefore, to the churches over which you yourself preside, as well as the bishops, presbyters, and deacons of other churches with whom you are acquainted, do you admonish all to be zealous in their attention to the buildings of the churches, and either to repair or enlarge those which at present exist, or, in cases of necessity, to erect new ones.

"We also empower you, and the others through you, to demand what is needful for the work, both from the provincial governors and from the Prætorian Præfect. For they have received instructions to be most diligent in obedience to your Holiness's orders." A copy of this charge was transmitted throughout all the provinces to the bishops of the several churches: the provincial governors received directions accordingly, and the imperial statute was speedily carried into effect.

CHAPTER XLVII

THE EMPEROR WROTE A LETTER ALSO IN CONDEMNATION OF IDOLATRY

MOREOVER the emperor, who continually made further progress in piety towards God, despatched an admonitory letter to the inhabitants of every province, respecting the error of idolatry into which his predecessors in power had fallen, in which he eloquently exhorts his subjects to acknowledge the Supreme God, and openly to profess their allegiance to His Christ as their Saviour. This letter also I have judged it necessary to translate from the Latin in his own handwriting into the present work, in order that we may hear, as it were, the voice of the emperor himself uttering the following sentiments in the audience of all mankind.

CHAPTER XLVIII

CONSTANTINE'S EDICT TO THE PEOPLE OF THE PROVINCES CONCERNING THE ERROR OF POLYTHEISM, COMMENCING WITH SOME GENERAL REMARKS ON VIRTUE AND VICE

"VICTOR CONSTANTINUS, MAXIMUS AUGUSTUS, to the people of the Eastern provinces.

"Whatever is comprehended under the sovereign laws of nature, is capable of conveying to all men an adequate idea of the forethought and intelligence which characterise the arrangements of God. Nor can any, whose minds are directed in the true path of knowledge to the attainment of that end, entertain a doubt that the just perceptions of sound reason, as well as those of the natural vision itself (the true perfection of each faculty having one and the same tendency), lead to the knowledge of God. Accordingly no wise man will ever be surprised when he sees the mass of mankind carried away by pursuits of an entirely opposite character. For the beauty of virtue would be useless and unperceived, did not vice display in contrast with it the course of perversity and folly. Hence it is that the one is crowned with reward, while the most high God is Himself the administrator of judgment to the other.

"And now I will endeavour to lay before you all, as explicitly as possible, the nature of my own hopes of future happiness.

CHAPTER XLIX

CONCERNING CONSTANTINE'S PIOUS FATHER, AND THE PERSECUTORS DIOCLETIAN AND MAXIMIAN

"THE former emperors I have been accustomed to regard as those with whom I could have no sympathy, on account of the savage cruelty of their character. Indeed, my father was the only one who uniformly practised the duties of humanity, and with admirable piety called for the blessing of God the Father on all his actions. For the rest, following the dictates of a perverted reason, they were more zealous of cruel than gentle measures; and this disposition they indulged without restraint, and thus marred the course of the true doctrine during the whole period of their reign. Nay, so violent did their malicious fury become, that in the midst of a profound peace, as regards both the religious and ordinary interests of men, they kindled as it were the flames of a civil war.

CHAPTER L

HOW THE PERSECUTION ORIGINATED FROM THE SILENCE OF THE ORACLE OF APOLLO, WHICH WAS ATTRIBUTED TO THE INFLUENCE OF "THE RIGHTEOUS MEN"

"ABOUT that time it is said that Apollo spoke from a deep and gloomy cavern, and with no human voice, and declared that the righteous men on earth were a bar to his speaking the truth, and accordingly that the oracles from the tripod were fallacious. Hence it was that he suffered his tresses to droop in token of grief, and mourned the evils which the loss of the oracular spirit would entail on mankind. But let us mark the consequences of this.

CHAPTER LI

CONSTANTINE, WHEN A YOUTH, UNDERSTOOD FROM HIM WHO DIRECTED THE PERSECUTION, THAT "THE RIGHTEOUS MEN" WERE THE CHRISTIANS

"I CALL now on Thee, most high God, to witness that, when very young, I heard him who at that time was chief of the sovereign rulers of the Roman empire (unhappy, truly unhappy as he was, and labouring under deep delusion of soul), make earnest inquiry of his attendants respecting these righteous ones on earth, and that one of the Pagan priests then present replied that they were the Christians. This answer he eagerly received, like some honied draught, and resolved to unsheath the sword which was ordained for the punishment of crime, against those whose holiness was beyond reproach. Immediately, therefore, he issued those sanguinary edicts, traced, if I may so express myself, with a sword's point dipped in blood; at the same time commanding his judges to tax their ingenuity for the invention of new and more terrible punishments.

CHAPTER LII

THE MANIFOLD FORMS OF TORTURE AND PUNISHMENT OPENLY PRACTISED AGAINST THE CHRISTIANS

"THEN indeed one might see with what perfect impunity those venerable worshippers of God were daily exposed, with continued and relentless cruelty, to outrages of the most grievous kind, and how that modesty of character which no enemy had ever treated with disrespect, became the mere sport of their infuriated fellow-citizens. Is there any punishment by fire, are there any instruments or modes of torture, which were not applied to all, without distinction of age or sex? Then, it may be truly said, the earth shed tears; the all encircling compass of heaven mourned because of the pollution of blood; and the very light of day itself was darkened, as it were, in grief and wonder at these scenes of horror.

CHAPTER LIII

HOW THE BARBARIANS KINDLY RECEIVED THE CHRISTIANS

"BUT is this all? Nay, the barbarians themselves may boast even now of the contrast their conduct presents to these cruel deeds; for they received and kept in gentlest captivity those who then fled from amongst us, and secured to them not merely safety from danger, but also the free exercise of their holy religion. And even now that lasting stain remains, which the flight of the Christians, at that time driven from the Roman world, and their reception by the barbarians, have branded on the Roman name.

CHAPTER LIV

HOW VENGEANCE OVERTOOK THOSE WHOM THE WORDS OF THE ORACLE HAD INDUCED TO RAISE THE PERSECUTION

"BUT why need I longer dwell on these lamentable events, and the general sorrow which in consequence pervaded the world? The perpetrators of this dreadful guilt are now no more: they have experienced a miserable end, and are consigned to unceasing punishment in the depths of the lower world. They encountered each other in the fatal arena of civil strife, and have left neither name nor race behind. And surely this calamity would never have befallen them, had not those impious words of the Pythian oracle exercised a delusive power and influence over their minds.

CHAPTER LV

CONSTANTINE GIVES GLORY TO GOD, CONFESSES THE EFFICACY OF THE STANDARD OF THE CROSS, AND PRAYS FOR THE CHURCHES AND PEOPLE

"AND now I beseech Thee, most mighty God, to be merciful and gracious to Thine Eastern nations, to Thy people in these provinces, bowed and broken as they are by protracted miseries; and vouchsafe them a remedy through Thy servant. Not without cause, O holy God, do I prefer this prayer to Thee, the Lord of all. Under Thy guidance have I devised and accomplished measures fraught with blessing: preceded by Thy sacred sign I have led Thy armies to victory: and still, on each occasion of public danger, I follow the same symbol of Thy perfections while advancing to meet the foe. Therefore have I dedicated to Thy service a soul duly attempered by love and fear. For Thy name I truly love, while I regard with reverence that power of which Thou hast given abundant proofs, to the confirmation and increase of my faith. I hasten then to devote all my powers to the restoration of that Church which is Thy most holy dwelling-place, and which those profane and impious men have marred by the rude and destroying hand of violence.

CHAPTER LVI

HE PRAYS THAT ALL MAY BE CHRISTIANS, BUT COMPELS NONE

"MY own desire is, for the general advantage of the world and all mankind, that Thy people should enjoy a life of peace and undisturbed concord. Let those, therefore, who are still blinded by error, be made welcome to the same degree of peace and tranquillity which they have who believe. For it may be that this restoration of equal privileges to all will have a powerful effect in leading them into the path of truth. Let no one molest another in this matter, but let every one be free to follow the bias of his own mind. Only let men of sound judgment be assured of this, that those only can live a life of holiness and purity, whom Thou callest to an acquiescence in Thy holy laws. With regard to those who will hold themselves aloof from us, let them have, if they please, their temples of lies: we have the glorious edifice of Thy truth, which Thou hast given us as our native home. We pray, however, that they too may receive the same blessing, and thus experience that heartfelt joy which unity of sentiment inspires.

CHAPTER LVII

HE RENDERS PRAISE TO GOD, WHO HAS GIVEN LIGHT BY HIS SON TO THOSE WHO WERE IN ERROR

"AND truly our worship is one of no novel or recent character, but such as Thou hast ordained in connexion with the honour due to Thyself from the time when, as we believe, this fair system of the universe was first fitly framed. And, although mankind have deeply fallen, and have been seduced by manifold errors, yet hast Thou revealed a pure light in the person of Thy Son (lest the power of evil should utterly prevail), and hast thus given testimony to all men concerning Thyself.

CHAPTER LVIII

HE STILL FURTHER PRAISES HIM FOR HIS GOVERNMENT OF THE MATERIAL WORLD

"THE truth of this is assured to us by Thy works. It is Thy power which removes our guilt, and makes us faithful. The sun and the moon have their settled course. The stars move in no uncertain orbits round this terrestrial globe. The revolution of the seasons recurs according to unerring laws. The solid fabric of the earth was established by Thy word: the winds receive their impulse at appointed times; and the course of the waters continues with ceaseless flow. The ocean is circumscribed by an immoveable barrier: in fine, whatever is comprehended within the compass of earth and sea, is all contrived for wondrous and important ends.

"Were it not so, were not all regulated by the determination of Thy mil, so great a diversity, so manifold a division of power, would doubtless have brought ruin on the whole course of this world's affairs. For those agencies which have maintained a mutual strife, would thus have carried to a more deadly length that hostility against the human race which they even now exercise, though unseen by mortal eyes.

CHAPTER LIX

PRAISE TO GOD, AS THE CONSTANT TEACHER OF GOOD THINGS

"ABUNDANT thanks, most mighty God, and Lord of all, be rendered to Thee on this behalf, that, the better knowledge of our nature is obtained from the diversified pursuits of man, the more are the precepts of Thy divine doctrine confirmed to those whose thoughts are directed aright, and who are sincerely devoted to true virtue. As for those who will not allow themselves to be cured of their error, let them not attribute this to any but themselves. For that remedy which is of sovereign and healing virtue is openly placed within the reach of all. Only let all beware lest they inflict an injury on that religion which experience itself testifies to be pure and undefiled. Henceforward, therefore, let us all enjoy in common the privilege placed within our reach, I mean the blessing of peace; and let us endeavour to keep our conscience pure from aught that might interrupt and mar this blessing.

CHAPTER LX

AN ADMONITION AT THE CLOSE OF THE EDICT, THAT NO ONE SHOULD DISTURB THE PEACE OF HIS NEIGHBOUR

"ONCE more, let none use that to the detriment of another which he may himself have received on conviction of its truth; but let every one, if it be possible, apply what he has understood and known to the benefit of his neighbour; if otherwise, let him relinquish the attempt. For it is one thing voluntarily to undertake the conflict for immortality, another to compel others to do so from the fear of punishment.

"These are our words; and we have enlarged on these topics more than our ordinary clemency would have dictated, because we were unwilling to dissemble or be false to the true faith; and the more so, since we understand there are some who say that the rites of the heathen temples, and the power of darkness, have been entirely removed. We should indeed have earnestly recommended such removal to all men, were it not that the rebellious spirit of those wicked errors still continues obstinately fixed in the minds of some, so as to discourage the hope of any general restoration of mankind to the ways of truth."

CHAPTER LXI

HOW CONTROVERSIES ORIGINATED AT ALEXANDRIA IN CONNEXION WITH ARIUS

IN this manner the emperor, like a powerful herald of God, addressed himself by his own letter to all the provinces, at the same time warning his subjects against the superstitious errors of idolatry, and encouraging them in the pursuit of true godliness. But in the midst of his joyful anticipations of the success of this measure, he received tidings of a most serious disturbance which had invaded the peace of the Church. This intelligence he heard with deep concern, and at once endeavoured to devise a remedy for the evil. The origin of this disturbance may be thus described. The people of God were in a truly flourishing state, and abounding in the practice of good works. No terror from without assailed them, but a bright and most profound peace, through the favour of God, encompassed His Church on every side. Meantime, however, the spirit of envy was watching to destroy our blessings, which at first crept in unperceived, but soon revelled without restraint in the midst of the assemblies of the saints. At length the same spirit reached the bishops themselves, and arrayed them in angry hostility against each other, on pretence of a jealous regard for the doctrines of Divine truth. Hence it was that a mighty fire was kindled as it were from a little spark, and which, originating in the first instance in the Alexandrian church, overspread the whole of Egypt and Libya, and the further Thebaid. Eventually it extended its ravages to the other provinces and cities of the empire; so that not only the prelates of the churches might be seen encountering each other in the strife of words, but the people themselves were completely divided, and embraced the tenets of opposing parties. Nay, so notorious did the scandal of these proceedings become, that the venerable mysteries of Divine revelation were exposed to the foulest insult and derision in the very theatres of the unbelievers.

CHAPTER LXII

CONCERNING THE SAME ARIUS, AND THE MELITIANS

THUS did the adverse parties at Alexandria maintain an obstinate conflict respecting questions of the highest and most mysterious kind. And at the same time others were at variance throughout Egypt and the Upper Thebaid, on account of a controversy which had been still earlier in existence: so that the churches were every where distracted by divisions. The body therefore being thus diseased, the whole of Libya caught the contagion; and the rest of the remoter provinces became affected with the same disorder. For the disputants at Alexandria sent emissaries to the bishops of the several provinces, who accordingly ranged themselves as partisans on either side, and shared in the same spirit of discord.

CHAPTER LXIII

THAT CONSTANTINE SENT A LETTER, WITH A VIEW TO THE RE-ESTABLISHMENT OF CONCORD

As soon as the emperor was informed of these facts (which he heard with much sorrow of heart, and considered them in the light of a calamity personally affecting himself), he forthwith selected from the Christians in his train one whom he well knew to be approved for the sobriety and genuineness of his faith, and who had before this time distinguished himself by the boldness of his religious profession, and sent him to act as mediator between the dissentient parties at Alexandria. He also made him the bearer of a most needful and appropriate letter to the original movers of the strife: and this letter, as exhibiting a specimen of his watchful care over God's people, it may be well to introduce into this our narrative of his life. Its purport was as follows.

CHAPTER LXIV

CONSTANTINE'S LETTER TO ALEXANDER THE BISHOP, AND ARIUS THE PRESBYTER

"VICTOR CONSTANTINUS, MAXIMUS AUGUSTUS, to Alexander and Arius.

"I call that God to witness (as well I may), who is the helper of my endeavours, and the Preserver of all men, that I had a two-fold reason for undertaking that duty which I have now effectually performed.

CHAPTER LXV

HIS CONTINUAL ANXIETY FOR PEACE

"MY design then was, first, to bring the diverse judgments formed by all nations respecting the Deity to a condition, as it were, of settled uniformity; and, secondly, to restore a healthy tone to the system of the world, then suffering under the malignant power of a grievous distemper. Keeping these objects in view, I looked forward to the accomplishment of the one with the secret gaze of the mental eye, while the other I endeavoured to secure by the aid of military power. For I was aware that, if I should succeed in establishing, according to my hopes, a common harmony of sentiment among all the servants of God, the general course of affairs would also experience a change correspondent to the pious desires of them all.

CHAPTER LXVI

HOW HE ADJUSTED THE CONTROVERSIES WHICH HAD ARISEN IN AFRICA

"FINDING, then, that the whole of Africa was pervaded by an intolerable spirit of madness and folly, through the influence of those whose wanton temerity had presumed to rend the religion of the people into diverse sects; I was anxious to allay the virulence of this disorder, and could discover no other remedy equal to the occasion, except in sending some of yourselves to aid in restoring mutual harmony among the disputants, after I had removed that common enemy of mankind who had interposed his lawless sentence for the prohibition of your holy synods.

CHAPTER LXVII

THAT CHRISTIANITY BEGAN IN THE EAST

"FOR since the power of Divine light, and the rule of our holy religion, which have illumined the world by their sacred radiance, proceeded in the first instance, through the favour of God, from the bosom, as it were, of the East, I naturally believed that you would be the first to promote the salvation of other nations, and resolved with all energy of purpose and diligence of inquiry to seek your aid. As soon therefore as I had secured my decisive victory and unquestionable triumph over my enemies, my first inquiry was concerning that object which I felt to be of paramount interest and importance.

CHAPTER LXVIII

BEING GRIEVED BY THE DISSENSIONS, HE RECOMMENDS A SPIRIT OF CONCORD

"BUT, O glorious Providence of God! how deep a wound did not my ears only, but my very heart receive in the report that divisions existed among yourselves more grievous still than those which continued in that country! so that you, through whose aid I had hoped to procure a remedy for the errors of others, are in a state which demands even more attention than theirs. And yet, having made a careful inquiry into the origin and foundation of these differences, I find the cause to be of a truly insignificant character, and quite unworthy of such fierce contention. Feeling myself, therefore, compelled to address you in this letter, and to appeal at the same time to your unanimity and sagacity, I call on Divine Providence to assist me in the task, while I interrupt your dissension in the character of a minister of peace. And with reason: for if I might expect (with the help of a higher Power) to be able without difficulty, by a judicious appeal to the pious feelings of those who heard me, to recall them to a better spirit, how can I refrain from promising myself a far easier and more speedy adjustment of this difference, when the cause which hinders general harmony of sentiment is intrinsically trifling and of little moment?

CHAPTER LXIX

ORIGIN OF THE DIFFERENCE BETWEEN ALEXANDER AND ARIUS—THESE QUESTIONS ARE NOT FIT SUBJECTS FOR CONTROVERSY

"I UNDERSTAND, then, that the occasion of your present controversy is to be traced to the following circumstances; that you, Alexander, demanded of the presbyters what opinion they severally maintained respecting a certain passage in the Divine law, or rather, I should say, that you asked them something connected with an unprofitable question; and then that you, Arius, inconsiderately gave utterance to objections which ought never to have been conceived at all, or if conceived, should have been buried in profound silence. Hence it was that a dissension arose between you; the meeting of the synod was prohibited; and the holy people, rent into diverse parties, no longer preserved the unity of the one body. Now therefore do ye both exhibit an equal degree of forbearance, and receive the advice which your fellow-servant feels himself justly entitled to give. What then is this advice? It was wrong in the first instance to propose such questions as these, or to reply to them when propounded. For those points of discussion which are enjoined by the authority of no law, but rather suggested by the contentious spirit which is fostered by misused leisure, even though they may be intended merely as an intellectual exercise, ought certainly to be confined to the region of our own thoughts, and neither hastily produced in the public assemblies of the saints, nor unadvisedly intrusted to the general ear. For how very few are there able either accurately to comprehend, or adequately to explain subjects so sublime and abstruse in their nature? Or, granting that one were fully competent for this, in how few ordinary minds will he succeed in producing conviction? Or who, again, in dealing with questions of such subtle nicety as these, can secure himself against a dangerous declension from the truth? It is incumbent therefore on us in these cases to be sparing of our words, lest, in case we ourselves are unable, through the feebleness of our natural faculties, to give a clear explanation of the subject before us, or, on the other hand, in case the slowness of our hearers' understandings disables them from arriving at an accurate apprehension of what we say, from one or other of these causes we reduce the people to the alternative either of blasphemy or schism.

CHAPTER LXX

AN EXHORTATION TO UNANIMITY

"LET therefore both the unguarded question and the inconsiderate answer receive your mutual forgiveness. For your difference has not arisen on any leading doctrines or precepts of the Divine law, nor have you introduced any new dogma respecting the worship of God. You are in truth of one and the same judgment: you may therefore well join in that communion which is the symbol of united fellowship.

CHAPTER LXXI

THERE SHOULD BE NO CONTENTION BECAUSE OF EXPRESSIONS IN THEMSELVES OF LITTLE MOMENT

"FOR as long as you continue to contend about these truly insignificant questions, it is not fitting that so large a portion of God's people should be under the direction of your judgment, since you are thus divided between yourselves. I believe it indeed to be not merely unbecoming, but positively evil, that such should be the case. But I will appeal to your good sense by a familiar instance to illustrate my meaning. You know that philosophers, while they all adhere to the general tenets of their respective sects, are frequently at issue on some particular assertion or statement: and yet, though they may differ as to the perfection of a principle, they are recalled to harmony of sentiment by the uniting power of their common doctrines. If this be true, is it not far more reasonable that you, who are the ministers of the Supreme God, should be of one mind respecting the profession of the same religion? But let us still more thoughtfully and with closer attention examine what I have said, and see whether it be right that, on the ground of some trifling and foolish verbal difference between ourselves, brethren should assume towards each other the attitude of enemies, and the august meeting of the synod be rent by profane disunion, because we will wrangle together on points so trivial and altogether unessential? Surely this conduct is unworthy of us, and rather characteristic of childish ignorance, than consistent with the wisdom of priests and men of sense. Let us withdraw ourselves with a good will from these temptations of the devil. Our great God and common Saviour has granted the same light to us all. Permit me, who am His servant, to bring my task to a successful issue, under the direction of His Providence, that I may be enabled through my exhortations, and diligence, and earnest admonition, to recall His people to the fellowship of one communion. For since you have, as I said, but one faith, and one sentiment respecting our religion, and since the Divine commandment in all its parts enjoins on us all the duty of maintaining a spirit of concord, let not the circumstance which has led to a slight difference between you, since it affects not the general principles of truth, be allowed to prolong any division or schism among you. And this I say without in any way desiring to force you to entire unity of judgment in regard to this truly idle question, whatever its real nature may be. For the dignity of your synod may be preserved, and the communion of your whole body maintained unbroken, however wide a difference may exist among you as to unimportant matters. For we are not all of us like-minded on every subject, nor is there such a thing as one disposition and judgment common to all alike. As far then as regards the Divine Providence, let there be one faith, and one understanding among you, one united judgment in reference to God. But as to your subtle disputations on questions of little or no significance, though you may be unable to harmonize in sentiment, such differences should be consigned to the secret custody of your own minds and thoughts. And now, let the precious bonds of common affection, let faith in the truth, let the honour due to God and the observance of His law continue immoveably established among you. Resume, then, your mutual feelings of affection and regard: permit the whole body of the people once more to unite in that embrace which should be natural to all; and do ye yourselves, having purified your souls, as it were, from every angry thought, once more return to your former fellowship. For it often happens that when a reconciliation is effected by the removal of the causes of enmity, friendship becomes even sweeter than it was before.

CHAPTER LXXII

THE EXCESS OF HIS PIOUS CONCERN CAUSED HIM TO SHED TEARS; AND HIS INTENDED JOURNEY TO THE EAST WAS POSTPONED BECAUSE OF THESE DISSENSIONS

"RESTORE me then my quiet days, and untroubled nights, that henceforth the joy of light undimmed by sorrow, the delight of a tranquil life, may continue to be my portion. Else must I needs mourn, with copious and constant tears, nor shall I be able to pass the residue of my days without disquietude. For while the people of God, whose fellow-servant I am, are thus divided amongst themselves by an unreasonable and pernicious spirit of contention, how is it possible that I shall be able to maintain tranquillity of mind? And I will give you a proof how great my sorrow has been on this behalf. Not long since I had visited Nicomedia, and intended forthwith to proceed from that city to the East. It was while I was on the point of hastening towards you, and was already among you in thought and desire, that the news of this matter arrested my intended progress, that I might not be compelled to witness that which I felt myself scarcely able even to hear. Open then for me henceforward by your unity of judgment that road to the regions of the East which your dissensions have closed against me, and permit me speedily to see the happiness both of yourselves and of all other provinces, and to render due acknowledgment to God in the language of praise and thanksgiving for the restoration of general concord and liberty to all."

CHAPTER LXXIII

THE CONTROVERSY CONTINUES WITHOUT ABATEMENT, EVEN AFTER THE RECEIPT OF THIS LETTER

IN this manner the pious emperor endeavoured by means of the foregoing letter to promote the peace of the Church of God. And the excellent man to whom it was intrusted performed his part not merely by communicating the letter itself, but also by seconding the views of him who sent it; for he was (as I have said) in all respects a person of pious character. The evil, however, was greater than could be remedied by a single letter, insomuch that the acrimony of the contending parties continually increased, and the effects of the mischief extended to all the Eastern provinces. Such were the fruits of the jealousy of that evil spirit who looked with an envious eye on the prosperity of the Church.

BOOK III

CHAPTER I

A COMPARISON OF CONSTANTINE'S PIETY WITH THE WICKEDNESS OF THE PERSECUTORS

IN this manner that Spirit who is the hater of good, actuated by envy at the blessing enjoyed by the Church, continued to raise against her the stormy troubles of intestine discord, in the midst of a period of peace and joy. Meanwhile, however, the divinely-favoured emperor engaged in no careless spirit in the duties which became his station, but exhibited in his whole conduct a direct contrast to those atrocities of which the cruel tyrants had been lately guilty, and thus triumphed over every enemy that opposed him. For in the first place, the tyrants, being themselves alienated from the true God, had enforced by every compulsion the worship of false deities: Constantine convinced mankind by actions as well as words, that these had but an imaginary existence, and exhorted them to acknowledge the only true God. They had derided His Christ with words of blasphemy: he assumed that as his safeguard against which they launched their impious invectives, and gloried in the symbol of the Saviour's passion. They had persecuted and driven into houseless exile, the servants of Christ: he recalled them every one, and restored them to their native homes. They had covered them with dishonour: he made their condition honourable and enviable in the eyes of all. The tyrants had shamefully plundered and sold the goods of godly men: Constantine not only replaced this loss, but still further enriched them with abundant presents. They had circulated injurious calumnies, through their written ordinances, against the prelates of the Church: he, on the contrary, conferred dignity on these individuals by personal marks of honour, and by his edicts and statutes raised them to higher distinction than before. They had utterly demolished and razed to the ground the houses of prayer: he commanded that those which still existed should be enlarged, and that new ones should be raised on a magnificent scale at the expense of the imperial treasury. They had ordered the inspired records to be burnt and destroyed: he decreed that copies of them should be multiplied, and magnificently adorned at the charge of the imperial treasury. They had strictly forbidden the prelates, any where or on any occasion, to convene synods; whereas he gathered them to his court from every province, invited them to his palace, gave them constant access to his person, and admitted them to a share of his imperial hospitality. The tyrants had honoured the demons with offerings: Constantine exposed their frauds, and continually distributed the now useless materials for sacrifice, to those who would apply them to a better use. They had ordered the pagan temples to be sumptuously adorned: he razed to their foundations those of them which had been the chief objects of superstitious reverence. They had subjected God's servants to the most ignominious punishments: he took vengeance on the persecutors, and inflicted on them just chastisement in the name of God, while he held the memory of His holy martyrs in constant veneration. They had driven God's worshippers from the imperial palaces: he placed full confidence in them at all times, and esteemed them more zealous and faithful than any beside. They, the victims of avarice, voluntarily subjected themselves as it were to the pangs of Tantalus: he with royal magnificence unlocked all his treasures, and distributed his gifts with rich and high-souled liberality. The tyrants had been stained with the guilt of countless murders, that they might plunder or confiscate the wealth of their victims; while throughout the reign of Constantine the sword of justice hung idle every where, and both people and municipal magistrates in every province, were rather constrained by a paternal authority than governed by the stringent power of the laws. Surely it must seem to all who duly regard these facts, that a new and fresh era of existence had begun to appear, and a light heretofore unknown suddenly to dawn from the midst of darkness on the human race: and all must confess that these things were entirely the work of God, who raised up this pious emperor to withstand the multitude of the ungodly.

CHAPTER II

FURTHER REMARKS ON CONSTANTINE'S PIETY, AND HIS OPEN PROFESSION OF THE CROSS

AND when we consider that their iniquities were without example, and the atrocities which they dared to perpetrate against the Church such as had never been heard of in any age of the world, well might God Himself bring before us something entirely new, and work thereby effects such as had hitherto been never either recorded or observed. And what miracle was ever more marvellous than the virtues of this our emperor, whom the wisdom of God has vouchsafed as a gift to the human race? For truly he maintained a continual testimony to His Christ with all boldness, and before all men; and so far was he from shrinking from an open profession of the Christian name, that he rather desired to make it manifest to all that he regarded this as his highest honour, whether it were by impressing on his face the salutary sign, or glorying in it as the trophy which led him on to victory.

CHAPTER III

OF HIS PICTURE SURMOUNTED BY A CROSS, AND HAVING BENEATH IT A WOUNDED DRAGON

AND besides this, he caused to be painted on a lofty tablet, and set up in the front of the portico of his palace, so as to be visible to all, a representation of the salutary sign placed above his head, and below it that hateful and savage adversary of mankind, who by means of the tyranny of the ungodly had wasted the Church of God, falling headlong, under the form of a dragon, to the abyss of destruction. For the sacred oracles in the books of God's prophets have described him as a dragon and a crooked serpent; and for this reason the emperor thus publicly displayed a painted resemblance of the dragon beneath his own and his children's feet, stricken through with a dart, and cast headlong into the depths of the sea.

In this manner he intended to represent the secret adversary of the human race, and to indicate that he was consigned to the gulf of perdition by virtue of the salutary trophy placed above his head. This allegory, then, was thus conveyed by means of the colours of a picture: and I am filled with wonder at what I may call the divine sagacity of the emperor, who thus vividly expressed what the prophets had foretold concerning this monster, that God would bring His great and strong and terrible sword against the dragon, the flying serpent; and would destroy the dragon that was in the sea. This it was of which the emperor gave a true and faithful representation in the picture above described.

CHAPTER IV

A FURTHER NOTICE OF THE CONTROVERSIES RAISED IN EGYPT THROUGH THE INSTRUMENTALITY OF ARIUS

IN such occupations as these he employed himself with pleasure: but the effects of that envious spirit which so disturbed the peace of the Churches of God in Alexandria, together with the Theban and Egyptian schism, continued to cause him no little anxiety of mind. For in fact, in every city bishops were engaged in obstinate conflict with bishops, and people rising against people; and almost, like the fabled Symplegades, coming into violent collision with each other. Nay, some were so far transported beyond the bounds of reason as to be guilty of reckless and outrageous conduct, and even to insult the statues of the emperor. This state of things had little power to excite his anger, but rather caused in him sorrow of spirit; for he deeply deplored the folly thus exhibited by misguided men.

CHAPTER V

OF THE DISSENSIONS RESPECTING THE CELEBRATION OF EASTER

BUT before this time another most virulent disorder had existed, and long afflicted the Church; I mean the difference respecting the salutary feast of Easter. For while one party asserted that the Jewish custom should be adhered to, the other affirmed that the exact recurrence of the period should be observed, without following the authority of those who were in error, and strangers to the grace of the gospel as well in this as in other respects.

Accordingly, the people being thus in every place divided, and the sacred observances of religion confounded for a long period (insomuch that the diversity of judgment in regard to the time for celebrating one and the same feast, caused the bitterest disunion between those who kept it, some afflicting themselves with fastings and austerities, while others devoted their time to festive relaxation), no one appeared who was capable of devising a remedy for the evil, because the controversy continued equally balanced between both parties. To God alone, the Almighty, was the healing of these differences an easy task; and Constantine appeared to be the only one on earth capable of being His minister for this good end. For as soon as he was made acquainted with the facts which I have described, and perceived that his letter to the Alexandrian Christians had failed to produce its due effect, he at once aroused the energies of his mind, and declared that he must prosecute to the utmost this war also against the secret adversary who was disturbing the peace of the Church.

CHAPTER VI

HE ORDERS A COUNCIL TO ASSEMBLE AT NICÆA

RESOLVED, therefore, to bring as it were a divine array against this enemy, he convoked a general council, and invited the speedy attendance of bishops from all quarters, in letters expressive of the honourable estimation in which he held them. Nor was this merely the issuing of a bare command, but the emperor's condescension contributed much to its being carried into effect: for he allowed some the use of the public means of conveyance, while he afforded to others an ample supply of horses for their transport. The place, too, selected for the synod, the city Nicœa in Bithynia (which derived its name from Victory), was appropriate to the occasion. As soon then as the imperial injunction was generally made known, all with the utmost celerity hastened to obey it, as though they would outstrip one another in a race: for they were impelled by the anticipation of a happy result to the conference, by the hope of enjoying present peace, and the desire of beholding something new and strange in the person of so admirable an emperor. Now when they were all assembled, it appeared evident that the proceeding was the work of God, inasmuch as men who had been most widely separated, not merely in sentiment, but also personally, and by difference of country, place, and nation, were here brought together, and comprised within the walls of a single city, forming as it were a vast garland of priests, composed of a variety of the choicest flowers.

CHAPTER VII

OF THE GENERAL COUNCIL, AT WHICH BISHOPS FROM ALL NATIONS WERE PRESENT

IN effect, the most distinguished of God's ministers from all the Churches which abounded in Europe, Africa, and Asia, were here assembled. And a single house of prayer, as though divinely enlarged, sufficed to contain at once Syrians and Cilicians, Phœnicians and Arabians, delegates from Palestine, and others from Egypt; Thebans and Libyans, with those who came from the region of Mesopotamia. A Persian bishop too was present at this conference, nor was even a Scythian found wanting to the number. Pontus, Galatia, and Pamphylia, Cappadocia, Asia, and Phrygia, furnished their most distinguished prelates; while those who dwelt in the remotest districts of Thrace and Macedonia, of Achaia and Epirus, were notwithstanding in attendance. Even from

Spain itself, one whose fame was widely spread took his seat as an individual in the great assembly. The prelate of the imperial city was prevented from attending by extreme old age; but his presbyters were present, and supplied his place. Constantine is the first prince of any age who bound together such a garland as this with the bond of peace, and presented it to Christ his Saviour as a thank-offering for the victories he had obtained over every foe, thus exhibiting in our own times a similitude of the apostolic company.

CHAPTER VIII

THE ASSEMBLY WAS COMPOSED, AS IN THE ACTS OF THE APOSTLES, OF INDIVIDUALS FROM VARIOUS NATIONS

FOR it is said that in the Apostles' age, devout men were gathered from every nation under heaven; among whom were Parthians, and Medes, and Elamites, and the dwellers in Mesopotamia, and in Judea, and Cappadocia, in Pontus and Asia, Phrygia and Pamphylia, in Egypt, and the parts of Libya about Cyrene; and strangers of Rome, Jews and proselytes, Cretes and Arabians. Now the defect of that assembly was, that not all who composed it were ministers of God: but in the present company, the number of bishops exceeded two hundred and fifty, while that of the presbyters and deacons in their train, and the crowd of acolytes and other attendants was altogether beyond computation.

CHAPTER IX

OF THE VIRTUE AND AGE OF THE TWO HUNDRED AND FIFTY BISHOPS

OF these ministers of God, some were distinguished by wisdom and eloquence, others by the gravity of their lives, and by patient fortitude of character, while others again united in themselves all these graces. There were among them men whose years demanded the tribute of respect and veneration: others were younger, and in the prime of bodily and mental vigour; and some had but recently entered on the course of their ministry. For the maintenance of all a sumptuous provision was daily furnished by the emperor's command.

CHAPTER X

MEETING IN THE PALACE, AT WHICH CONSTANTINE APPEARED, AND TOOK HIS SEAT IN THE ASSEMBLY

Now when the appointed day arrived on which the council met for the final solution of the questions in dispute, each member attended to deliver his judgment in the central building of the palace, which appeared to exceed the rest in magnitude. On each side of the interior of this were many seats disposed in order, which were occupied by those who had been invited to attend, according to their rank. As soon, then, as the whole assembly had seated themselves with becoming gravity, a general silence prevailed, in expectation of the emperor's arrival. And first of all three of his immediate family entered in succession, and others also preceded his approach, not of the soldiers or guards who usually accompanied him, but only friends who avowed the faith of Christ. And now, all rising at the signal which indicated the emperor's entrance, at last he himself proceeded through the midst of the assembly, like some heavenly messenger of God, clothed in raiment which glittered as it were with rays of light, reflecting the glowing radiance of a purple robe, and adorned with the brilliant splendour of gold and precious stones. Such was the external appearance of his person; and with regard to his mind, it was evident that he was distinguished by piety and godly fear. This was indicated by his downcast eyes, the blush on his countenance, and the modesty of his gait. For the rest of his personal excellencies, he surpassed all present in height of stature and beauty of form, as well as in majestic dignity of mien, and invincible strength and vigour. All these graces, united to a suavity of manner, and a serenity becoming his imperial station, declared the excellence of his mental qualities to be above all praise. As soon as he had advanced to the upper end of the seats, at first he remained standing, and when a low chair of wrought gold had been set for him, he waited until the bishops had beckoned to him, and then sat down, and after him the whole assembly did the same.

CHAPTER XI

SILENCE OF THE COUNCIL, AFTER SOME WORDS SPOKEN BY THE BISHOP EUSEBIUS

THE bishop who occupied the chief place in the right division of the assembly then rose, and, addressing the emperor, delivered a concise speech, in a strain of praise and thanksgiving to Almighty God on his behalf. When he had resumed his seat, silence ensued, and all regarded the emperor with fixed attention; on which he looked serenely round on the assembly with a cheerful aspect, and, having collected his thoughts, in a calm and gentle tone gave utterance to the following words.

CHAPTER XII

CONSTANTINE'S ADDRESS TO THE COUNCIL, IN PRAISE OF PEACE

"IT was once my chief desire, dearest friends, to enjoy the spectacle of your united presence; and now that this desire is fulfilled, I feel myself bound to render thanks to God the universal King, because, in addition to all His other benefits, he has granted me a blessing higher than all the rest, in permitting me to see you not only all assembled together, but all united in a common harmony of sentiment. I pray therefore that no malignant adversary may henceforth interfere to mar our happy state; I pray that, now the impious hostility of the tyrants has been for ever removed by the power of God our Saviour, that spirit who delights in evil may devise no other means for exposing the divine records to blasphemous calumny: for, in my judgment, intestine strife within the Church of God is far more evil and dangerous than any kind of war or conflict; and these our differences appear to me more grievous than any outward trouble. Accordingly, when, by the will and with the co-operation of God, I had been victorious over my enemies, and thought that nothing more remained but to render thanks to Him, and sympathize in the joy of those whom he had restored to freedom through my instrumentality; as soon as I heard that intelligence which I had least expected to receive, I mean the news of your dissension, I judged it to be of no secondary importance, but with the earnest desire that a remedy for this evil also might be found through my means, I immediately sent to require your presence. And now I rejoice in beholding your assembly; but I feel that my desires will be most completely fulfilled when I can see you all united in one judgment, and that common spirit of peace and concord prevailing amongst you all, which it becomes you, as consecrated to the service of God, to commend to others. Delay not, then, dear friends: delay not, ye ministers of God, and faithful servants of Him who is our common Lord and Saviour: begin from this moment to discard the causes of that disunion which has existed among you, and remove the perplexities of controversy by embracing the principles of peace. For by such conduct you will at the same time be acting in a manner most pleasing to the supreme

God, and you will confer an exceeding favour on me who am your fellow-servant."

CHAPTER XIII

IN WHAT MANNER HE LED THE DISSENTIENT BISHORS TO UNITE IN HARMONY OF SENTIMENT

AS soon as the emperor had spoken these words in the Latin tongue, which another present rendered into Greek, he gave permission to those who presided in the council to deliver their opinions. On this some began to accuse their neighbours, who defended themselves, and recriminated in their turn. In this manner numberless assertions were put forth by each party, and a violent controversy arose at the very commencement. Notwithstanding this, the emperor gave patient audience to all alike, and received every proposition with steadfast attention, and by occasionally assisting the argument of each party in turn, he gradually disposed even the most vehement disputants to a reconciliation. At the same time, by the affability of his address to all, and his use of the Greek language (with which he was not altogether unacquainted), he appeared in a truly attractive and amiable light, persuading some, convincing others by his reasonings, praising those who spoke well, and urging all to unity of sentiment, until at last he succeeded in bringing them to one mind and judgment respecting every disputed question.

CHAPTER XIV

UNANIMOUS DECLARATION OF THE COUNCIL CONCERNING FAITH, AND THE CELEBRATION OF EASTER

THE result was that they were not only united as concerning the faith, but that the time for the celebration of the salutary feast of Easter was agreed on by all. Those points also which were sanctioned by the resolution of the whole body were committed to writing, and received the signature of each several member: and then the emperor, believing that he had thus obtained a second victory over the adversary of the Church, proceeded to solemnize a triumphal festival in honour of God.

CHAPTER XV

CONSTANTINE ENTERTAINS THE BISHOPS ON THE OCCASION OF HIS VICENNALIA

ABOUT this time he completed the twentieth year of his reign. On this occasion public festivals were celebrated by the people of the provinces generally, but the emperor himself invited and feasted with those ministers of God whom he had reconciled, and thus offered as it were through them a suitable sacrifice to God. Not one of the bishops was wanting at the imperial banquet, the circumstances of which were splendid beyond description. Detachments of the body guard and other troops surrounded the entrance of the palace with drawn swords, and through the midst of these the men of God proceeded without fear into the innermost of the imperial apartments, in which some were the emperor's own companions at table, while others reclined on couches arranged on either side. One might have thought that a picture of Christ's kingdom was thus shadowed forth, and that the scene was less like reality, than a dream.

CHAPTER XVI

PRESENTS TO THE BISHOPS, AND LETTERS ADDRESSED TO THE PEOPLE GENERALLY

AFTER the celebration of this brilliant festival, the emperor courteously received all his guests, and generously added to the favours he had already bestowed by personally presenting gifts to each individual according to his rank. He also gave information of the proceedings of the synod to those who had not been present, by a letter in his own hand-writing. And this letter also I will inscribe as it were on a tablet by inserting it in this my narrative of his life. It was as follows:—

CHAPTER XVII

CONSTANTINE'S LETTER TO THE CHURCHES RESPECTING THE COUNCIL AT NICÆA

"CONSTANTINUS AUGUSTUS, to the Churches.

"Having had full proof, in the general prosperity of the empire, how great the favour of God has been towards us, I have judged that it ought to be the first object of my endeavours, that unity of faith, sincerity of love, and community of feeling in regard to the worship of Almighty God, might be preserved among the highly favoured multitude who compose the Catholic Church. And, inasmuch as this object could not be effectually and certainly secured, unless all, or at least the greater number of the bishops were to meet together, and a discussion of all particulars relating to our most holy religion to take place; for this reason as numerous an assembly as possible has been convened, at which I myself was present, as one among yourselves (and far be it from me to deny that which is my greatest joy, that I am your fellow-servant), and every question received due and full examination, until that judgment which God, who sees all things, could approve, and which tended to unity and concord, was brought to light, so that no room was left for further discussion or controversy in relation to the faith.

CHAPTER XVIII

HE SPEAKS OF THEIR UNANIMITY RESPECTING THE FEAST OF EASTER, AND AGAINST THE PRACTICE OF THE JEWS

"AT this meeting the question concerning the most holy day of Easter was discussed, and it was resolved by the united judgment of all present, that this feast ought to be kept by all and in every place on one and the same day. For what can be more becoming or honourable to us than that this feast, from which we date our hopes of immortality, should be observed unfailingly by all alike, according to one ascertained order and arrangement? And first of all, it appeared an unworthy thing that in the celebration of this most holy feast we should follow the practice of the Jews, who have impiously defiled their hands with enormous sin, and are therefore deservedly afflicted with blindness of soul. For we have it in our power, if we abandon their custom, to prolong the due observance of this ordinance to future ages, by a truer order, which we have preserved from the very day of the passion until the present time. Let us then have nothing in common with the detestable Jewish crowd; for we have received from our Saviour a different way. A course at once legitimate and honourable lies open to our most holy religion. Beloved brethren, let us with one consent adopt this course, and withdraw ourselves from all participation in their baseness. For their boast is absurd indeed, that it is not in our power without instruction from them to observe these things. For how should they be capable of forming a sound judgment, who, since their parricidal guilt in slaying their Lord, have been subject to the direction, not of reason, but of ungoverned passion, and are swayed by every impulse of the mad spirit that is in them? Hence it is that on this point as well as others they have no perception of the truth, so that, being altogether ignorant of the true adjustment of this question, they sometimes celebrate Easter twice in the same year. Why then should we follow those who are confessedly in grievous error? Surely we shall never consent to keep this feast a second time in the same year. But supposing these reasons were not of sufficient weight, still it would be incumbent on your Sagacities to strive and pray continually that the purity of your souls may not seem in any thing to be sullied by fellowship with the customs of these most wicked men. We must consider, too, that a discordant judgment in a case of such importance, and respecting such a solemnity of our religion, must needs be contrary to the Divine will. For our Saviour has left us one feast in commemoration of the day of our deliverance, I mean the day of His most holy passion; and He has willed that His Catholic Church should be one, the members of which, however scattered in many and diverse places, are yet cherished by one pervading spirit, that is, by the will of God. And let your Holinesses' sagacity reflect how grievous and scandalous it is that on the self-same days some should be engaged in fasting, others in festive enjoyment; and again, that after the days of Easter some should lend their countenance to banquets and amusements, while others are fulfilling the appointed fasts. It is, then, plainly the will of Divine Providence (as I suppose you all clearly see), that this usage should receive fitting correction, and be reduced to one uniform rule.

CHAPTER XIX

HE HOLDS OUT FOR THEIR IMITATION THE EXAMPLE OF THE GREATER PART OF THE WORLD

"SINCE, therefore, it was needful that this matter should be rectified, so that we might have nothing in common with that nation of parricides who slew their Lord; and since that arrangement is consistent with propriety which is observed by all the churches of the western, southern, and northern parts of the world, and by some of the eastern also: for these reasons all are unanimous on this present occasion in thinking it worthy of adoption. And I myself have undertaken that this decision should meet with the approval of your Sagacities, in the hope that your Wisdoms will gladly admit that practice which is observed at once in the city of Rome, and in Africa; throughout Italy, and in Egypt; in Spain, the Gauls, Britain, Libya, and the whole of Greece; in the dioceses of Asia and Pontus, and in Cilicia, with entire unity of judgment. And you will consider not only that the number of churches is far greater in the regions I have enumerated than in any other, but also that it is most fitting that all should unite in desiring that which sound reason appears to demand, and in avoiding all participation in the perjured conduct of the Jews. In fine, that I may express my meaning in as few words as possible, it has been determined by the common judgment of all, that the most holy feast of Easter should be kept on one and the same day. For on the one hand a discrepancy of opinion on so sacred a question is unbecoming, and on the other it is surely best to act on a decision which is free from error.

CHAPTER XX

HE RECOMMENDS OBEDIENCE TO THE DECREES OF THE COUNCIL

"RECEIVE, then, with all willingness this truly Divine injunction, and regard it as the gift of God. For whatever is determined in the holy assemblies of the bishops is to be regarded as indicative of the Divine will. As soon, therefore, as you have communicated these proceedings to all our beloved brethren, you are bound from that time forward to adopt for yourselves, and to enjoin on others the arrangement above mentioned, and the due observance of this most sacred day; that whenever I come into the presence of your love (which I have long desired), I may have it in my power to celebrate the holy feast with you on the same day, and may rejoice with you on all accounts, when I behold the cruel power of Satan removed by Divine aid through the agency of our endeavours, while your faith, and peace, and concord every where flourish. God preserve you, beloved brethren!"

The emperor transmitted a faithful copy of this letter to every province, wherein they who read it might discern as in a mirror the pure sincerity of his thoughts, and of his piety toward God.

CHAPTER XXI

HE EXHORTS THE BISHOPS, ON THEIR DEPARTURE, TO PRESERVE A SPIRIT OF CONCORD

AND now, when the council was on the point of being finally dissolved, he summoned all the bishops to meet him on an appointed day, and on their arrival addressed them in a farewell speech, in which he recommended them to be diligent in the maintenance of peace, and the avoidance of contentious disputations, amongst themselves. He cautioned them also against a spirit of jealousy, should any one of their number appear pre-eminent for wisdom and eloquence, bidding them esteem the excellence of one a blessing common to all. On the other hand he reminded them that the more gifted should forbear to exalt themselves to the prejudice of their humbler brethren, since it is God's prerogative to judge of real superiority. Rather should they considerately condescend to the weaker, remembering that absolute perfection in any case is a rare quality indeed. Each, then, should be willing to accord indulgence to the other for slight offences, to forgive and pass over mere human errors; holding mutual harmony in the highest honour, that no occasion of mockery might be given by their dissensions to those who are ever ready to blaspheme the word of God: for whose benefit indeed we should do all in our power, as for those who might be saved, were our state and conduct exhibited before them in an attractive light. Meantime they should be well aware of the fact, that the testimony given is by no means productive of blessing to all, since some who hear are glad to secure the supply of their mere bodily necessities, while others court the patronage of their superiors; some fix their affection on those who treat them with hospitable kindness, others again, being honoured with presents, love their benefactors in return; but few are they who really desire the word of testimony, and rare indeed is it to find a friend of truth. Hence the necessity of endeavouring to meet the case of all, and, physician-like, to administer to each that which may tend to the health of the soul, to the end that the saving doctrine may be fully honoured by all. Of this kind was the former part of his exhortation; and in conclusion he enjoined them to offer diligent supplications to God on his behalf. Having thus taken leave of them, he gave them all permission to return to their respective countries; and this they did with joy, and thenceforward that unity of judgment at which they had arrived in the emperor's presence continued to prevail, and those who had long been divided were bound together as members of the same body.

CHAPTER XXII

HAVING HONOURABLY DISMISSED SOME, HE WROTE LETTERS TO OTHERS, BESTOWING LIKEWISE PRESENTS IN MONEY

FULL of joy therefore at this success, the emperor presented as it were fair and pleasant fruits in the way of letters to those who had not been present at the council. He commanded also that ample gifts of money should be bestowed on all the people, both in the country and the cities, being pleased thus to honour the festive occasion of the twentieth anniversary of his reign.

CHAPTER XXIII

HE WRITES TO THE EGYPTIANS, EXHORTING THEM TO PEACE

AND now, when all else were at peace, among the Egyptians alone an implacable contention still raged, so as once more to disturb the emperor's tranquillity, though not to excite his anger. For indeed he treated the contending parties with all respect, as fathers, nay rather, as prophets of God; and again he summoned them to his presence, and again patiently acted as mediator between them, and honoured them with gifts. He communicated also the result of his arbitration by letter, confirming and sanctioning the decrees of the council, and calling on them to strive earnestly for concord, and not to distract and rend the Church, but to keep before them the thought of God's judgment on this behalf. And these injunctions he sent by a letter written with his own hand.

CHAPTER XXIV

HE WRITES FREQUENT LETTERS OF A RELIGIOUS CHARACTER TO THE BISHOPS AND PEOPLE

BUT besides these, his writings are very numerous on kindred subjects, and he was the author of a multitude of letters, some to the bishops, in which he laid injunctions on them tending to the advantage of the churches of God; and sometimes, thrice blessed as he was, he addressed the people of the churches generally, calling them his own brethren and fellow-servants. But perhaps we may hereafter find leisure to collect these despatches in a separate form, in order that the integrity of our present history may not be impaired by their insertion.

CHAPTER XXV

HE ORDERS THE ERECTION OF A CHURCH AT JERUSALEM, IN THE HOLY PLACE OF OUR SAVIOUR'S RESURRECTION

AFTER these things, the pious emperor addressed himself to another work truly worthy of record, in the province of Palestine. What then was this work? He judged it incumbent on him to render the blessed locality of our Saviour's resurrection an object of attraction and veneration to all. He issued immediate injunctions, therefore, for the erection in that spot of a house of prayer: and this he did, not on the mere natural impulse of his own mind, but feeling his spirit directed thereto by the Saviour Himself.

CHAPTER XXVI

HOW THE HOLY SEPULCHRE HAD BEEN COVERED WITH RUBBISH AND PROFANED WITH IDOLS BY THE UNGODLY

FOR it had been in time past the endeavour of impious men (or rather let me say of the whole race of evil spirits through their means), to consign to the darkness of oblivion that divine monument of immortality to which the radiant angel had descended from heaven, and rolled away the stone for those who still had stony hearts, and who supposed that the living One still lay among the dead; and had declared glad tidings to the women also, and removed their stony-hearted unbelief by the conviction that He whom they sought was alive. This sacred cave, then, certain impious and godless persons had thought to remove entirely from the eyes of men, supposing in their folly that thus they should be able effectually to obscure the truth. Accordingly they brought a quantity of earth from a distance with much labour, and covered the entire spot; then, having raised this to a moderate height, they paved it with stone, concealing the holy cave beneath this massive mound. Then, as though their purpose had been effectually accomplished, they prepare on this foundation a truly dreadful sepulchre of souls, by building a gloomy shrine of lifeless idols to the impure spirit whom they call Venus, and offering detestable oblations therein on profane and accursed altars. For they supposed that their object could no otherwise be fully attained, than by thus burying the sacred cave beneath these foul pollutions. Unhappy men! they were unable to comprehend how impossible it was that their attempt should remain unknown to Him who had been crowned with victory over death, any more than the blazing sun, when he rises above the earth, and holds his wonted course through the midst of heaven, is unseen by the whole race of mankind. Indeed, His saving power, shining with still greater brightness, and illumining, not the bodies, but the souls of men, was already filling the world with the effulgence of its own light. Nevertheless, these devices of impious and wicked men against the truth had prevailed for a long time, nor had any one of the governors, or military commanders, or even of the emperors themselves ever yet appeared, with ability to abolish these daring impieties, save only our prince, who enjoyed the favour of the King of kings. And now, acting as he did under the guidance of His Spirit, he could not consent to see the sacred spot of which we have spoken thus buried, through the devices of the adversaries, under every kind of impurity, and abandoned to obscenity and neglect; nor would he yield to the malice of those who had contracted this guilt, but gave orders that the place should be thoroughly purified, thinking that the parts which had been most polluted by the enemy ought to receive special tokens, through his means, of the greatness of the Divine favour. As soon, then, as his commands were issued, these engines of deceit were cast down from their proud eminence to the very ground, and the dwelling-places of error, with the statues and the evil spirits which they represented, were overthrown and utterly destroyed.

CHAPTER XXVII

CONSTANTINE COMMANDS THE MATERIALS OF THE IDOL-TEMPLE, AND THE SOIL ITSELF, TO BE REMOVED AND THROWN TO A DISTANCE

NOR did the emperor's zeal stop here; but he gave further orders that the materials of what was thus destroyed, both stone and timber, should be removed and thrown as far from the spot as possible; and this command also was speedily executed. The emperor, however, was not satisfied with having proceeded thus far: once more, fired with holy ardour, he directed that the ground itself should be dug up to a considerable depth, and the soil which had been polluted by the foul impurities of demon worship transported to a far distant place.

CHAPTER XXVIII

DISCOVERY OF THE MOST HOLY SEPULCHRE

THIS also was accomplished without delay. But as soon as the original surface of the ground, beneath the covering of earth, appeared, immediately, and contrary to all expectation, the venerable and hallowed monument of our Saviour's resurrection was discovered. Then indeed did this most holy cave present a faithful similitude of His return to life, in that, after lying buried in darkness, it again emerged to light, and afforded to all who came to witness the sight, a clear and visible proof of the wonders of which that spot had once been the scene, a testimony to the resurrection of the Saviour clearer than any voice could give.

CHAPTER XXIX

HE WRITES CONCERNING THE ERECTION OF A CHURCH, BOTH TO THE GOVERNORS OF THE PROVINCES, AND TO THE BISHOP MACARIUS

IMMEDIATELY after the transactions I have recorded, the emperor sent forth injunctions which breathed a truly pious spirit, at the same time granting ample supplies of money, and commanding that a house of prayer worthy of the worship of God should be erected near the Saviour's tomb on a scale of rich and royal greatness. This object he had indeed for some time kept in view, and had foreseen, as if by the aid of a superior intelligence, that which should afterwards come to pass. He laid his commands, therefore, on the governors of the Eastern provinces, that by an abundant and unsparing expenditure they should secure the completion of the work on a scale of noble and ample magnificence. He also despatched the following letter to the bishop who at that time presided over the church at Jerusalem, in which he clearly asserted the saving doctrine of the faith, writing in these terms.

CHAPTER XXX

CONSTANTINE'S LETTER TO MACARIUS RESPECTING THE BUILDING OF A MEMORIAL OF OUR SAVIOUR'S DEATH

"VICTOR CONSTANTINUS, MAXIMUS AUGUSTUS, to Macarius.

"Such is our Saviour's grace, that no power of language seems adequate to describe the wondrous circumstance to which I am about to refer. For, that the monument of His most holy Passion, so long ago buried beneath the ground, should have remained unknown for so long a series of years, until its reappearance to His servants now set free through the removal of him who was the common enemy of all, is a fact which truly surpasses all admiration. For if all who are accounted wise throughout the world were to unite in their endeavours to say somewhat worthy of this event, they would be unable to attain their object in the smallest degree. Indeed, the nature of this miracle as far transcends the capacity of human reason as heavenly things are superior to the interests of men. For this cause it is ever my first, and indeed my only object, that, as the authority of the truth is evincing itself daily by fresh wonders, so our souls may all become more zealous, with all sobriety and earnest unanimity, for the honour of the Divine law. I desire, therefore, especially, that you should be persuaded of that which I suppose is evident to all beside, namely, that I have no greater care than how I may best adorn with a splendid structure that sacred spot, which, under Divine direction, I have disencumbered as it were of the heavy weight of foul idol worship; a spot which has been accounted holy from the beginning in God's judgment, but which now appears holier still, since it has brought to light a clear assurance of our Saviour's passion.

CHAPTER XXXI

HE DESIRED THAT THE BUILDING SHOULD SURPASS ALL THE CHURCHES IN THE WORLD IN THE BEAUTY OF ITS WALLS, ITS COLUMNS, AND MARBLES

"IT will be well, therefore, for your Sagacity to make such arrangements and provision of all things needful for the work, that not only the church itself as a whole may surpass all others whatsoever in beauty, but that the details of the building may be of such a kind that the fairest structures in any city of the empire may be excelled by this. And with respect to the erection and decoration of the walls, this is to inform you that our friend Dracilianus, the deputy of the Prætorian Præfects, and the governor of the province, have received a charge from us. For our pious directions to them are to the effect that artificers and labourers, and whatever they shall understand from your Sagacity to be needful for the advancement of the work, shall forthwith be furnished by their care. And as to the columns and marbles, whatever you shall judge, after actual inspection of the plan, to be especially precious and serviceable, be diligent to send information to us in writing, in order that whatever materials and in whatever quantity we shall esteem from your letter to be needful, may be procured from every quarter, as required.

CHAPTER XXXII

DIRECTIONS TO THE PRESIDENTS CONCERNING THE BEAUTIFYING OF THE ROOF; ALSO CONCERNING THE WORKMEN, AND MATERIALS

"WITH respect to the roof of the church, I wish to know from you whether in your judgment it should be ceiled, or finished with any other kind of workmanship. If the ceiling be adopted, it may also be ornamented with gold. For the rest, your Holiness will give information as early as possible to the beforementioned magistrates how many labourers and artificers, and what expenditure of money is required. You will also be careful to send us a report without delay, not only respecting the marbles and columns, but the ceiling also, should this appear to you to be the most beautiful form. God preserve you, beloved brother!"

CHAPTER XXXIII

HOW THE CHURCH OF OUR SAVIOUR WAS BUILT, WHICH ANSWERED TO THE NEW JERUSALEM PROPHESIED OF IN SCRIPTURE

THIS was the emperor's letter; and his directions were at once carried into effect. Accordingly, on the very spot which witnessed the Saviour's sufferings, a new Jerusalem was constructed, over against the one so celebrated of old, which, since the foul stain of guilt brought on it by the murder of the Lord, had experienced the last extremity of desolation, the effect of Divine judgment on its impious people. It was opposite this city that the emperor now began to rear a monument to the Saviour's victory over death, with rich and lavish magnificence. And it may be that this was that second and new Jerusalem spoken of in the predictions of the prophets, concerning which such abundant testimony is given in the divinely inspired records.

First of all, then, he adorned the sacred cave itself, as the chief part of the whole work, and the hallowed monument at which the angel radiant with light had once declared to all that regeneration which was first manifested in the Saviour's person.

CHAPTER XXXIV

DESCRIPTION OF THE FABRIC OF THE HOLY SEPULCHRE

THIS monument, therefore, first of all, as the chief part of the whole, the emperor's zealous magnificence beautified with rare columns, and profusely enriched with the most splendid decorations of every kind.

CHAPTER XXXV

DESCRIPTION OF THE ATRIUM AND PORTICOS

THE next object of his attention was a space of ground of great extent, and open to the pure air of heaven. This he adorned with a pavement of finely polished stone, and enclosed it on three sides with porticos of great length.

CHAPTER XXXVI

DESCRIPTION OF THE WALLS, ROOF, DECORATION, AND GILDING, OF THE BODY OF THE CHURCH

FOR at the side opposite to the sepulchre, which was the eastern side, the church itself was erected; a noble work rising to a vast height, and of great extent both in length and breadth. The interior of this structure was floored with marble slabs of various colours; while the external surface of the walls, which shone with polished stones exactly fitted together, exhibited a degree of splendour in no respect inferior to that of marble. With regard to the roof, it was covered on the outside with lead, as a protection against the rains of winter. But the inner part of the roof, which was finished with sculptured fretwork, extended in a series of connected compartments, like a vast sea, over the whole church; and, being overlaid throughout with the purest gold, caused the entire building to glitter as it were with rays of light.

CHAPTER XXXVII

DESCRIPTION OF THE DOUBLE PORTICOS ON EITHER SIDE, AND OF THE THREE EASTERN GATES

BESIDES this were two porticos on each side, with upper and lower ranges of pillars, corresponding in length with the church itself; and these also had their roofs ornamented with gold. Of these porticos, those which were exterior to the church, were supported by columns of great size, while those within these, rested on piles of stone beautifully adorned on the surface. Three gates, placed exactly east, were intended to receive those who entered the church.

CHAPTER XXXVIII

DESCRIPTION OF THE HEMISPHERE, THE TWELVE COLUMNS, AND THEIR BOWLS

OPPOSITE these gates the crowning part of the whole was the hemisphere, which rose to the very summit of the church. This was encircled by twelve columns, (according to the number of the apostles of our Saviour,) having their capitals embellished with silver bowls of great size, which the emperor himself presented as a splendid offering to his God.

CHAPTER XXXIX

DESCRIPTION OF THE ATRIUM, THE COURTS, AND PORCHES

IN the next place he enclosed the atrium, which occupied the space leading to the entrances in front of the church. This comprehended, first the court, then the porticos on each side, and lastly the gates of the court. After these, in the midst of the open market-place, the entrance gates of the whole work, which were of exquisite workmanship, afforded to passers by on the outside a view of the interior which could not fail to inspire astonishment.

CHAPTER XL

OF THE NUMBER OF HIS OFFERINGS

THIS temple, then, the emperor erected as a conspicuous monument of the Saviour's resurrection, and embellished it throughout on an imperial scale of magnificence. He further enriched it with numberless offerings of inexpressible beauty, consisting of gold, silver, and precious stones, in various forms; the skilful and elaborate arrangement of which, in regard to their magnitude, number, and variety, we have not leisure at present to describe particularly.

CHAPTER XLI

OF THE ERECTION OF CHURCHES IN BETHLEHEM, AND ON THE MOUNT OF OLIVES

IN the same country he discovered other places, venerable as being the localities of two sacred caves: and these also he adorned with lavish magnificence. In the one case, he rendered due honour to that which had been the scene of the first manifestation of our Saviour's divine presence, when He submitted to be born in mortal flesh; while in the case of the second cavern he hallowed the remembrance of His ascension to heaven from the mountain top. And while he thus nobly testified his reverence for these places, he at the same time eternized the memory of his mother, who had been the instrument of conferring so valuable a benefit on mankind.

CHAPTER XLII

THAT HELENA AUGUSTA, CONSTANTINE'S MOTHER, HAVING VISITED THIS LOCALITY FOR DEVOTIONAL PURPOSES, BUILT THESE CHURCHES

FOR this empress, having resolved to discharge the duties of pious devotion to the Supreme God, and feeling it incumbent on her to render thanksgivings with prayers on behalf both of her own son, now so mighty an emperor, and of his sons, her own grandchildren, the divinely favoured Cæsars, with youthful alacrity (though now advanced in years, yet gifted with no common degree of wisdom), had hastened to survey this venerable land; and at the same time to visit the eastern provinces, cities, and people, with a truly imperial solicitude. As soon, then, as she had rendered due reverence to the ground which the

Saviour's feet had trodden, according to the prophetic word which says "Let us worship at the place whereon His feet have stood," she immediately bequeathed the fruit of her piety to future generations.

CHAPTER XLIII

A FURTHER NOTICE OF THE CHURCHES AT BETHLEHEM

FOR without delay she dedicated two churches to the God whom she adored, one at the grotto which had been the scene of the Saviour's birth; the other on the mount of His ascension. For He who was "God with us" had submitted to be born even in a cave of the earth, and the place of His nativity was called Bethlehem by the Hebrews. Accordingly the pious empress honoured with rare memorials the scene of her travail who bore this heavenly child, and beautified the sacred cave with all possible splendour. The emperor himself soon after testified his reverence for the spot by princely offerings, and added to his mother's magnificence by costly presents of silver and gold, and embroidered curtains. Once more, his imperial mother raised a stately structure on the Mount of Olives also, in memory of His ascent to heaven who is the Saviour of mankind, erecting a sacred church or temple on the very summit of the mount. And indeed authentic history informs us that in a cave on this very spot the Saviour imparted mysterious and secret revelations to His disciples. And here also the emperor testified his reverence for the King of kings, by diverse and costly offerings. Thus did Helena Augusta, the pious mother of a pious emperor, erect these two noble and beautiful monuments of devotion, worthy of everlasting remembrance, to the honour of God her Saviour, and as proofs of her holy zeal: and thus did she receive from her son the countenance and aid of his imperial power. Nor was it long ere this aged lady reaped the due reward of her labours. After passing the whole period of her life, even to declining age, in the greatest prosperity, and exhibiting both in word and deed abundant fruits of obedience to the divine precepts, and having enjoyed in consequence an easy and tranquil existence, with unimpaired powers of body and mind, at length she obtained from God, an end befitting her pious course, and a recompense of her good deeds even in this present life.

CHAPTER XLIV

OF HELENA'S GENEROSITY, AND BENEFICENT ACTS

FOR on the occasion of a circuit which she made of the eastern provinces, with circumstances of royal splendour, she bestowed abundant proofs of her liberality as well on the inhabitants of the several cities collectively, as on individuals who approached her, at the same time that she scattered largesses among the soldiery with a liberal hand. But especially abundant were the gifts she bestowed on the naked and friendless poor. To some she gave money, to others an ample supply of clothing: she liberated some from imprisonment, or from the bitter servitude of the mines; others she delivered from unjust oppression, and others again, she restored from exile to their native land.

CHAPTER XLV

HER PIOUS CONDUCT IN THE CHURCHES

WHILE, however, her character derived lustre from such deeds as I have described, she was far from neglecting personal piety toward God. She might be seen continually frequenting His Church, while at the same time she adorned the houses of prayer with splendid offerings, not overlooking the churches of the smallest cities. In short, this admirable woman was to be seen, in simple and modest attire, mingling with the crowd of worshippers, and testifying her devotion to God by a uniform course of pious conduct.

CHAPTER XLVI

SHE MAKES HER WILL, AND DIES AT THE AGE OF EIGHTY YEARS

AND when at length, at the close of a long life, she was called to inherit a happier lot, having arrived at the eightieth year of her age, and being very near the time of her departure, she prepared and executed her last will in favour of her only son, the emperor and sole monarch of the world, and her grandchildren, the Cæsars his sons, to whom severally she bequeathed whatever property she possessed in any part of the world. Having thus disposed of her earthly affairs, this thrice blessed woman breathed her last in the presence of her illustrious son, who was in attendance at her side, and clasped her hands:

so that, to those who rightly discerned the truth, she seemed to experience a real change and transition from an earthly to a heavenly existence, since her soul, remoulded as it were into an incorruptible and angelic essence, was received up into her Saviour's presence.

CHAPTER XLVII

HOW CONSTANTINE BURIED HIS MOTHER, AND HOW HE HONOURED HER DURING HER LIFE

HER body, too, was honoured with special tokens of respect, being escorted on its way to the imperial city by a vast train of guards, and there deposited in a royal tomb. Such were the last days of our emperor's mother, a person worthy of being had in perpetual remembrance, both for her own practical piety, and because she had given birth to so extraordinary and admirable an offspring. And well may his character be styled blessed, for his filial piety as well as on other grounds. He rendered her through his influence so devout a worshipper of God (though not previously so), that she seemed to have been instructed from the first by the Saviour of mankind: and besides this, he had honoured her so fully with imperial dignities, that in every province, and in the very ranks of the soldiery, she was spoken of under the titles of Augusta, and empress, and her likeness was impressed on golden coins. He had even granted her authority over the imperial treasures, to use and dispense them according to her own will and discretion in every case; for this enviable distinction also she received at the hands of her son. Hence it is that among the qualities which shed a lustre on his memory, we may rightly include that surpassing degree of filial affection whereby he rendered full obedience to the Divine precepts which enjoin due honour from children to their parents. In this manner, then, the emperor executed in Palestine the noble works I have above described: and indeed in every province he raised new churches on a far more imposing scale than those which had existed before his time.

CHAPTER XLVIII

HE BUILDS CHURCHES IN HONOUR OF MARTYRS, AND ABOLISHES IDOLATRY AT CONSTANTINOPLE

AND being fully resolved to distinguish the city which bore his name with especial honour, he embellished it with numerous sacred edifices, both memorials of martyrs on the largest scale, and other buildings of the most splendid kind, not only within the city itself, but in its vicinity: and thus at the same time he rendered honour to the memory of the martyrs, and consecrated his city to the martyrs' God. Being filled, too, with Divine wisdom, he determined to purge the city which was to be distinguished by his own name from idolatry of every kind, that henceforth no statues might be worshipped there in the temples of those falsely reputed to be gods, nor any altars defiled by the pollution of blood: that there might be no sacrifices consumed by fire, no demon festivals, nor any of the other ceremonies usually observed by the slaves of superstition.

CHAPTER XLIX

REPRESENTATION OF THE CROSS IN THE PALACE, AND OF DANIEL AT THE PUBLIC FOUNTAINS

ON the other hand one might see the fountains in the midst of the forum graced with figures representing the good Shepherd (well known to those who study the sacred oracles), and that of Daniel also with the lions, forged in brass, and resplendent with plates of gold. Indeed, so large a measure of Divine love possessed the emperor's soul, that in the principal apartment of the imperial palace itself, on a vast tablet displayed in the centre of its gilded ceiling, he caused the symbol of our Saviour's Passion to be fixed, composed of a variety of precious stones richly inwrought with gold: and this symbol the pious prince seemed to have intended to be as it were the safeguard of the empire itself.

CHAPTER L

HE ERECTS CHURCHES IN NICOMEDIA, AND IN OTHER CITIES

HAVING thus embellished the city which bore his name, he next distinguished the metropolis of Bithynia by the erection of a stately and magnificent church, being desirous of raising in this city also, in honour of his Saviour and at his own charges, a memorial of his victory over his own enemies and the adversaries of God. He also decorated the principal cities of the other provinces with sacred edifices of great beauty; as, for example, in the case of that metropolis of the East which derived its name from Antiochus, in which, as the head of that portion of the empire, he consecrated to the service of God a church of unparalleled size and beauty. The entire building was encompassed by an enclosure of great extent, within which the church itself rose to a vast elevation, being of an octagonal form, and surrounded on all sides by many chambers, courts, and upper and lower apartments; the whole richly adorned with a profusion of gold, brass, and other materials of the most costly kind.

CHAPTER LI

HE ORDERS A CHURCH TO BE BUILT AT MAMBRE

SUCH were the principal sacred edifices erected by the emperor's command. But having heard that the self-same Saviour who erewhile had appeared on earth had in ages long since past afforded a manifestation of His Divine presence to holy men of Palestine near the oak of Mambre, he ordered that a house of prayer should be built there also in honour of the God who had thus appeared. Accordingly the imperial commission was transmitted to the provincial governors by letters addressed to them individually, enjoining a speedy completion of the appointed work. He sent moreover to the writer of this history an eloquent admonition, a copy of which I think it well to insert in the present work, in order to convey a just idea of his pious diligence and zeal. To express, then, his displeasure at the evil practices which he had heard were usual in the place just referred to, he addressed me in the following terms.

CHAPTER LII

CONSTANTINE'S LETTER TO EUSEBIUS CONCERNING MAMBRE

"VICTOR CONSTANTINUS, MAXIMUS AUGUSTUS, to Macarius, and the rest of the bishops in Palestine.

"One benefit, and that of no ordinary importance, has been conferred on us by my truly pious mother-in-law, in that she has made known to us by letter that abandoned folly of impious men which has hitherto escaped detection by you: so that the criminal conduct thus overlooked may now obtain, through our means, that attention and correction which are absolutely needed, however tardily applied. For surely it is a grave impiety indeed, that holy places should be defiled by the stain of unhallowed impurities. What then is this, dearest brethren, which, though it has eluded your sagacity, she of whom I speak was impelled by a pious sense of duty to disclose?

CHAPTER LIII

THAT OUR SAVIOUR APPEARED IN THIS PLACE TO ABRAHAM

"SHE assures me, then, that the place which takes its name from the oak of Mambre, where we find that Abraham dwelt, is defiled by certain of the slaves of superstition in every possible way. She declares that idols which should be utterly destroyed have been erected on the site of that tree; that an altar is near the spot; and that impure sacrifices are continually performed. Now since it is evident that these practices are equally inconsistent with the character of our times, and unworthy the sanctity of the place itself, I wish your Gravities to be informed that the illustrious Count Acacius, our friend, has received instructions by letter from me, to the effect that every idol which shall be found in the place above-mentioned shall immediately be consigned to the flames; that the altar be utterly demolished; and that if any one, after this our mandate, shall be guilty of impiety of any kind in this place, he shall be visited with condign punishment. The place itself we have directed to be adorned with an unpolluted structure, I mean a church; in order that it may become a fitting place of assembly for holy men. Meantime, should any breach of these our commands occur, it should be made known to our clemency without the least delay by letters from you, that we may direct the person detected to be dealt with, as a transgressor of the law, in the severest manner. For you are not ignorant that the Supreme God first appeared to Abraham, and conversed with him, in that place. There it was that the observance of the Divine law first began; there first the Saviour Himself, with the two angels, vouchsafed to Abraham a manifestation of His presence; there God first appeared to men; there He gave promise to Abraham concerning his future seed, and straightway fulfilled that promise; there He foretold that he should be the father of a multitude of nations. For these reasons, it seems to me right that this place should not only be kept pure through our diligence from all defilement, but restored also to its pristine sanctity; that nothing hereafter may be done there except the performance of fitting service to Him who is the Almighty God, and our Saviour, and Lord of all. And this service it is incumbent on you to care for with due attention, if your Gravities be willing (and of this I feel confident), to gratify my wishes, which are especially interested in the worship of God. May He preserve you, beloved brethren!"

CHAPTER LIV

THE IDOL TEMPLES AND IMAGES EVERY WHERE DESTROYED

ALL these things the emperor diligently performed to the praise of the saving power of Christ, and thus made it his constant aim to glorify his Saviour God. On the other hand he used every means to rebuke the superstitious errors of the heathen. Hence the entrances of their temples in the several cities were left exposed to the weather, being stripped of their doors at his command; the tiling of others was removed, and their roofs destroyed. From others again the venerable statues of brass, of which the superstition of antiquity had boasted for a long series of years, were exposed to view in all the public places of the imperial city: so that here a Pythian, there a Sminthian Apollo, excited the contempt of the beholder; while the Delphic tripods were deposited in the circus, and the Muses of Helicon in the palace itself. In short, the city of Constantinople was every where filled with brazen statues of the most exquisite workmanship, which had been dedicated in every province, and which the deluded victims of superstition had long vainly honoured as gods with numberless victims and burnt sacrifices, though now at length they learnt to renounce their error, when the emperor held up the very objects of their worship to be the ridicule and sport of all beholders. With regard to those images which were of gold, he dealt with them in a different manner. For as soon as he understood that the ignorant multitudes were inspired with a vain and childish dread of these bugbears of error, wrought in gold and silver, he judged it right to remove these also (like stumbling-stones thrown in the way of men walking in the dark), and henceforward to open a plain and unobstructed road to all. Having formed this resolution, he considered no military force needful for the repression of the evil: a few of his own friends sufficed for this service, and these he sent by a simple expression of his will to visit each several province. Accordingly, sustained by confidence in the emperor's pious intentions and their own personal devotion to God, they passed through the midst of numberless tribes and nations, abolishing this ancient error in every city and country. They ordered the priests themselves, amidst general laughter and scorn, to bring their gods from their dark recesses to the light of day: they then stripped them of their ornaments, and exhibited to the gaze of all the unsightly reality which had been hidden beneath a painted exterior. Lastly, whatever part of the material appeared valuable they scraped off and melted in the fire to prove its worth, after which they secured and set apart whatever they judged needful for their purpose, leaving to the superstitious worshippers that which was altogether useless, as a memorial of their shame. Meanwhile our admirable prince was himself engaged in a work similar to what we have described. For at the same time that these costly images of the dead were stripped, as we have said, of their precious materials, he also attacked those composed of brass; causing those to be dragged from their places with ropes and as it were carried away captive, whom the dotage of antiquity had esteemed as gods.

CHAPTER LV

OVERTHROW OF AN IDOL TEMPLE, AND ABOLITION OF LICENTIOUS PRACTICES, AT APHACA IN PHŒNICIA

THE emperor's next care was to kindle, as it were, a brilliant torch, by the light of which he directed his imperial gaze around, to see if any hidden vestiges of error might still exist. And as the keen-sighted eagle in its heaven-ward flight, is able to descry from its lofty height the most distant objects on the earth, so did he, while residing in the imperial palace of his own fair city, discover as from a watch-tower a hidden and fatal snare of souls in the province of Phœnicia. This was a grove and temple, not situated in the midst of any city, nor in any public place (as mostly is the case with a view to splendour of effect), but apart from the beaten and frequented road, at Aphaca, on part of the summit of Mount Libanus, and dedicated to the foul demon known by the name of Venus. It was a school of wickedness for all the abandoned votaries of sensuality and impurity. Here men undeserving of the name forgot the dignity of their sex, and propitiated the demon by their effeminate conduct; here too unlawful commerce of women and adulterous intercourse, with other horrible and infamous practices, were perpetrated in this temple as in a place beyond the scope and restraint of law. Meantime these evils remained unchecked by the presence of any observer, since no one of fair character ventured to visit such scenes. These proceedings, however, could not escape the vigilance of our august emperor, who, having himself inspected them with characteristic forethought, and judging that such a temple was unfit for the light of heaven, gave orders that the building with its offerings should be utterly destroyed. Accordingly, in obedience to the imperial command, these engines of an abandoned superstition were immediately abolished, and the hand of military force was made instrumental in purging the impurities of the place. And now those who had heretofore lived without restraint found an inducement to modesty in the emperor's threat of punishment, as did also those superstitious Gentiles who had boasted in their fancied wisdom, but now obtained experimental proof of their own vanity and folly.

CHAPTER LVI

DESTRUCTION OF THE TEMPLE OF ÆSCULAPIUS AT ÆGÆ

FOR since it happened that many of these pretenders to wisdom were deluded votaries of the demon worshipped in Cilicia, whom thousands regarded with reverence as the possessor of saving and healing power, who sometimes appeared to those who passed the night in his temple, sometimes restored the diseased to health (though in reality he was a destroyer of souls, who drew his easily deluded worshippers from the true Saviour to involve them in impious error), the emperor, consistently with his practice, and desire to advance the worship of Him who is at once a jealous God and the true Saviour, gave directions that this temple also should be razed to the ground. In prompt obedience to this command, a band of soldiers laid this building, the object of admiration even to noble philosophers, prostrate in the dust, together with its unseen inmate, neither demon nor god, but rather a deceiver of souls, who had seduced mankind for so long a series of years. And thus he who had promised to others deliverance from misfortune and distress, could find no means for his own security, any more, than when (as fables feign) he was scorched by the lightning's stroke. Our emperor's pious deeds, however, had in them nothing fabulous or feigned; but by virtue of the manifested power of his Saviour, this temple as well as others was so utterly overthrown, that not a vestige of the former follies was left behind.

CHAPTER LVII

HOW THE GENTILES ABANDONED IDOL WORSHIP, AND TURNED TO THE KNOWLEDGE OF GOD

HENCE it was that, of those who had been the slaves of superstition, when they saw with their own eyes the exposure of the delusion by which they had been enthralled, and beheld the actual ruin of the temples and images in every place, some applied themselves to the saving doctrine of Christ; while others, though they declined to take this step, yet reprobated the senseless creed of their fathers, and laughed those falsities to scorn, which they had so long been accustomed to regard as gods. Indeed, what other feelings could possess their minds, when they witnessed the thorough uncleanness concealed beneath the fair exterior of the objects of their worship? Beneath this were found either the bones of dead men or dry skulls, fraudulently obtained by designing impostors, or filthy rags full of abominable impurity, or a bundle of hay or stubble. On seeing all these things heaped together within their lifeless images, they denounced their fathers' folly and their own, especially when neither in the secret recesses of the temples nor in the statues themselves could any inmate be found; neither demon, nor utterer of oracles, neither god nor prophet, as they had heretofore supposed: nay, not even a dim and shadowy phantom could be seen. Accordingly, every gloomy cavern, every hidden recess, afforded easy access to the emperor's emissaries: the inaccessible and secret chambers, the innermost shrines of the temples, were trampled by the soldiers' feet; and thus the mental blindness which had prevailed for so many ages over the gentile world became clearly apparent to the eyes of all.

CHAPTER LVIII

CONSTANTINE DESTROYS THE TEMPLE OF VENUS AT HELIOPOLTS, AND BUILDS THE FIRST CHURCH IN THAT CITY

SUCH actions as I have described may well be reckoned among the emperor's noblest achievements, as also the wise arrangements which he made respecting each particular province. We may instance the Phœnician city Heliopolis, in which those who dignify licentious pleasure with a distinguishing title of honour, had permitted their wives and daughters to commit shameless fornication. But now a new statute, breathing the very spirit of modesty, proceeded from the emperor, which peremptorily forbade the continuance of former practices. And besides this, he sent them also written exhortations, as though he had been especially ordained by God for this end, that he might instruct all men in the principles of charity. Hence, he disdained not to communicate by letter even with these persons, urging them to seek diligently the knowledge of God. At the same time he followed up his words by corresponding deeds, and erected even in this city a church of great size and magnificence: so that an event unheard of before in any age, now for the first time came to pass, namely, that a city which had hitherto been wholly given up to superstition now obtained the privilege of a church of God, with presbyters and deacons, and its people were placed under the presiding care of a bishop consecrated to the service of the supreme God. And further, the emperor, being anxious that here also as many as possible might be won to the profession of the truth, bestowed abundant provision for the necessities of the poor, desiring even thus to invite them to seek the doctrines of salvation, as though he were almost adopting the words of him who said, "Whether in pretence, or in truth, let Christ be preached."

CHAPTER LIX

OF THE DISTURBANCES RAISED AT ANTIOCH ON ACCOUNT OF EUSTATHIUS

IN the midst, however, of the general happiness occasioned by these events, and while the Church of God was every where and every way flourishing throughout the empire, once more that spirit of envy, who ever watches for the ruin of the good, prepared himself to combat the greatness of our prosperity, in the expectation, perhaps, that the emperor himself, provoked by our tumults and disorders, might eventually become estranged from us. Accordingly, he kindled a furious controversy at Antioch, and thereby involved the church in that place in a series of tragic calamities, which had well nigh occasioned the total overthrow of the city. The members of the Church were divided into two opposite parties; while the people, including even the magistrates and soldiery, regarded each other with feelings of bitter hostility; so that the contest would have been decided by the sword, had not the watchful providence of God, as well as dread of the emperor's displeasure, controlled the fury of the multitude. On this occasion too, the emperor, acting the part of a preserver and physician of souls, applied with much forbearance the remedy of persuasion to those who needed it. He gently pleaded, as it were by an embassy, with his people, sending among them one of the best approved and most faithful of those who were honoured with the dignity of Count; at the same time that he exhorted them to a peaceable spirit by repeated letters, and instructed them in the practice of true godliness. Having prevailed by these remonstrances, he excused their conduct in his subsequent letters, alleging that he had himself heard the merits of the case from him on whose account the disturbance had arisen. And these letters of his, which are replete with learning and instruction of no ordinary kind, I should have inserted in this present work, were it not that they might affix a mark of dishonour to the character of the persons accused. I will therefore omit these, being unwilling to revive the memory of past grievances, and will only annex those to my present narrative which he wrote to testify his satisfaction at the re-establishment of peace and concord among the rest, In these letters, he cautioned them against any desire to claim the ruler of another district as their own (through whose intervention peace had been restored), and exhorted them, consistently with the usage of the Church, to choose him as their bishop, whom the common Saviour of all should point out as suited for the office. His letter, then, is addressed to the people and to the bishops, severally, in the following terms.

CHAPTER LX

CONSTANTINE'S LETTER TO THE ANTIOCHIANS, DIRECTING THEM NOT TO WITHDRAW EUSEBIUS FROM CÆSAREA, BUT TO SEEK FOR ANOTHER BISHOP

"VICTOR CONSTANTINUS, MAXIMUS AUGUSTUS, to the people of Antioch.

"How pleasing to the wise and intelligent portion of mankind is the concord which exists among you! And I myself, brethren, am disposed to love you with an enduring affection, inspired both by religion, and by your own manner of life and zeal on my behalf. It is by the exercise of right understanding and sound discretion, that we are enabled really to enjoy our blessings. And what can become you so well as this discretion? No wonder, then, if I affirm that your maintenance of the truth has tended rather to promote your security than to draw on you the hatred of others. Indeed, amongst brethren, whom the selfsame disposition to walk in the ways of truth and righteousness promises, through the favour of God, to register among His pure and holy family, what can be more honourable than gladly to acquiesce in the prosperity of all men? Especially since the precepts of the Divine law prescribe a better direction to your proposed intention, and we ourselves desire that your judgment should be confirmed by proper sanction. It may be that you are surprised, and at a loss to understand the meaning of this introduction to my present address. The cause of it I will not hesitate to explain without reserve. I confess, then, that on reading your records I perceived, by the highly eulogistic testimony which they bear to Eusebius bishop of Cæsarea (whom I have myself long well known and esteemed for his learning and moderation), that you are strongly attached to him, and desire to appropriate him as your own prelate. What thoughts, then, do you suppose that I entertain on this subject, desirous as I am to seek for and act on the strict principles of right? What anxiety do you imagine this desire of yours has caused me? O holy faith, who givest us in our Saviour's words and precepts a model, as it were, of what our life should be, how hardly wouldst thou thyself resist the course of sin, were it not that thou refusest to subserve the purposes of gain! In my own judgment, he whose first object is the maintenance of peace, seems to be superior to Victory herself; and where a right and honourable course lies open to one's choice, surely no one would hesitate to adopt it. I ask then, brethren, why do we so decide as to inflict an injury on others by our choice? Why do we covet those objects which will destroy the credit of our own character? I myself highly esteem the individual whom ye judge worthy of your respect and affection: notwithstanding, it cannot be right that those principles should be entirely disregarded which should be authoritative and binding on all alike; for example, that each should be content with the limits assigned them, and that all should enjoy their proper privileges: nor can it be right, in considering the claims of rival candidates, to suppose but that not one only, but many, may appear worthy of comparison with this person. For as long as no violence or harshness are suffered to disturb the dignities of the church, they continue to be on an equal footing, and worthy of the same consideration every where. Nor is it reasonable that an inquiry into the qualifications of one person should be made to the detriment of others; since the judgment of all churches, whether reckoned of greater or less importance in themselves, is equally capable of receiving and maintaining the Divine ordinances, so that one is in no way inferior to another (if we will but boldly declare the truth), in regard to that standard of practice which is common to all. If this be so, we must say that you will be chargeable, not with retaining this prelate, but with wrongfully removing him; your conduct will be characterized rather by violence than justice; and whatever may be generally thought by others, I dare clearly and boldly affirm that this measure will furnish ground of accusation against you, and will provoke factious disturbances of the most mischievous kind: for even timid flocks can shew the use and power of their teeth, when the watchful care of their shepherd declines, and they find themselves bereft of his accustomed guidance. If this then be really so, if I am not deceived in my judgment, let this, brethren, be your first consideration (for many and important considerations will immediately present themselves, if you adopt my advice), whether, should you persist in your intention, that mutual kindly feeling and affection which should subsist among you will suffer no diminution? In the next place, remember that Eusebius, who came among you for the purpose of offering disinterested counsel, now enjoys the reward which is due to him in the judgment of heaven; for he has received no ordinary recompense in the high testimony you have borne to his equitable conduct. Lastly, in accordance with your usual sound judgment, do ye exhibit a becoming diligence in selecting the person of whom you stand in need, carefully avoiding all factious and tumultuous clamour; for such clamour is always wrong, and from the collision of discordant elements both sparks and flame will arise. I protest, as I desire to please God and you, and to enjoy a happiness commensurate with your kind wishes, that I love you, and the quiet haven of your gentleness, now that you have cast from you that which defiled, and received in its place at once sound morality and concord, firmly planting in the vessel the sacred standard, and guided, as one may say, by a helm of iron in your course onward to the light of heaven. Receive then on board that merchandise which is incorruptible, since all impurity has been drained, as it were, from the vessel; and be careful henceforth so to secure the enjoyment of all your present blessing, that you may not seem at any future time either to have determined any measure on the impulse of inconsiderate or ill-directed zeal, or in the first instance rashly to have entered on an inexpedient course. May God preserve you, beloved brethren!"

CHAPTER LXI

THE EMPEROR'S LETTER TO EUSEBIUS, ON THE OCCASION OF HIS REFUSING THE BISHOPRIC OF ANTIOCH

"VICTOR CONSTANTINUS, MAXIMUS AUGUSTUS, to Eusebius.

"I have most carefully perused your letter, and perceive that you have strictly conformed to the rule enjoined by the discipline of the church. Now to abide by that which appears at the same time pleasing to God, and accordant with apostolical tradition, is a proof of true piety: and you have reason to deem yourself happy on this behalf, that you are counted worthy, in the judgment, I may say, of all the world, to have the oversight of the whole church. For the desire which all feel to claim you for their own, undoubtedly enhances your enviable fortune in this respect. Notwithstanding, your Prudence, whose resolve it is to observe the ordinances of God and the apostolic rule of the church, has done excellently well in declining the bishopric of the Church at Antioch, and desiring to continue in that Church of which you first received the oversight by the will of God. I have written on this subject to the people of Antioch, and also to your colleagues in the ministry who had themselves consulted me in regard to this question; on reading which letters, your Holiness will easily discern, that (inasmuch as justice itself opposed their claims) I have written to them under divine direction. It will be necessary that your Prudence should be present at their conference, in order that this decision may be ratified in the Church at Antioch. God preserve you, beloved brother!"

CHAPTER LXII

CONSTANTINE'S LETTER TO THE COUNCIL, DEPRECATING THE REMOVAL OF EUSEBIUS FROM CÆSAREA

"VICTOR CONSTANTINUS, MAXIMUS AUGUSTUS, to Theodotus, Theodorus, Narcissus, Aëtius, Alpheus, and the rest of the bishops who are at Antioch.

"I have perused the letters written by your Prudences, and highly approve of the wise resolution of your colleague in the ministry, Eusebius. Having, moreover, been informed of the circumstances of the case, partly by your letters, partly by those of our illustrious friends Acacius and Strategius, after sufficient investigation I have written to the people of Antioch, suggesting the course which will be at once pleasing to God and advantageous for the Church. A copy of this I have ordered to be subjoined to this present letter, in order that ye yourselves may know what I thought fit, as an advocate of the cause of justice, to write to that people: since I find in your letter this proposal, that, in consonance with the choice of the people, sanctioned by your own desire, Eusebius the holy bishop of Cæsarea should preside over and take the charge of the Church at Antioch. Now the letters of Eusebius himself on this subject appeared to be strictly accordant with the order prescribed by the Church. Nevertheless it is expedient that your Prudences should be made acquainted with my opinion also. For I am informed that Euphronius the presbyter, who is a citizen of Cæsarea in Cappadocia, and George of Arethusa, likewise a presbyter, and appointed to that office by Alexander at Alexandria, are men of tried faith. It was right, therefore, to intimate to your Prudences, that in proposing these men and any others whom you may deem worthy the episcopal dignity, you should decide this question in a manner conformable to the tradition of the apostles. For in that case, your Prudences will be able, according to the rule of the Church and apostolic tradition, to direct this election in the manner which true ecclesiastical discipline shall prescribe. God preserve you, beloved brethren!"

CHAPTER LXIII

HOW HE DISPLAYED HIS ZEAL FOR THE EXTIRPATION OF HERESIES

SUCH were the exhortations to maintain the integrity of the divine religion which the emperor addressed to the rulers of the churches. Having by these means banished dissension, and reduced the Church of God to a happy uniformity of doctrine, he next proceeded to a different duty, feeling it incumbent on him to extirpate another sort of impious persons, as pernicious enemies of the human race. These were pests of society, who ruined whole cities under the specious garb of religious decorum; men whom our Saviour's warning voice somewhere terms false prophets and ravenous wolves: "Beware of false prophets, who will come to you in sheep's clothing, but inwardly they are ravening wolves. Ye shall know them by their fruits." Accordingly, by an order transmitted to the governors of the several provinces, he effectually banished all such offenders. In addition to this ordinance he addressed to them personally a severely awakening admonition, exhorting them to an earnest repentance, that they might still find a haven of safety in the true Church of God. Hear, then, in what manner he addressed them in this letter.

CHAPTER LXIV

CONSTANTINE'S EDICT AGAINST THE HERETICS

"VICTOR CONSTANTINUS, MAXIMUS AUGUSTUS, to the heretics.

"Understand now, by this present statute, ye Novatians, Valentinians, Marcionites, Paulians, ye who are called Cataphrygians, and all ye who devise and support heresies by means of your private assemblies, with what a tissue of falsehood and vanity, with what destructive and venomous errors, your doctrines are inseparably interwoven; so that through you the healthy soul is stricken with disease, and the living becomes the prey of everlasting death. Ye haters and enemies of truth and life, in league with destruction! All your counsels are opposed to the truth, but familiar with deeds of baseness; fit subjects for the fabulous follies of the stage: and by these ye frame falsehoods, oppress the innocent, and withhold the light from them that believe. Ever trespassing under the mask of godliness, ye fill all things with defilement: ye pierce the pure and guileless conscience with deadly wounds, while ye withdraw, one may almost say, the very light of day from the eyes of men. But why should I particularise, when to speak of your criminality as it deserves demands more time and leisure than I can give? For so long and unmeasured is the catalogue of your offences, so hateful and altogether atrocious are they, that a single day would not suffice to recount them all. And indeed it is well to turn one's ears and eyes from such a subject, lest by a description of each particular evil, the pure sincerity and freshness of one's own faith be impaired. Why then do I still bear with such abounding evil; especially since this protracted clemency is the cause that some who were sound are become tainted with this pestilent disease? Why not at once strike, as it were, at the root of so great a mischief by a public manifestation of displeasure?

CHAPTER LXV

THE HERETICS ARE DEPRIVED OF THEIR PLACES OF ASSEMBLY, AND THEIR MEETINGS SUPPRESSED

"FORASMUCH, then, as it is no longer possible to bear with your pernicious errors, we give warning by this present statute that none of you henceforth presume to assemble yourselves together. We have directed, accordingly, that you be deprived of all the houses in which you are accustomed to hold your assemblies: and our care in this respect extends so far as to forbid the holding of your superstitious and senseless meetings, not in public merely, but in any private house or place whatsoever. Let those of you, therefore, who are desirous of embracing the true and pure religion, take the far better course of entering the catholic Church, and uniting with it in holy fellowship, where by you will be enabled to arrive at the knowledge of the truth. In any case, the delusions of your perverted understandings must entirely cease to mingle with and mar the felicity of our present times; I mean the impious and wretched double-mindedness of heretics and schismatics. For it is an object worthy of that prosperity which we enjoy through the favour of God, to endeavour to bring back those who in time past were living in the hope of future blessing, from all irregularity and error to the right path, from darkness to light, from vanity to truth, from death to salvation. And in order that this remedy may be applied with effectual power, we have commanded (as before said), that you be positively deprived of every gathering point for your superstitious meetings, I mean all the houses of prayer (if such be worthy of the name) which belong to heretics, and that these be made over without delay to the catholic Church; that any other places be confiscated to the public service, and no facility whatever be left for any future gathering; in order that from this day forward none of your unlawful assemblies may presume to appear in any public or private place. Let this edict be made public."

CHAPTER LXVI

ON THE DISCOVERY OF PROHIBITED BOOKS AMONG THE HERETICS, MANY OF THEM RETURN TO THE CATHOLIC CHURCH

THUS were the lurking-places of the heretics broken up by the emperor's command, and the savage beasts they harboured (I mean the chief authors of their impious doctrines) driven to flight. Of those whom they had deceived, some, intimidated by the emperor's threats, with a false and time-serving disguise of their real sentiments, crept secretly into the Church. For since the law directed that search should be made for their books, those of them who practised evil and forbidden arts were detected, and these were ready to secure their own safety by dissimulation of every kind. Others, however, there were, who voluntarily and with real sincerity embraced a better hope. Meantime the prelates of the several churches continued to make strict inquiry, utterly rejecting those who attempted an entrance under the specious disguise of false pretences, while those who came with sincerity of purpose were proved for a time, and after sufficient trial numbered with the congregation. Such was the treatment of those who stood charged with rank heresy: those, however, who maintained no impious doctrine, but had been separated from the one body through the influence of schismatic advisers, were received without difficulty or delay. Accordingly, numbers thus revisited (as it were) their own country after an absence in a foreign land, and acknowledged the Church as a mother from whom they had wandered long, and to whom they now returned with joy and gladness. Thus the members of the entire body became united, and compacted in one harmonious whole; and the one catholic Church, at unity with itself, shone with full lustre, while no heretical or schismatic body any where continued to exist. And the credit of having achieved this mighty work our Heaven-protected emperor alone, of all who had gone before him, was able to attribute to himself.

BOOK IV

CHAPTER I

CONSTANTINE CONFERS NUMEROUS HONOURS IN THE WAY OF PRESENTS AND PROMOTIONS

WHILE thus variously engaged in promoting the extension and glory of the Church of God, and striving by every measure to commend the Saviour's doctrine, the emperor was far from neglecting secular affairs; but in this respect also he was unwearied in bestowing benefits of every kind and in quick succession on the people of every province. On the one hand he manifested a paternal anxiety for the general welfare of his subjects; on the other he would distinguish individuals of his own acquaintance with various marks of honour; conferring his benefits in every instance in a truly noble spirit. No one could request a favour from the emperor, and fail of obtaining what he sought: no one expected a boon from him, and found that expectation vain. Some received presents in money, others in land; some obtained the Prætorian præfecture, others senatorial, others again consular rank: many were appointed provincial governors: others were made counts of the first, second, or third order: in numberless instances the title of Most Illustrious, and many other distinctions were conferred; for the emperor devised new dignities, that he might invest a larger number with the tokens of his favour.

CHAPTER II

REMISSION OF A FOURTH PART OF THE TRIBUTES

THE extent to which he studied the general happiness and prosperity may be understood from a single instance, most beneficial and universal in its application, and still gratefully remembered. He remitted a fourth part of the yearly tribute paid for land, and bestowed it on the owners of the soil; so that if we compute this yearly reduction, we shall find that the cultivators enjoyed their produce free of tribute every fourth year. This privilege being established by law, and secured for the time to come, has given occasion for the emperor's beneficence to be held, not merely by the then present generation, but by their children and descendants, in perpetual remembrance.

CHAPTER III

EQUALISATION OF THE MORE OPPRESSIVE TAXES

AND whereas some persons found fault with the surveys of land which had been made under former emperors, and complained that their property was unduly burdened; acting in this case also on the principles of justice, he sent commissioners to equalise the tribute, and to secure indemnity to those who had made this appeal.

CHAPTER IV

HIS LIBERALITY, FROM HIS PRIVATE RESOURCES, TO THE LOSERS IN SUITS OF A PECUNIARY NATURE

IN cases of judicial arbitration, in order that the loser by his decision might not quit his presence less contented than the victorious litigant, he himself bestowed, and from his own private means, in some cases lands, in others money, on the defeated party. In this manner he took care that the loser, as having appeared in his presence, should be as well satisfied as the gainer of the cause; for he considered that no one ought in any case to retire dejected and sorrowful from an interview with such a prince. Thus it happened that both parties returned from the scene of trial with glad and cheerful countenances, while the emperor's noble-minded liberality excited universal admiration.

CHAPTER V

DEFEAT AND CONQUEST OF THE SCYTHIANS THROUGH THE STANDARD OF THE SAVIOUR'S CROSS

AND why should I relate even briefly and incidentally, how he subjected barbarous nations to the Roman power; how he was the first who subjugated the Scythian and Sarmatian tribes, which had never learned submission, and compelled them, how unwilling soever, to own the sovereignty of Rome? For the emperors who preceded him had actually rendered tribute to the Scythians: and Romans, by an annual payment, had confessed themselves servants to barbarians; an indignity which our emperor could no longer bear, nor think it consistent with his victorious career to continue the payment his predecessors had made. Accordingly, with full confidence in his Saviour's aid, he raised his conquering standard against these enemies also, and soon reduced them all to obedience; coercing by military force those who fiercely resisted his authority, while, on the other hand, he conciliated the rest by wisely conducted embassies, and reclaimed them to a state of order and civilization from their lawless and savage life. Thus the Scythians at length learned to acknowledge subjection to the power of Rome.

CHAPTER VI

CONQUEST OF THE SARMATIANS, CONSEQUENT ON THE REBELLION OF THEIR SLAVES

WITH respect to the Sarmatians, God Himself brought them beneath the rule of Constantine, and subdued a nation swelling with barbaric pride in the following manner. Being attacked by the Scythians, they had intrusted their slaves with arms, in order to repel the enemy. These slaves first overcame the invaders, and then, turning their weapons against their masters, drove them all from their native land. The expelled Sarmatians found that their only hope of safety was in Constantine's protection: and he, whose familiar habit it was to save mens' lives, received them all within the confines of the Roman empire. Those who were capable of serving, he incorporated with his own troops: to the rest he allotted lands to cultivate for their own support: so that they themselves acknowledged that their past misfortune had produced a happy result, in that they now enjoyed Roman liberty in the place of savage barbarism. In this manner God added to his dominions many and various barbaric tribes.

CHAPTER VII

AMBASSADORS FROM DIFFERENT BARBAROUS NATIONS RECEIVE PRESENTS FROM THE EMPEROR

INDEED, ambassadors were continually arriving from all nations, bringing for his acceptance their most precious gifts. So that I myself have sometimes stood near the entrance of the imperial palace, and observed a conspicuous array of barbarians in attendance, differing from each other in costume and decorations, and equally unlike in the fashion of their hair and beard. Their aspect truculent and terrible, their bodily stature prodigious: some of a red complexion, others white as snow, others again of an intermediate colour. For in the number of those I have referred to might be seen specimens of the Blemmyan tribes, of the Indians, and the Ethiopians, "that widely-divided race, remotest of mankind." All these in due succession (like some painted pageant), presented to the emperor those gifts which their own nation held in most esteem; some offering crowns of gold, others diadems set with precious stones; some bringing fair-haired boys, others barbaric vestments embroidered with gold and flowers: some appeared with horses, others with shields and long spears, with arrows and bows, thereby offering their services and alliance for the emperor's acceptance. These presents he separately received and carefully laid aside, acknowledging them in so munificent a manner as at once to enrich those who bore them. He also honoured the noblest among them with Roman offices of dignity; so that many of them thenceforward preferred to continue their residence among us, and felt no desire to revisit their native land.

CHAPTER VIII

HE WRITES TO THE KING OF PERSIA, WHO HAD SENT HIM AN EMBASSY, ON BEHALF OF THE CHRISTIANS IN HIS REALM

THE king of the Persians also having testified a desire to form an alliance with Constantine, by sending an embassy and presents as assurances of peace and friendship, the emperor, in negotiating this treaty, far surpassed the monarch who had first done him honour, in the magnificence with which he acknowledged his gifts. Having heard, too, that there were many churches of God in Persia, and that large numbers there were gathered into the fold of Christ, full of joy at this intelligence, he resolved to extend his anxiety for the general welfare to that country also, as one whose aim it was to care for all alike in every nation.

CHAPTER IX

LETTER OF CONSTANTINE AUGUSTUS TO SAPOR KING OF THE PERSIANS, CONTAINING A TRULY PIOUS CONFESSION OF GOD AND CHRIST

COPY OF HIS LETTER TO THE KING OF PERSIA

#"BY keeping the Divine faith, I am made a partaker of the light of truth: guided by the light of truth, I advance in the knowledge of the Divine faith. Hence it is that (as my actions themselves evince), I profess the most holy religion; and this worship I declare to be that which teaches me deeper acquaintance with the most holy God; aided by whose Divine power, beginning from the very borders of the ocean, I have aroused each nation of the world in succession to a well-grounded hope of security; so that those which, groaning in servitude to the most cruel tyrants, and yielding to the pressure of their daily sufferings, had well nigh been utterly destroyed, have been restored through my agency to a far happier state. This God I confess that I hold in unceasing honour and remembrance; this God I delight to contemplate with pure and guileless thoughts in the height of His glory.

CHAPTER X

THE WRITER DENOUNCES IDOLS, AND PRAISES GOD

"THIS God I invoke with bended knees, and recoil with horror from the blood of sacrifices, from their foul and detestable odours, and from every earth-born magic fire: for the profane and impious superstitions which are defiled by these rites have cast down and consigned to perdition many, nay, whole nations of the Gentile world. For He who is Lord of all cannot endure that those blessings which, in His own loving-kindness and consideration of the wants of men, He has revealed for the use of all, should be perverted to serve the lusts of any. His only demand from man is purity of mind and an undefiled spirit; and by this standard He weighs the actions of virtue and godliness. For His pleasure is in works of moderation and gentleness: He loves the meek, and hates the turbulent spirit: delighting in faith, He chastises unbelief: by Him all presumptuous power is broken down, and He avenges the insolence of the proud. While the arrogant and haughty are utterly overthrown, He requites the humble and forgiving with deserved rewards: even so does He highly honour and strengthen with His special help a kingdom justly governed, and maintains a prudent king in the tranquillity of peace.

CHAPTER XI

REMARKS CONDEMNATORY OF THE TYRANTS AND PERSECUTORS; AND ON THE CAPTIVITY OF VALERIAN

"I CANNOT, then, my brother, believe that I err in acknowledging this one God, the author and parent of all things: whom many of my predecessors in power, led astray by the madness of error, have ventured to deny, but who were all visited with a retribution so terrible and so destructive, that all succeeding generations have held up their calamities as the most effectual warning to any who desire to follow in their steps. Of the number of these I believe him to have been, whom the lightning-stroke of Divine vengeance drove forth from hence, and banished to your dominions, and whose disgrace contributed to the fame of your much boasted triumph.

CHAPTER XII

HE DECLARES THAT, HAVING WITNESSED THE FALL OF THE PERSECUTORS, HE NOW REJOICES AT THE PEACE ENJOYED BY THE CHRISTIANS

"AND it is surely a happy circumstance that the punishment of such persons as I have described should have been publicly manifested in our own times. For I myself have witnessed the end of those who lately harassed the worshippers of God by their impious edicts. And for this abundant thanksgivings are due to Him through whose excellent Providence all who observe His holy laws are gladdened by the renewed enjoyment of peace. Hence I am fully persuaded that every thing is in the best and safest posture, since God is vouchsafing, through the influence of their pure and faithful religious service, and their unity of judgment respecting His Divine character, to gather all men to Himself.

CHAPTER XIII

HE BESPEAKS HIS AFFECTIONATE INTEREST FOR THE CHRISTIANS IN HIS COUNTRY

"IMAGINE, then, with what joy I heard tidings so accordant with my desire, that the fairest districts of Persia are to a great extent honoured by the presence of that class of men on whose behalf alone I am at present speaking, I mean the Christians. I pray, therefore, that both you and they may enjoy abundant prosperity, and that your blessings and theirs may be in equal measure; for thus you will experience the mercy and favour of that God who is the Lord and Father of all. And now, because your power is great, I commend these persons to your protection; because your piety is eminent, I commit them to your care. Cherish them with your wonted humanity and kindness; for by this proof of faith you will secure an immeasurable benefit both to yourself and us."

CHAPTER XIV

HOW THE ZEALOUS PRAYERS OF CONSTANTINE PROCURED PEACE TO THE CHRISTIANS

THUS, the nations of the world being every where guided in their course as it were by the skill of a single pilot, and acquiescing in the administration of him who governed as the servant of God, the peace of the Roman Empire continued undisturbed, and all classes of his subjects enjoyed a life of tranquillity and repose. At the same time the emperor, who was convinced that the prayers of godly men contributed powerfully to the maintenance of the public welfare, felt himself constrained zealously to seek such prayers, and not only himself implored the help and favour of God, but charged the prelates of the churches to offer supplications on his behalf.

CHAPTER XV

HE CAUSES HIMSELF TO BE REPRESENTED ON HIS COINS, AND IN HIS PORTRAITS, IN THE ATTITUDE OF PRAYER

HOW deeply his soul was impressed by the power of divine faith may be understood from the circumstance that he directed his likeness to be stamped on the golden coin of the empire with the eyes uplifted as in the posture of prayer to God: and this money became current throughout the Roman world. His portrait also at full length was placed over the entrance gates of the palaces in some cities, the eyes upraised to heaven, and the hands outspread as if in prayer.

CHAPTER XVI

HE FORBIDS BY LAW THE PLACING HIS LIKENESS IN IDOL TEMPLES

IN this manner he represented himself, even through the medium of painting, as habitually engaged in prayer to God. At the same time he forbade, by an express enactment, the setting up of any resemblance of himself in any idol temple, that not even the mere lineaments of his person might receive contamination from the error of forbidden superstition.

CHAPTER XVII

OF HIS PRAYERS IN THE PALACE, AND HIS READING THE HOLY SCRIPTURES

STILL nobler proofs of his piety might be discerned by those who marked how he modelled as it were his very palace into a Church of God, and himself afforded a pattern of zeal to those assembled therein: how he took the sacred scriptures into his hands, and devoted himself to the study of those divinely inspired oracles; after which he would offer up regular prayers with all the members of his imperial court.

CHAPTER XVIII

HE ENJOINS THE GENERAL OBSERVANCE OF THE LORD'S DAY, AND THE DAY BEFORE THE SABBATH

HE ordained, too, that one day should be regarded as a special occasion for prayer: I mean that which is truly the first and chief of all, the day of our Lord and Saviour. The entire care of his household was intrusted to deacons and other ministers consecrated to the service of God, and distinguished by gravity of life and every other virtue: while his trusty body guard, strong in affection and fidelity to his person, found in their emperor an instructor in the practice of piety, and like him held the Lord's salutary day in honour, and performed on that day the devotions which he loved. The same observance was recommended by this blessed prince to all classes of his subjects; his earnest desire being gradually to lead all mankind to the worship of God. Accordingly he enjoined on all the subjects of the Roman empire to observe the Lord's day, as a day of rest, and also to honour the day which precedes the sabbath; in memory, I suppose, of what the Saviour of mankind is recorded to have achieved on that day. And since his desire was to teach his whole army zealously to honour the Saviour's day (which derives its name from light, and from the sun), he freely granted to those among them who were partakers of the divine faith, leisure for attendance on the services of the Church of God, in order that they might be able, without impediment, to perform their religious worship.

CHAPTER XIX

HE DIRECTED EVEN HIS PAGAN SOLDIERS TO PRAY ON THE LORD'S DAY

WITH regard to those who were as yet ignorant of divine truth, he provided by a second statute that they should appear on each Lord's day on an open plain near the city, and there, at a given signal, offer to God with one accord a prayer which they had previously learnt. He admonished them that their confidence should not rest in their spears, or armour, or bodily strength, but that they should acknowledge the supreme God as the giver of every good, and of victory itself; to whom they were bound to offer their prayers with due regularity, uplifting their hands toward heaven, and raising their mental vision higher still to the King of heaven, on whom they should call as the Author of victory, their Preserver, Guardian, and Helper. The emperor himself prescribed the prayer to be used by all his troops, commanding them to pronounce the following words in the Latin tongue.

CHAPTER XX

THE FORM OF PRAYER GIVEN BY CONSTANTINE TO HIS SOLDIERS

"WE acknowledge Thee the only God: we own Thee as our King, and implore Thy succour. By Thy favour have we gotten the victory: through Thee are we mightier than our enemies. We render thanks for Thy past benefits, and trust Thee for future blessings. Together we pray to Thee, and beseech Thee long to preserve to us, safe and triumphant, our emperor Constantine and his pious sons."

Such was the duty to be performed on Sunday by his troops, and such the prayer they were instructed to offer up to God.

CHAPTER XXI

HE ORDERS THE SIGN OF THE CROSS TO BE ENGRAVEN ON HIS SOLDIERS' SHIELDS

AND not only so, but he also caused the sign of the salutary trophy to be impressed on the very shields of his soldiers; and commanded that his embattled forces should be preceded in their march, not by golden images, as heretofore, but only by the standard of the cross.

CHAPTER XXII

OF HIS ZEAL IN PRAYER, AND THE HONOUR HE PAID TO THE FEAST OF EASTER

THE emperor himself, as a sharer in the holy mysteries of our religion, would seclude himself daily at a stated hour in the innermost chambers of his palace; and there, in solitary converse with his God, would kneel in humble supplication, and entreat the blessings of which he stood in need. But especially at the salutary feast of Easter, his religious diligence was redoubled; he fulfilled as it were the duties of a hierophant with every energy of his mind and body, and outvied all others in the zealous celebration of this feast. He changed, too, the holy night vigil into a brightness like that of day, by causing waxen tapers of great length to be lighted throughout the city: besides which, torches every where diffused their light, so as to impart to this mystic vigil a brilliant splendour beyond that of day. As soon as day itself returned, in imitation of our Saviour's gracious acts, he opened a liberal hand to his subjects of every nation, province, and people, and lavished abundant bounties on all.

CHAPTER XXIII

HE FORBIDS IDOLATROUS WORSHIP, BUT HONOURS MARTYRS AND THEIR FESTIVALS

SUCH were his sacred ministrations in the service of his God. At the same time, his subjects, both civil and military, throughout the empire, found a barrier every where opposed against idol worship, and every kind of sacrifice forbidden. A statute was also passed, enjoining the due observance of the Lord's day, and transmitted to the governors of every province, who undertook, at his command, to respect the days commemorative of martyrs, and duly to honour the festivals of the Church: and all these intentions were fulfilled to the emperor's entire satisfaction.

CHAPTER XXIV

HE DESCRIBES HIMSELF AS A BISHOP, IN CHARGE OF AFFAIRS EXTERNAL TO THE CHURCH

HENCE it was not without reason that once, on the occasion of his entertaining a company of bishops, he let fall the expression, "that he himself too was a bishop," addressing them in my hearing in the following words: "You are bishops whose jurisdiction is within the Church: I also am a bishop, ordained by God to overlook whatever is external to the Church." And truly his measures corresponded with his words; for he watched over his subjects with an episcopal care, and exhorted them as far as in him lay to follow a godly life.

CHAPTER XXV

PROHIBITION OF SACRIFICES, OF PROFANE MYSTERIES, AND COMBATS OF GLADIATORS: ALSO SUPPRESSION OF THE IMPIOUS PRIESTHOOD OF THE NILE

CONSISTENTLY with this zeal he issued successive laws and ordinances, forbidding any to offer sacrifice to idols, to consult diviners, to erect images, or to pollute the cities with the sanguinary combats of gladiators. And inasmuch as the Egyptians, especially those of Alexandria, had been accustomed to honour their river through a priesthood composed of effeminate men, a further law was passed commanding the extermination of these as a corrupt and vicious class of persons, that no one might thenceforward be found tainted with the like impurity. And whereas the superstitious inhabitants apprehended that the river would in consequence withhold its customary flood, God Himself showed His approval of the emperor's law by ordering all things in a manner quite contrary to their expectation. For those who had defiled the cities by their vicious conduct were indeed seen no more; but the river, as if the country through which it flowed had been purified to receive it, rose higher than ever before, and completely overflowed the country with its fertilizing streams: thus effectually admonishing the deluded people to turn from the impure with abhorrence, and ascribe their prosperity to Him alone who is the Giver of all good.

CHAPTER XXVI

AMENDMENT OF THE LAW IN FORCE RESPECTING CHILDLESS PERSONS, AND OF THE LAW OF WILLS

SO numerous, indeed, were the benefits of this kind conferred by the emperor on every province, as to afford ample materials to any who might desire to record them. Among these may be instanced those laws which he entirely remodelled, and established on a more equitable basis: the nature of which reform may be briefly and easily explained. The childless were punished under the old law with the forfeiture of their hereditary property. This merciless statute, which dealt with persons thus circumstanced as positive criminals, the emperor annulled, and regulated this question on the principles of equity and justice. Wilful transgressors, he argued, should be chastised with the penalties their crimes deserve. But nature herself denies children to many, who long, perhaps, for a numerous offspring, but are disappointed of their hope by bodily infirmity. Others continue childless, not from any dislike of posterity, but because their ardent love of philosophy renders them averse to the conjugal union. Women, too, consecrated to the service of God, have maintained a pure and spotless virginity, and have devoted themselves, soul and body, to a life of entire chastity and holiness. What then? Should this conduct be deemed worthy of punishment, or rather of admiration and praise; since to desire this state is in itself honourable, and to maintain it surpasses the power of unassisted nature? Surely those whose bodily infirmity destroys their hope of offspring are worthy of pity, not of punishment: and he who devotes himself to a higher object calls not for chastisement, but especial admiration. On such principles of sound reason did the emperor rectify the defects of this law. Again, with regard to the wills of dying persons, the old laws had ordained that they should be expressed, even at the latest breath, as it were, in certain definite words, and had prescribed the exact form and terms to be employed. This practice had occasioned many fraudulent attempts to hinder the intentions of the deceased from being carried into full effect. As soon as our emperor was aware of these abuses, he reformed this law likewise, declaring that a dying man ought to be permitted to indicate his last wishes in as few words as possible and in whatever terms he pleased; and to set forth his will in any written form; or even by word of mouth, provided it were done in the presence of proper witnesses, who might be competent faithfully to discharge their trust.

CHAPTER XXVII

AMONG OTHER ENACTMENTS, HE FORBIDS THE JEWS TO POSSESS CHRISTIAN SLAVES, AND AFFIRMS THE VALIDITY OF THE DECISIONS OF COUNCILS

HE also passed a law to the effect that no Christian should remain in servitude to a Jewish master, on the ground that it could not be right that those whom the Saviour had ransomed should be subjected to the yoke of slavery by a people who had slain the prophets and the Lord Himself. If any were found hereafter in these circumstances, the slave was to be set at liberty, and the master punished by a fine.

He likewise added the sanction of his authority to the decisions of bishops passed at their synods, and forbade the provincial governors to rescind any of their decrees: for he rated the priests of God at a higher value than any judge whatever. These and a thousand similar provisions did he enact for the benefit of his subjects; but to give a special description of them, such as might convey an accurate idea of his imperial wisdom in these respects, would be a work of some time: nor need I now relate at length, how, as a devoted servant of the Supreme God, he employed himself throughout the day in seeking objects for his beneficence, and how equally and universally kind he was to all.

CHAPTER XXVIII

HIS OFFERINGS TO THE CHURCHES, AND DISTRIBUTIONS OF MONEY TO THE VIRGINS, AND TO THE POOR

HIS liberality, however, was most especially exercised on behalf of the churches of God. In some cases he granted lands, in others he issued supplies of food for the support of the poor, of orphan children, and widows; besides which, he evinced much care and forethought in fully providing the naked and destitute with clothing. He distinguished, however, with most special honour those who had devoted their lives to the practice of Divine philosophy. Hence his respect, little short of veneration, for God's most holy and ever virgin quire; for he felt assured that the God to whom such persons devoted themselves was Himself an inmate of their souls.

CHAPTER XXIX

OF CONSTANTINE'S DISCOURSES AND DECLAMATIONS

FOR himself, he sometimes passed sleepless nights in furnishing his mind with Divine knowledge: and much of his time was spent in composing discourses, many of which he delivered in public; for he conceived it to be incumbent on him to govern his subjects by appealing to their reason, and to secure in all respects a rational obedience to his authority. Hence he would sometimes himself convoke an assembly, on which occasions vast multitudes attended, in the hope of hearing an emperor sustain the part of a philosopher. And if in the course of his speech any occasion offered of touching on sacred topics, he immediately stood erect, and with a grave aspect and subdued tone of voice seemed reverently to be initiating his auditors in the mysteries of the Divine doctrine: and when they greeted him with shouts of acclamation, he would direct them by his gestures to raise their eyes to heaven, and reserve their admiration for the Supreme King alone, and honour Him with adoration and praise. He usually divided the subjects of his address, first thoroughly exposing the error of polytheism, and proving the superstition of the Gentiles to be mere fraud, and a cloak for impiety. He then would assert the sole sovereignty of God; passing thence to His Providence, both general and particular. Proceeding next to the dispensation of salvation, he would demonstrate its necessity, and adaptation to the nature of the case; entering next in order on the doctrine of the Divine judgment. And here especially he appealed most powerfully to the consciences of his hearers, while he denounced the rapacious and violent, and those who were slaves to an inordinate thirst of gain. Nay, he caused some of his own acquaintance who were present to feel the severe lash of his words, and to stand with downcast eyes in the consciousness of guilt, while he testified against them in the clearest and most impressive terms that they would have an account to render of their deeds to God. He reminded them that God Himself had given him the empire of the world, portions of which he himself, acting on the same Divine principle, had intrusted to their government; but that all would in due time be alike summoned to give account of their actions to the Supreme Sovereign of all. Such was his constant testimony; such the subjects of his admonition and instruction. And he himself both felt and uttered these sentiments in the genuine confidence of faith: but his hearers were little disposed to learn, and deaf to sound advice; receiving his words indeed with loud applause, but induced by insatiable cupidity practically to disregard them.

CHAPTER XXX

HE ATTEMPTS TO SHAME A COVETOUS PERSON, BY MARKING OUT BEFORE HIM THE MEASURE OF A GRAVE

ON one occasion he thus personally addressed one of his courtiers: "How far, my friend, are we to carry our inordinate desires?" Then drawing the dimensions of a human figure with a lance which he happened to have in his hand, he continued: "Though thou couldst obtain the whole wealth of this world, yea, the whole world itself, thou wilt carry with thee at last no more than this little spot which I have marked out, if indeed even that be thine." Such were the words and actions of this blessed prince; and though at the time he failed to reclaim any from their evil ways, yet notwithstanding the course of events afforded evident proof that his admonitions rather resembled the Divine oracles than mere ordinary words.

CHAPTER XXXI

HE IS DERIDED BECAUSE OF HIS EXCESSIVE CLEMENCY

MEANTIME, since there was no fear of capital punishment to deter from the commission of crime, for the emperor himself was uniformly inclined to clemency, and none of the provincial governors visited offences with their proper penalties, this state of things drew with it no small degree of blame on the general administration of the empire; whether justly or not, let every one form his own judgment: for myself, I only ask permission to record the fact.

CHAPTER XXXII

OF CONSTANTINE'S ORATION WHICH HE WROTE TO THE ASSEMBLY OF THE SAINTS

THE emperor was in the habit of composing his orations in the Latin tongue, from which they were translated into Greek by interpreters appointed for this special service. One of the discourses thus translated I intend to annex, by way of specimen, to this present work (that one, I mean, which he inscribed to the assembly of the saints, and dedicated to the Church of God), that no one may have ground for deeming my testimony on this head mere empty praise.

CHAPTER XXXIII

HE LISTENED IN A STANDING POSTURE TO EUSEBIUS'S DECLAMATION IN HONOUR OF OUR SAVIOUR'S SEPULCHRE

ONE act, however, I must by no means omit to record, which this admirable prince performed in my own presence. On one occasion, emboldened by the confident assurance I entertained of his piety, I had begged permission to pronounce a discourse on the subject of our Saviour's sepulchre in his hearing. With this request he most readily complied, and in the midst of a large number of auditors, in the interior of the palace itself, he stood and listened with the rest. I entreated him (but in vain) to seat himself on the imperial throne which stood near: he continued with fixed attention to weigh the topics of my discourse, and gave his own testimony to the truth of the theological doctrines it contained. After some time had passed, the oration being of considerable length, I was myself desirous of concluding; but this he would not permit, and exhorted me to proceed to the very end. On my again entreating him to sit, he in his turn admonished me to desist, saying that it was not right to listen in a careless manner to the discussion of doctrines relating to God; and again, that this posture was good and profitable to himself, since it argued a becoming reverence to stand while listening to sacred truths. Having, therefore, concluded my discourse, I returned home, and resumed my usual occupations.

CHAPTER XXXIV

HE WRITES TO EUSEBIUS RESPECTING EASTER, AND THE SACRED BOOKS OF SCRIPTURE

EVER careful for the welfare of the churches of God, the emperor addressed me personally in a letter on the means of providing copies of the inspired oracles, and also on the subject of the most holy feast of Easter. For I had myself dedicated to him an exposition of the mystical import of that feast; and the manner in which he honoured me with a reply may be understood by any one who reads the following letter.

CHAPTER XXXV

CONSTANTINE'S LETTER TO EUSEBIUS, IN PRAISE OF HIS DISCOURSE CONCERNING EASTER

"VICTOR CONSTANTINUS, MAXIMUS AUGUSTUS, to Eusebius.

"It is indeed an arduous task, and beyond the power of language itself, worthily to treat of the mysteries of Christ, and to explain in a fitting manner the controversy respecting the feast of Easter, its origin as well as its precious and toilsome accomplishment. For it is not in the power even of those who are able to apprehend them, adequately to describe the things of God. I am, notwithstanding, filled with admiration of your learning and zeal, and have not only myself read your work with pleasure, but have given directions, according to your own desire, that it be communicated to many sincere followers of our holy religion. Seeing, then, with what pleasure we receive favours of this kind from your Sagacity, be pleased to gladden us more frequently with those compositions, to the practice of which, indeed, you confess yourself to have been trained from an early period, so that I am urging a willing man (as they say), in exhorting you to your customary pursuits. And certainly the high and confident judgment we entertain is a proof that the person who has translated your writings into the Latin tongue is in no respect incompetent to the task, impossible though it be that such version should fully equal the excellence of the works themselves. God preserve you, beloved brother." Such was his letter on this subject: and that which related to the providing of copies of the scriptures for reading in the churches was to the following purport.

CHAPTER XXXVI

CONSTANTINE'S LETTER TO EUSEBIUS ON THE PREPARATION OF COPIES OF THE SCRIPTURES

"VICTOR CONSTANTINUS, MAXIMUS AUGUSTUS, to Eusebius.

"It happens, through the favouring providence of God our Saviour, that great numbers have united themselves to the most holy church in the city which is called by my name. It seems, therefore, highly requisite, since that city is rapidly advancing in prosperity in all other respects, that the number of churches should also be increased. Do you, therefore, receive with all readiness my determination on this behalf. I have thought it expedient to instruct your Prudence to order fifty copies of the sacred scriptures (the provision and use of which you know to be most needful for the instruction of the Church) to be written on prepared parchment in a legible manner, and in a commodious and portable form, by transcribers thoroughly practised in their art. The procurator of the diocese has also received instructions by letter from our Clemency to be careful to furnish all things necessary for the preparation of such copies; and it will be for you to take special care that they be completed with as little delay as possible. You have authority also, in virtue of this letter, to use two of the public carriages for their conveyance, by which arrangement the copies when fairly written will most easily be forwarded for my personal inspection; and one of the deacons of your church may be intrusted with this service, who, on his arrival here, shall experience my liberality. God preserve you, beloved brother!"

CHAPTER XXXVII

HOW THE COPIES WERE PROVIDED

SUCH were the emperor's commands, which were followed by the immediate execution of the work itself, which we sent him in magnificent and elaborate volumes of a threefold and fourfold form. This fact is attested by another letter, which the emperor wrote in acknowledgment, in which, having heard that the city Constantia in our country, the inhabitants of which had been more than commonly devoted to superstition, had been impelled by a sense of religion to abandon their past idolatry, he testified his joy, and approval of their conduct.

CHAPTER XXXVIII

THE PORT OF GAZA IS MADE A CITY FOR ITS PROFESSION OF CHRISTIANITY, AND RECEIVES THE NAME OF CONSTANTIA

FOR in fact the place now called Constantia, in the province of Palestine, having embraced the saving religion, was distinguished both by the favour of God, and by special honour from the emperor, being now for the first time raised to the rank of a city, and receiving the more honoured name of his pious sister in exchange for its former appellation.

CHAPTER XXXIX

A PLACE IN PHŒNICIA ALSO IS MADE A CITY, AND IN OTHER CITIES IDOLATRY IS ABOLISHED, AND CHURCHES BUILT

A SIMILAR change was effected in several other cities; for instance, in that town of Phœnicia which received its name, Constantina, from that of the emperor, and the inhabitants of which committed their innumerable idols to the flames, and adopted in their stead the principles of the saving faith. Numbers, too, in the other provinces, both in the cities and the country, became willing inquirers after the saving knowledge of God; destroyed as worthless things the images of every kind which they had heretofore held most sacred; voluntarily demolished the lofty temples and shrines which contained them; and, renouncing their former sentiments (or rather errors), commenced and completed entirely new churches. But since it is not so much my province to give a circumstantial detail of the actions of this pious prince, as it is theirs who have been privileged to enjoy his society at all times, I shall content myself with briefly recording such facts as have come to my own personal knowledge, before I proceed to notice the last days of his life.

CHAPTER XL

HAVING CONFERRED THE DIGNITY OF CÆSARS ON HIS THREE SONS AT THE THREE DECENNIAL PERIODS OF HIS REIGN, HE DEDICATED THE CHURCH AT JERUSALEM

BY this time the thirtieth year of his reign was completed. In the course of this period, his three sons had been admitted at different times as his colleagues in the empire. The first, who bore his father's name, obtained this distinction about the tenth year of his reign. Constantius, the second son, so called from his grandfather, was proclaimed Cæsar about the twentieth, while Constans, the third (whose name expresses the firmness and stability of his character), was advanced to the same dignity at the thirtieth anniversary of his father's reign. Having thus reared a threefold offspring, a Trinity, as it were, of pious sons, and having received them severally at each decennial period to a participation in his imperial authority, he judged the festival of his Tricennalia to be a fit occasion for thanksgiving to the Sovereign Lord of all, at the same time believing that the dedication of the church which his zealous magnificence had erected at Jerusalem might advantageously be performed.

CHAPTER XLI

IN THE MEANTIME HE ORDERS A COUNCIL TO BE CONVENED AT TYRE, BECAUSE OF CONTROVERSIES RAISED IN EGYPT

MEANWHILE that spirit of envy which is the enemy of all good, like a dark cloud intercepting the sun's brightest rays, endeavoured to mar the joy of this festivity, by again raising contentions to disturb the tranquillity of the Egyptian Churches. Our divinely favoured emperor, however, once more convened a synod composed of many bishops, and set them as it were in armed array (like the host of God) against this malignant spirit, having commanded their presence from the whole of Egypt and Libya, from Asia, and from Europe, in order, first, to decide the questions in dispute, and afterwards to perform the dedication of the sacred edifice above mentioned. He enjoined them, by the way, to adjust their differences at the capital city of Phœnicia, reminding them that they had no right, while harbouring feelings of mutual animosity, to engage in the service of God, since His law expressly forbids those who are at variance to offer their gift until they have first become reconciled and mutually disposed to peace. Such were the salutary precepts which the emperor continually kept vividly before his own mind, and in accordance with which he admonished them to undertake their present duties in a spirit of perfect unanimity and concord, in a letter to the following purport.

CHAPTER XLII

CONSTANTINE'S LETTER TO THE COUNCIL AT TYRE

"VICTOR CONSTANTINUS, MAXIMUS AUGUSTUS, to the holy Council at Tyre.

"Surely it would best consist with and best become the prosperity of these our times, that the Catholic Church should be undivided, and the servants of Christ be at this present moment clear from all reproach. Since, however, there are those who, carried away by a baleful and furious spirit of contention (for I will not charge them with intentionally leading a life unworthy of their profession), are endeavouring to create that general confusion which, in my judgment, is the most pernicious of all evils; I exhort you (forward as you already are) to meet together and form a synod without delay: to defend those who need protection; to administer remedies to your brethren who are in peril; to recall the divided members to unity of judgment; to rectify errors while opportunity is yet allowed: that thus you may restore to so many provinces that due measure of concord which, strange and sad anomaly! the arrogance of a few individuals has destroyed. And I believe that all are alike persuaded that this course is at the same time pleasing to Almighty God (as well as the highest object of my own desires), and will bring no small honour to yourselves, should you be successful in restoring peace. Delay not, then, but hasten with redoubled zeal to terminate the present dissensions in a manner becoming the occasion, by assembling together in that spirit of true sincerity and faith which the Saviour whom we serve demands from us, I may almost say with an audible voice, on all occasions. No proof of pious zeal on my part shall be wanting. Already have I done all to which my attention was directed by your letters. I have sent to those bishops whose presence you desired, that they may share your counsels. I have despatched Dionysius, a man of consular rank, who will both remind those prelates of their duty who are bound to attend the Council with you, and will himself be there to superintend the proceedings, but especially to maintain good order. Meantime should any one (though I deem it most improbable) venture on this occasion to violate my command, and refuse his attendance, a messenger shall be despatched forthwith to banish that person in virtue of an imperial edict, and to teach him that it does not become him to resist an emperor's decrees when issued in defence of truth. For the rest, it will be for your Holinesses, unbiassed either by enmity or favour, but consistently with ecclesiastical and apostolic order, to devise a fitting remedy, whether it be for positive offences or for unpremeditated errors; in order that you may at once free the Church from all reproach, relieve my anxiety, and, by restoring the blessings of peace to those who are now divided, procure the highest honour for yourselves. God preserve you, beloved brethren!"

CHAPTER XLIII

BISHOPS FROM EVERY PROVINCE ATTENDED THE DEDICATION OF THE CHURCH AT JERUSALEM

No sooner had these injunctions been carried into effect, than another emissary arrived with despatches from the emperor, and an urgent admonition to the Council to hasten their journey to Jerusalem without delay. Accordingly they all took their departure from the province of Phœnicia, and proceeded to their destination, availing themselves of the public means of transport. Thus Jerusalem became the gathering point for distinguished prelates from every province, and the whole city was thronged by a vast assemblage of the servants of God. The Macedonians had sent the bishop of their metropolis; the Pannonians and Mœsians the fairest of God's youthful flock among them. A holy prelate from Persia too was there, deeply versed in the sacred oracles; while Bithynian and Thracian bishops graced the Council with their presence; nor were the most illustrious from Cilicia wanting, nor the chief of the Cappadocians, distinguished above all for learning and eloquence. In short, the whole of Syria and Mesopotamia, Phœnicia and Arabia, Palestine, Egypt, and Libya, with the dwellers in the Thebaid, all contributed to swell the mighty concourse of God's ministers, followed as they were by vast numbers from every province, and each attended by an imperial escort. Officers of trust had also been sent from the palace itself, with instructions to heighten the splendour of the festival at the emperor's expense.

CHAPTER XLIV

OF THEIR RECEPTION BY THE NOTARY MACARIUS; THE DISTRIBUTION OF MONEY TO THE POOR; AND OFFERINGS TO THE CHRUCH

THE director and chief of these officers was a most useful servant of the emperor, a man eminent for faith and piety, and thoroughly acquainted with the Divine word, who had been honourably conspicuous by his profession of godliness during the time of the tyrants' power, and therefore was deservedly intrusted with the arrangement of the present proceedings. Accordingly, in faithful obedience to the emperor's commands, he received the assembly with courteous hospitality, and entertained them with feasts and banquets on a scale of great splendour. He also distributed lavish supplies of money and clothing among the naked and destitute, and the multitudes of both sexes who suffered from want of food and the common necessaries of life. Finally, he enriched and beautified the church itself throughout with offerings of imperial magnificence, and thus fully accomplished the service he had been commissioned to perform.

CHAPTER XLV

VARIOUS DISCOURSES BY THE ASSEMBLED BISHOPS; ALSO BY EUSEBIUS THE WRITER OF THIS HISTORY

MEANTIME the festival derived additional lustre both from the prayers and discourses of the ministers of God, some of whom extolled the pious emperor's willing devotion to the Saviour of mankind, and dilated on the magnificence of the edifice which he had raised to His memory. Others afforded, as it were, an intellectual feast to the ears of all present, by public disquisitions on the sacred doctrines of our religion. Others interpreted passages of holy Scripture, and unfolded their hidden meaning; while such as were unequal to these efforts presented a bloodless sacrifice and mystical service to God in the prayers which they offered for general peace, for the Church of God, for the emperor himself as the instrumental cause of so many blessings, and for his pious sons. I myself too, unworthy as I was of such a privilege, pronounced various public orations in honour of this solemnity, wherein I partly explained by a written description the details of the imperial edifice, and partly endeavoured to gather from the prophetic visions apt illustrations of the symbols it displayed. Thus joyfully was the festival of dedication celebrated in the thirtieth year of our emperor's reign.

CHAPTER XLVI

EUSEBIUS AFTERWARDS REPEATED HIS DESCRIPTION OF THE CHURCH, AND HIS ORATION ON THE TRICENNALIA, BEFORE CONSTANTINE HIMSELF

THE structure of the church of our Saviour, the form of His sacred cave, the splendour and elegance of the work itself, and the numberless offerings in gold, and silver, and precious stones, I have described to the best of my ability, and dedicated to the emperor in a separate treatise, which on a fitting opportunity I shall append to this present work. I shall add to it also that oration on his Tricennalia which shortly afterwards, having travelled to the city which bears his name, I delivered in the emperor's own presence. This was the second opportunity afforded me of glorifying the Supreme God in the imperial palace itself: and on this occasion my pious hearer evinced the greatest joy, as he afterwards testified, when he entertained the bishops then present, and loaded them with distinctions of every kind.

CHAPTER XLVII

THE COUNCIL AT NICÆA WAS HELD IN THE TWENTIETH, THE DEDICATION OF THE CHURCH AT JERUSALEM IN THE THIRTIETH YEAR OF CONSTANTINE'S REIGN

THIS second synod the emperor convened at Jerusalem, being the greatest of which we have any knowledge, next to the first which he had summoned at the famous Bithynian city. That indeed was a triumphal assembly, held in the twentieth year of his reign, an occasion of thanksgiving for victory over his enemies in the very city which bears the name of Victory. The present meeting added lustre to the thirtieth anniversary, during which the emperor dedicated the church at the sepulchre of our Saviour, as a peace-offering to God the Giver of all good.

CHAPTER XLVIII

CONSTANTINE TESTIFIES HIS AVERSION TO EXCESSIVE PRAISE

AND now that all these ceremonies were completed, and the divine qualities of the emperor's character continued to be the theme of universal praise, one of God's ministers presumed so far as in his own presence to pronounce him blessed, as having been counted worthy to hold absolute and universal empire in this life, and as being destined to share the empire of the Son of God in the world to come. These words, however, Constantine heard with indignation, and forbade the speaker to hold such language, exhorting him rather to pray earnestly on his behalf, that whether in this life or in that which is to come, he might be found worthy to be a servant of God.

CHAPTER XLIX

MARRIAGE OF HIS SON CONSTANTIUS CÆSAR

ON the completion of the thirtieth year of his reign he solemnized the marriage of his second son, having concluded that of his first-born long before. This was an occasion of great joy and festivity, the emperor himself attending on his son at the ceremony, and entertaining the guests of both sexes (the men and women in distinct and separate companies) with sumptuous hospitality. Rich presents likewise were liberally distributed among the cities and people.

CHAPTER L

AN EMBASSY ARRIVES, WITH PRESENTS, FROM THE INDIANS

ABOUT this time ambassadors from the Indians, who inhabit the distant regions of the East, arrived with presents consisting of many varieties of brilliant precious stones, and animals differing in species from those known to us. These offerings they presented to the emperor, thus allowing that his sovereignty extended even to the Indian Ocean, and that the princes of their country, who rendered homage to him both by paintings and statues, acknowledged his imperial and paramount authority. Thus the Eastern Indians now submitted to his sway, as the Britons of the Western Ocean had done at the commencement of his reign.

CHAPTER LI

CONSTANTINE DIVIDES THE EMPIRE BETWEEN HIS THREE SONS, WHOM HE HAD INSTRUCTED IN THE ARTS OF GOVERNMENT AND THE DUTIES OF RELIGION

HAVING thus established his power in the opposite extremities of the world, he divided the whole extent of his dominions, as though he were allotting a patrimonial inheritance to the dearest objects of his regard, among his three sons. To the eldest he assigned his grandfather's portion; to the second, the empire of the East; to the third, the countries which lie between these two divisions. And being desirous of furnishing his children with an inheritance truly valuable and salutary to their souls, he had been careful to imbue them with true religious principles, being himself their guide to the knowledge of sacred things, and also appointing men of approved piety to be their instructors. At the same time he assigned them the most accomplished teachers of secular learning, by some of whom they were taught the arts of war, while they were trained by others in political, and by others again in legal science. To each moreover was granted a truly royal retinue, consisting of infantry, spearmen, and body guards, with every other kind of military force; commanded respectively by captains, tribunes, and generals, of whose warlike skill and devotion to his sons the emperor had had previous experience.

CHAPTER LII

HIS PIOUS INSTRUCTIONS AFTER THEY HAD REACHED MATURITY

AS long as the Cæsars were of tender years, they were aided by suitable advisers in the management of public affairs; but on their arrival at the age of manhood their father's instructions alone sufficed. When present, he proposed to them his own example, and admonished them to follow his pious course: in their absence he furnished them by letter with rules of conduct suited to their imperial station, the first and greatest of which was an exhortation to value the knowledge and worship of the Sovereign Lord of all more than any wealth, nay, more than empire itself. At length he permitted them to direct the public administration of the empire without control, making it his first request that they would care for the interests of the Church of God, and boldly profess themselves disciples of Christ. Thus trained, and excited to obedience not so much by precept as by their own voluntary desire for virtue, his sons more than fulfilled the admonitions of their father, devoting their earnest attention to the service of God, and observing the ordinances of the Church even in the palace itself, with all the members of their households. For their father's forethought had provided that all the attendants of his sons should be Christians. And not only so, but the military officers of highest rank, and those who had the control of public business, were professors of the same faith: for the emperor placed confidence in the fidelity of men devoted to the service of God, as in a strong and sure defence. It was after our thrice blessed prince had completed these arrangements, and thus secured order and tranquillity throughout the empire, that God, the Dispenser of all blessings, judged it to be the fitting time to translate him to a better inheritance, and summoned him to pay the debt of nature.

CHAPTER LIII

HAVING REIGNED ABOUT THIRTY TWO YEARS, AND LIVED ABOVE SIXTY, HE STILL ENJOYED SOUND BODILY HEALTH

HE completed the time of his reign in two and thirty years, wanting a few months and days, and his whole life extended to about twice that period. At this age he still possessed a sound and vigorous body, free from all blemish, and of more than youthful vivacity; a noble mien, and strength equal to any exertion; so that he was able to join in martial exercises, to ride, endure the fatigues of travel, engage in battle, and erect trophies over his conquered enemies, besides gaining those bloodless victories by which he was wont to triumph over those who opposed him.

CHAPTER LIV

HIS EXTREME BENEVOLENCE WAS ABUSED BY SOME AS AN ENCOURAGEMENT TO AVARICE AND HYPOCRISY

IN like manner his mental qualities reached the highest point of human perfection. Indeed he was distinguished by every excellence of character, but especially by benevolence; a virtue, however, which subjected him to censure from many, in consequence of the baseness of wicked men, who ascribed their own crimes to the emperor's forbearance. In truth I can myself bear testimony to the grievous evils which prevailed during these times; I mean the violence of rapacious and unprincipled men, who preyed on all classes of society alike, and the scandalous hypocrisy of those who crept into the Church, and assumed the name and character of Christians. His own benevolence and goodness of heart, the genuineness of his own faith, and his truthfulness of character, induced the emperor to credit the profession of these reputed Christians, who craftily preserved the semblance of sincere affection for his person. The confidence he reposed in such men sometimes forced him into conduct unworthy of himself, of which envy took advantage to cloud in this respect the lustre of his character.

CHAPTER LV

CONSTANTINE EMPLOYED HIMSELF IN COMPOSITION OF VARIOUS KINDS TO THE CLOSE OF HIS LIFE

THESE offenders, however, were soon overtaken by divine chastisement. To return to our emperor. He had so thoroughly trained his mind in the art of reasoning that he continued to the last to compose discourses on various subjects, to deliver frequent orations in public, and to instruct his hearers in the sacred doctrines of religion. He was also habitually engaged in legislating both on political and military questions; in short, in devising whatever might be conducive to the general welfare of the human race. It is well worthy of remark, that, very shortly before his departure, he pronounced a funeral oration before his usual auditory, in which he spoke at length on the immortality of the soul, the state of those who had persevered in a life of godliness, and the blessings which God has laid up in store for them that love Him. On the other hand lie made it appear by copious and conclusive arguments what the end of those will be who have pursued a contrary career, describing in vivid language the final ruin of the ungodly. His powerful testimony on these subjects seemed so far to touch the consciences of those around him, that one of the self-imagined philosophers, of whom he asked his opinion of what he had heard, bore testimony to the truth of his words, and accorded a real, though reluctant tribute of praise, to the arguments by which he had exposed the worship of a plurality of Gods. By converse such as this with his friends before his death, the emperor seemed as it were to smooth and prepare the way for his transition to a happier life.

CHAPTER LVI

HE IS ATTENDED BY BISHOPS ON AN EXPEDITION AGAINST THE PERSIANS, AND TAKES WITH HIM A TENT IN THE FORM OF A CHURCH

IT is also worthy of record that about the time of which I am at present writing, the emperor, having heard of an insurrection of some barbarians in the East, observed that the conquest of this enemy was still in store for him, and resolved on an expedition against the Persians. Accordingly he proceeded at once to put his forces in motion, at the same time communicating his intended march to the bishops who happened to be at his court, some of whom he judged it right to take with him as companions, and as needful coadjutors in the service of God. They, on the other hand, cheerfully declared their willingness to follow in his train, disclaiming any desire to leave him, and engaging to battle with and for him by supplication to God on his behalf. Full of joy at this answer to his request, he unfolded to them his projected line of march; after which he caused a tent of great splendour, representing in shape the figure of a church, to be prepared for his own use in the approaching war. In this he intended to unite with the bishops in offering prayers to the God from whom all victory proceeds.

CHAPTER LVII

HIS FAVOURABLE RECEPTION OF AN EMBASSY FROM THE PERSIANS. HE KEEPS THE NIGHT VIGIL WITH OTHERS AT THE FEAST OF EASTER

IN the mean while the Persians, hearing of the emperor's warlike preparations, and not a little terrified at the prospect of an engagement with his forces, dispatched an embassy to pray for conditions of peace. These overtures the emperor, himself a sincere lover of peace, at once accepted, and readily entered on friendly relations with that people. At this time, the great festival of Easter was at hand; on which occasion he rendered the tribute of his prayers to God, and passed the night in watching with the assembled worshippers.

CHAPTER LVIII

BUILDING OF A CHURCH IN HONOUR OF THE APOSTLES AT CONSTANTINOPLE

AFTER this he proceeded to erect a church in memory of the apostles, in the city which bears his name. This building he carried to a vast height, and brilliantly decorated by encasing it from the foundation to the roof with marble slabs of various colours. He also formed the inner roof of finely fretted work, and overlaid it throughout with gold. The external covering, which protected the building from the weather, was of brass instead of tiles; and this too was splendidly and profusely adorned with gold, and reflected the sun's rays with a brilliancy which dazzled the distant beholder. The dome was entirely encompassed by a finely carved tracery, wrought in brass and gold.

CHAPTER LIX

FURTHER DESCRIPTION OF THE SAME CHURCH

SUCH was the magnificence with which the emperor was pleased to beautify this church. The building was surrounded by an open area of great extent, the four sides of which were terminated by porticos which enclosed the area and the church itself. Adjoining these porticos were ranges of stately chambers, with baths and lodging rooms, and many other apartments adapted to the use of those who had charge of the place.

CHAPTER LX

HE ALSO ERECTED HIS OWN SEPULCHRAL MONUMENT IN THIS CHURCH

ALL these edifices the emperor consecrated with the desire of perpetuating the memory of the apostles of our Saviour. He had, however, another object in erecting this building: an object at first unknown, but which afterwards became evident to all. He had in fact made choice of this spot in the prospect of his own death, anticipating with extraordinary fervour of faith that his body would share their title with the apostles themselves, and that he should thus even after death become the subject, with them, of the devotions which should be performed to their honour in this place. He accordingly caused twelve coffins to be set up in this church, like sacred pillars in honour and memory of the apostolic number, in the centre of which his own was placed, having six of theirs on either side of it. Thus, as I said, he had provided with prudent foresight an honourable resting-place for his body after death, and, having long before secretly formed this resolution, he now consecrated this church to the apostles, believing that this tribute to their memory would be of no small advantage to his own soul. Nor did God disappoint him of that which he so ardently expected and desired. For after he had completed the first services of the feast of Easter, and had passed this sacred day of our Lord in a manner which made it an occasion of joy and gladness to himself and to all; the God through whose aid he performed all these acts, and whose zealous servant he continued to be even to the end of life, was pleased at a happy time to translate him to a higher and better sphere of being.

CHAPTER LXI

HIS SICKNESS AT HELENOPOLIS, AND PRAYERS RESPECTING HIS BAPTISM

AT first he experienced some slight interruption of his usual health, which was soon followed by positive disease. In consequence of this he visited the hot baths of his own city; and thence proceeded to that which bore the name of his mother. Here he passed some time in the church of the martyrs, and offered up supplications and prayers to God. Being at length convinced that his life was drawing to a close, he felt the time was come at which he should seek to expiate the errors of his past career, firmly believing that whatever sins he had committed as a mortal man, his soul would be purified from them through the efficacy of the mysterious words and the salutary waters of baptism. Impressed with these thoughts, he poured forth his supplications and confessions to God, kneeling on the pavement in the church itself, in which he also now for the first time received the imposition of hands with prayer. After this he proceeded as far as the suburbs of Nicomedia, and there, having summoned the bishops to meet him, addressed them in the following words.

CHAPTER LXII

CONSTANTINE'S APPEAL TO THE BISHOPS, REQUESTING THEM TO CONFER UPON HIM THE RITE OF BAPTISM

"THE time is arrived which I have long hoped for, with an earnest desire and prayer that I might obtain the salvation of God. The hour is come in which I too may receive the blessing of that seal which confers immortality; the hour in which I may partake of the impression of the salutary sign. I had thought to do this in the waters of the river Jordan, wherein our Saviour, for our example, is recorded to have been baptized: but God, who knows what is expedient for us, is pleased that I should receive this blessing here. Be it so, then, without delay: for should it be His will who is Lord of life and death, that my existence here should be prolonged, and should I be destined henceforth to associate with the people of God, and unite with them in prayer as a member of His Church, I will prescribe to myself from this time such a course of life as befits His service." After he had thus spoken, the prelates performed the sacred ceremonies in the usual manner, and, having given him the necessary instructions, made him a partaker of the mystic ordinance. Thus was Constantine the first of all sovereigns who was regenerated and perfected in a church dedicated to the martyrs of Christ; thus gifted with the Divine seal of baptism, he rejoiced in spirit, was renewed, and filled with heavenly light: his soul was gladdened by reason of the fervency of his faith, and astonished at the manifestation of the power of God. At the conclusion of the ceremony he arrayed himself in imperial vestments, white and brilliant as the light, and reclined on a couch of the purest white, refusing to clothe himself with the purple any more.

CHAPTER LXIII

AFTER HIS BAPTISM HE RENDERS THANKS TO GOD

HE then lifted his voice and poured forth a strain of thanksgiving to God; after which he added these words. "Now I know that I am truly blessed: now I feel assured that I am accounted worthy of immortality, and am made a partaker of Divine light." He further expressed his compassion for the unhappy condition of those who were strangers to such blessings as he enjoyed: and when the tribunes and generals of his army appeared in his presence with lamentations and tears at the prospect of their bereavement, and with prayers that his days might yet be prolonged, he assured them in reply that he was now in possession of true life; that none but himself could know the value of the blessings he had received; so that he was anxious rather to hasten than to defer his departure to God. He then proceeded to complete the needful arrangement of his affairs, bequeathing an annual donation to the Roman inhabitants of his imperial city; apportioning the inheritance of his empire, like a patrimonial estate, among his own children; in short, making every other disposition according to his own judgment and desire.

CHAPTER LXIV

CONSTANTINE'S DEATH AT NOON ON THE FEAST OF PENTECOST

ALL these events occurred during a most important festival, I mean the august and holy solemnity of Pentecost, which is distinguished by a period of seven weeks, and crowned with that one day on which the holy Scriptures attest the reception of our common Saviour into heaven, and the descent of the Holy Spirit among men. In the course of this feast the emperor received the privileges I have described; and on the last day of all, which one might justly call the feast of feasts, he was removed about mid-day to the presence of his God, leaving his mortal remains to his fellow mortals, and carrying into fellowship with God that part of his being which was capable of understanding and loving Him. Such was the close of Constantine's mortal life. Let us now attend to the circumstances which followed this event.

CHAPTER LXV

LAMENTATIONS OF THE SOLDIERY AND THEIR OFFICERS

IMMEDIATELY the assembled spearmen and bodyguard rent their garments, and prostrated themselves on the ground, striking their heads, and uttering lamentations and cries of sorrow, calling on their imperial lord and master, or rather, like fond and affectionate children, on their father, while their tribunes and centurions addressed him as their preserver, protector, and benefactor. The rest of the soldiery also came in respectful order to mourn as a flock the removal of their good shepherd. The people meanwhile ran wildly throughout the city, some expressing the inward sorrow of their hearts by loud cries, others appearing confounded with grief: each mourning the event as a calamity which had befallen himself, and bewailing his death as though they felt themselves bereft of a blessing common alike to all.

CHAPTER LXVI

REMOVAL OF THE BODY FROM NICOMEDIA TO THE PALACE AT CONSTANTINOPLE

AFTER this the soldiers lifted the body from its couch, and laid it in a golden coffin, which they enveloped in a covering of purple, and removed to the city which was called by his own name. Here it was placed in an elevated position in the principal chamber of the imperial palace, and surrounded by candles burning in candlesticks of gold, presenting a marvellous spectacle, and such as no mortal had exhibited on earth since the world itself began. For in the central apartment of the imperial palace, the body of the emperor lay in its elevated resting-place, arrayed in the symbols of sovereignty, the diadem and purple robe, and encircled by a numerous retinue of attendants, who watched around it incessantly night and day.

CHAPTER LXVII

HE RECEIVED THE SAME HONOURS FROM THE COUNTS AND OTHER OFFICERS AS BEFORE HIS DEATH

THE military officers, too, of the highest rank, the counts, and the whole order of magistrates, who had been accustomed to do obeisance to their emperor before his death, continued to fulfil this duty without any change, entering the chamber at the appointed times, and saluting their coffined sovereign with bended knee, as though he were still alive. After them the senators appeared, and all who had been distinguished by any honourable office, and rendered the same homage. These were followed by multitudes of every rank, who came with their wives and children to witness the spectacle. These honours continued to be rendered for a considerable time, the soldiers having resolved thus to guard the body until his sons should arrive, and take on themselves the conduct of their father's funeral. No mortal had ever, like this blessed prince, continued to reign even after death, and to receive the same homage as during his life: he only, of all who have ever lived, obtained this reward from God: a suitable reward, since he alone of all sovereigns had in all his actions honoured the Supreme God and His Christ, and God Himself accordingly was pleased that even his mortal remains should still retain imperial authority among men; thus indicating to all who were not utterly devoid of understanding the immortal and endless empire which his soul was destined to enjoy.

CHAPTER LXVIII

RESOLUTION OF THE ARMY TO CONFER THENCE-FORWARD THE TITLE OF AUGUSTUS ON HIS SONS

MEANWHILE the tribunes selected from the troops under their command those officers whose fidelity and zeal had long been known to the emperor, and despatched them to the Cæsars with intelligence of the late event. This service they accordingly performed. As soon, however, as the soldiery throughout the provinces received the tidings of the emperor's decease, they all, as if by a supernatural impulse, resolved with one consent (as though their great emperor had been yet alive) to acknowledge none other than his sons as sovereigns of the Roman world: and these they soon after determined should no longer retain the name of Cæsar, but should each be honoured with the title of Augustus, a name which indicates the highest supremacy of imperial power. Such were the measures adopted by the army; and these resolutions they communicated to each other by letter, so that the unanimous desire of the legions became known at the same point of time throughout the whole extent of the empire.

CHAPTER LXIX

MOURNING ROR CONSTANTINE AT ROME; AND PAINTINGS IN MEMORY OF HIS DEATH

ON the arrival of the news of the emperor's death in the imperial city, the Roman senate and people felt the announcement as the heaviest and most afflictive of all calamities, and gave themselves up to an excess of grief. The baths and markets were closed, the public spectacles, and all other recreations in which men of leisure are accustomed to indulge, were interrupted. Those who had erewhile lived in luxurious ease, now walked the streets in gloomy sadness, while all united in blessing the name of the deceased, as the friend of heaven, and truly worthy of the imperial dignity. Nor was their sorrow expressed only in words: they proceeded also to honour him, by the dedication of paintings to his memory, with the same respect as before his death. The design of these pictures embodied a representation of heaven itself, and depicted the emperor reposing in an ethereal mansion above the celestial vault. They too declared his sons to be his only successors in the imperial power and the title of Augustus, and begged with earnest entreaty that they might be permitted to receive the body of their emperor, and perform his obsequies in the imperial city.

CHAPTER LXX

HIS BURIAL BY HIS SON CONSTANTIUS AT CONSTANTINOPLE

THUS did the citizens of Rome testify their respect for the memory of him who had been honoured by God. The second of his sons, however, who had by this time arrived, proceeded to celebrate his father's funeral in the city which bears his name, himself heading the procession, which was preceded by detachments of soldiers in military array, and followed by vast multitudes, the body itself being surrounded by companies of spearmen and heavy-armed infantry. On the arrival of the procession at the church dedicated to the apostles of our Saviour, the coffin was there entombed. Such honour did the youthful emperor Constantius render to his deceased parent, both by his presence, and by the due performance of this sacred ceremony.

CHAPTER LXXI

SACRED SERVICE IN THE CHURCH OF THE APOSTLES ON THE OCCASION OF CONSTANTINE'S FUNERAL

AS soon as Constantius had withdrawn himself with the military train, the ministers of God came forward, with the multitude and the whole congregation of the faithful, and performed the rites of Divine worship with prayer. At the same time the tribute of their praises was given to the character of this blessed prince, whose body rested on a lofty and conspicuous monument, and the whole multitude united with the priests of God in offering prayers for his soul with many tears, thus performing an office consonant with the desires of the pious deceased. In this respect also the favour of God was manifested to His servant, in that he not only bequeathed the succession of the empire to his own beloved sons, but that the earthly tabernacle of his thrice blessed soul, according to his own earnest wish, was permitted to share the monument of the apostles; was associated with the honour of their name, and with that of the people of God; was honoured by the performance of the sacred ordinances and mystic service; and enjoyed a participation in the prayers of the saints. Thus, too, he continued to possess imperial power even after death, controlling, as though with renovated life, a universal dominion, and retaining in his own name, as Victor, Maximus, Augustus, the sovereignty of the Roman world.

CHAPTER LXXII

AN ALLUSION TO THE PHŒNIX

WE cannot compare him with that bird of Egypt, the only one, as they say, of its kind, which dies, self-sacrificed, in the midst of aromatic perfumes, and, rising from its own ashes with new life, soars aloft in the same form which it had before. Rather did he resemble his Saviour, who, as the sown corn which is multiplied from a single grain, had yielded abundant increase through the blessing of God, and had overspread the world with His fruit. Even so did our thrice blessed prince become multiplied, as it were, through the succession of his sons. His statue was erected along with theirs in every province; and the name of Constantine was owned and honoured even after the close of his mortal life.

CHAPTER LXXIII

CONSTANTINE IS REPRESENTED ON COINS IN THE ACT OF ASCENDING TO HEAVEN

A COINAGE was also struck which bore the following device. On one side appeared the figure of our blessed prince, with the head closely veiled: the reverse exhibited him sitting as a charioteer, drawn by four horses, with a hand stretched downward from above to receive him up to heaven.

CHAPTER LXXIV

THE GOD WHOM HE HAD HONOURED DESERVEDLY HONOURED HIM IN RETURN

SUCH are the proofs by which the Supreme God has made it manifest to us, in the person of him who alone of all sovereigns had openly professed the Christian faith, how great a difference He perceives between those whose privilege it is to worship Him and His Christ, and those who have chosen the contrary part, who provoked His enmity by daring to assail His Church, and whose calamitous end, in every instance, afforded tokens of His displeasure, as manifestly as the death of Constantine conveyed to all men an evident assurance of His Divine love.

CHAPTER LXXV

HE SURPASSED ALL PRECEDING EMPERORS IN DEVOTION TO GOD

STANDING, as he did, alone and pre-eminent among the Roman emperors as a worshipper of God; alone as the bold proclaimer to all men of the doctrine of Christ; having alone rendered honour, as none before him had ever done, to His Church; having alone abolished utterly the superstitious worship of a plurality of gods, and discountenanced idolatry in every form: so, both during life and after death, was he accounted worthy of such honours as none can say have been attained to by any other; so that no one, whether Greek or Barbarian, nay, of the ancient Romans themselves, has ever been presented to us as worthy of comparison with him.

THE ORATION OF THE EMPEROR CONSTANTINE, WHICH HE ADDRESSED "TO THE ASSEMBLY OF THE SAINTS"

CHAPTER I

PRELIMINARY REMARKS ON THE FEAST OF EASTER: AND HOW THE WORD OF GOD, HAVING CONFERRED MANIFOLD BENEFITS ON MANKIND, RECEIVED A BASE AND TREACHEROUS RETURN

THAT light which far outshines the day and the radiance of the sun, first pledge of resurrection, and renovation of bodies long since dissolved, the spring of promise, the path which leads to everlasting life—in a word, the day of the Passion—is arrived, best beloved Doctors, and ye, my friends who are assembled here—ye blessed multitudes, who worship Him who is the Author of all worship, and praise Him continually with heart and voice, according to the precepts of His holy word. But thou, Nature, parent of all things, what blessing like to this hast thou ever accomplished for mankind? Nay rather, what is in any sense thy workmanship, since He who formed the universe is Himself the Author of thy being? For it is He who has arrayed thee in thy beauty; and the beauty of Nature is life according to Nature's laws. But principles quite opposed to Nature have mightily prevailed; in that men have agreed in withholding His rightful worship from the Lord of all, believing that the order of the universe depended, not on His providence, but on the blind uncertainty of chance: and this notwithstanding the clearest announcement of the truth by His inspired prophets, whose words should have claimed belief, but were in every way resisted by that impious wickedness which hates the light of truth, and loves the obscure mazes of darkness. Nor was this error unaccompanied by violence and cruelty, especially in that the will of princes encouraged the blind impetuosity of the multitude, or rather itself led the way in the career of reckless folly. Such principles as these, confirmed by the practice of many generations, became the source of terrible evils in those early times: but no sooner had the radiance of the Saviour's presence appeared, than justice took the place of wrong, a calm succeeded the confusion of the storm, and the predictions of the prophets were all fulfilled. For after He had enlightened the world by the glorious discretion and purity of His character, and had ascended to the mansions of His Father's house, He founded His Church on earth, as a holy temple of virtue, an immortal, imperishable temple, wherein the worship due to the Supreme Father and to Himself should be piously performed. But what did the insane malice of the nations hereupon devise? Their effort was to reject the grace of Christ, and to ruin that Church which was ordained for the salvation of all, though they thus ensured the overthrow of their own superstition. Once more then unholy sedition, once more war and strife prevailed, with stubborn discontent, luxurious riot, and that craving for wealth which now soothes its victims with specious hope, now strikes them with groundless fear; a craving which is contrary to nature, and the very characteristic of Vice herself. Let her, however, lie prostrate in the dust, and own the victorious power of Virtue; and let her rend and tear herself, as well she may, in the bitterness of repentance. But let us now proceed to speak of topics which pertain to the Divine doctrine.

CHAPTER II

AN APPEAL TO THE CHURCH AND HIS AUDIENCE GENERALLY, TO PARDON AND CORRECT THE ERRORS OF HIS SPEECH

HEAR then, thou master of the sacred vessel, possessor of virgin purity, and thou Church, the cherisher of tender and inexperienced age, guardian of truth and gentleness, through whose perennial fountain the streams of salvation flow! Be ye too my indulgent hearers, who worship God sincerely, and are therefore the objects of His care: attending, not to the language, but the truth of what is said; not to him who speaks, but rather to the pious zeal which hallows his discourse! For how shall language have power to charm, while the real sentiments of the speaker remain unknown? It may be, indeed, that I essay great things; the love of God which animates my soul, a love which overpowers natural reserve, is my plea for the bold attempt. On you, then, I call, who are best instructed in the mysteries of God, to aid me with your counsel, to follow me with your thoughts, and correct whatever shall savour of error in my words, expecting no display of perfect knowledge, but graciously accepting the sincerity of my endeavour. And may the Spirit of the Father and the Son accord His mighty aid, while I utter the words which He shall dictate and suggest to my thoughts. For if any one, whether in the practice of eloquence, or any other art, expects to produce a finished work without the help of God, both the author and his efforts will be found alike imperfect; while he has no cause to fear, no room for discouragement, who has once been blessed with the inspiration of Heaven. And now let me pray your indulgence for the length of this preface, and proceed at once to the main subject of my discourse.

CHAPTER III

THAT GOD IS THE FATHER OF THE WORD, AND THE CREATOR OF ALL THINGS: AND THAT MATERIAL OBJECTS COULD NOT CONTINUE TO EXIST, WERE THEIR CAUSES DIFFERENT

GOD, who is ever above all existence, and the good which all things desire, has no origin, and therefore no beginning, being Himself the originator of all things which receive existence. But He who proceeds from Him is again united to Him; and this separation from and union with Him is not local, but intellectual in its character. For this generation was accompanied by no diminution of the Father's substance (as existence is derived according to the ordinary course of nature), but was consequent upon that disposition of Divine Providence which manifested the Saviour to be the director of this visible world, and all the works contained therein. From hence, then, is the source of existence and life to all things which are within the compass of this world; hence proceed the soul, and every sense; hence those faculties through which the actions prompted by the senses are perfectly performed. What, then, is the object of this argument? To prove that there is One director of all things that exist, and that all things, whether in heaven or on earth, both natural and organized bodies, are subject to His single sovereignty. For if the dominion of these things, numberless as they are, were in the hands, not of one but of many, there must be a partition and distribution of the elements, and the old fables would be true; jealousy, too, and ambition, striving for superior power, would shake the harmonious concord of the whole, while each of the many masters would regulate in a manner different from the rest the portion subject to his control. The fact, however, that this universal order is ever one and the same, is the proof that it is under the care of a superior Power, and that its origin cannot be ascribed to chance. Else how could the author of universal nature ever be known? To whom first, or last, could prayers and supplications be addressed? Whom could I choose as the object of my worship, without being guilty of impiety towards the rest? Again, if haply I desired to obtain some temporal blessing, should I not, while expressing my gratitude to the Power who favoured my request, convey a reproach to him who opposed it? Or to whom should I pray, when desiring to know the cause of my calamity, and to obtain deliverance? Or let us suppose that the answer is given by oracles and prophecies, but that the case is not within the scope of their authority, being the province of some other deity. Where then is mercy? where is the provident care of God for the human race? Unless, indeed, some more benevolent Power, assuming a hostile attitude against another who has no such feeling, be disposed to accord me his protection. Hence anger, division, mutual censure, and finally universal confusion, would ensue, while each departed from his proper sphere of action, dissatisfied, through ambitious love of power, with his allotted portion. What then would be the result of these things? Surely this discord among the heavenly powers would prove destructive to the interests of earth: the orderly alternation of times and seasons would disappear; the successive productions of the earth would be enjoyed no more; the day itself, and the repose of night which follows it, would cease to be. But enough on this subject: let us once more resume that species of reasoning which admits of no reply.

CHAPTER IV

ON THE ERROR OF IDOLATROUS WORSHIP

WHATEVER has had a beginning, has also an end. Now that which is a beginning in respect of time, is called a generation: and whatever is by generation is subject to corruption, and its beauty is impaired by the lapse of time. How, then, can they whose origin is from corruptible generation, be immortal? Again, this supposition has gained credit with the ignorant multitude, that marriages, and the birth of children, are usual among the gods. Granting, then, such offspring to be immortal, and continually produced, the race must of necessity multiply to excess: and if this were so, where is the heaven, or the earth, which could contain so vast and still increasing a multitude of gods? But what shall we say of those men who represent these celestial beings as joined in incestuous union with their sister goddesses, and charge them with adultery and impurity? We declare, further, with all confidence, that the very honours and worship which these deities receive from men are accompanied by acts of wantonness and profligacy. Once more; the experienced and skilful statuary, having formed the conception of his design, perfects his work according to the rules of art; and in a little while, as if forgetful of himself, idolizes his own creation, and adores it as an immortal god, while yet he admits that himself, the author and maker of the image, is a mortal man. Nay, they even shew the graves and monuments of those whom they deem immortal, and bestow divine honours on the dead: not knowing that that which is truly blessed and incorruptible needs no distinction which perishable men can give: for that Being, who is seen by the mental eye, and conceived by the intellect alone, requires to be distinguished by no external form, and admits no figure to represent its character and likeness. But the honours of which we speak are given to those who have yielded to the power of death: they once were men, and tenants, while they lived, of a mortal body.

CHAPTER V

THAT CHRIST, THE SON OF GOD, CREATED ALL THINGS, AND HAS APPOINTED TO EVERY THING THE TERM OF ITS EXISTENCE

BUT why do I defile my tongue with unhallowed words, when my object is to sound the praises of the true God? Rather let me cleanse myself, as it were, from this bitter draught by the pure stream which flows from the everlasting fountain of the virtue of that God who is the object of my praise. Be it my special province to glorify Christ, as well by the actions of my life, as by that thanksgiving which is due to Him for the manifold and signal blessings which He has bestowed. I affirm, therefore, that He has laid the foundations of this universe; that He created the race of men, and ordered all these things consistently with His own wisdom. And immediately He transferred our newly created parents (ignorant at first, according to His will, of good and evil) to a happy region, abounding in flowers and fruits of every kind. At length, however, He appointed them a seat on earth befitting creatures endued with reason; and then unfolded to their faculties, as intelligent beings, the knowledge of good and evil. Then, too, He bade the race increase; and each healthy region of the world, as far as the bounds of the circumambient ocean, became the dwelling-place of men; while with this increase of numbers the invention of the useful arts went hand in hand. Meantime the various species of inferior animals increased in due proportion, each kind discovering some characteristic quality, the special gift of nature: the tame distinguished by gentleness and obedience to man; the wild by strength and swiftness, and an instinctive foresight which warned them to escape from peril. The gentler animals He placed entirely beneath man's protecting care, but entailed on him the necessity of strife with those of fiercer nature. He next created the feathered race, manifold in number, diverse in character and habits; brilliant with every variety of colour, and endued with native powers of melody. Finally, having arranged with wise discrimination whatever else the compass of this world contains, and having assigned to every creature the stated term of its existence, He thus completed the beautiful order of the perfect whole.

CHAPTER VI

THE FALSITY OF THE GENERAL OPINION RESPECTING FATE IS PROVED BY THE CONSIDERATION OF HUMAN LAWS, AND BY THE WORKS OF CREATION, THE COURSE OF WHICH IS NOT FORTUITOUS, BUT ACCORDING TO A DEFINITE ARRANGEMENT WHICH EVINCES THE DESIGN OF THE CREATOR

THE great majority, however, in their folly, ascribe the regulation of the universe to nature, while some imagine fate, or accident, to be the cause. With regard to those who attribute the control of all things to fate, they know not that in using this term they utter a mere word, but designate no active power, nor anything which has real and substantial existence. For what can this fate be, considered in itself, if nature be the first cause of all things? Or what shall we suppose nature itself to be, if the law of fate be inviolable? Indeed, the very assertion that there is a law of fate implies that such law is the work of a legislator: if therefore fate itself be a law, it must be a law devised by God. All things, therefore, are subject to God, and nothing is beyond the sphere of His power. If it be said that fate is the will of God, and is so considered, we admit the fact. But in what respect do justice, or self-control, or the other virtues, depend on fate? From whence, if so, do their contraries, as injustice and intemperance, proceed? For vice has its origin from nature, not from fate; and virtue is the due regulation of natural character and disposition. But, granting that the varied results of actions (whether right or erroneous in themselves) depend on fortune or fate: in what sense can the general principle of justice, the principle of rendering to every one his due, be ascribed to fate? Or how can it be said that laws, encouragements to virtue and dissuasives from what is evil, praise, blame, punishment, in short whatever operates as a motive to virtue, and deters from the practice of vice, derive their origin from fortune or accident, and not rather from that justice which is a characteristic attribute of the God of providence? For the events which befall men are consequent upon the tenour of their lives. Hence pestilence or sedition, famine and plenty, succeed in turn, declaring plainly and emphatically that all these things are regulated with reference to our course of life. For the Divine Being delights in goodness, but turns with aversion from all impiety; looks with acceptance on the humble spirit, but abhors presumption, and that pride which exalts itself above what becomes a creature. And though the proofs of these truths are clear and manifest to our sight, they appear in a still stronger light, when we collect, and as it were concentrate our thoughts within ourselves, and ponder their causes with deep attention. I say, then, that it becomes us to lead a life of sobriety and gentleness, not suffering our thoughts to rise proudly above our natural condition, and ever mindful that God is near us, and is the observer of all our actions. But let us still further examine the statement, that the order of the universe depends on chance or accident. Are we then to suppose that the stars and other heavenly bodies, the earth and sea, fire and wind, water and air, the succession of the seasons, the recurrence of summer and winter, that all these have an undesigned and fortuitous existence, and not rather that they proceed from the creative hand of God? Some, indeed, are so senseless as to say that most of these things have been devised by mankind for their own benefit. Let it be admitted that this opinion has a semblance of reason in regard to earthly and corruptible things (though nature herself supplies every good with a lavish hand); can we believe that things which are immortal and unchangeable are the inventions of men? These, indeed, and all things else which are beyond the reach of our senses, and comprehended by the intellect alone, receive their being, not from the material life of man, but from the spiritual and eternal essence of God. Again, the orderly arrangement of these things is the work of His providence: for instance, the brightness which the day derives from the radiance of the sun; the succession of night at his setting, and the starry host by which night itself is redeemed from total darkness. And what shall we say of the moon, which when most distant from, and opposite to the sun, is filled with light, but wanes in proportion to the nearness of her approach to him? Do not these things manifestly evince the intelligence and sagacious wisdom of God? Add to this that needful warmth of the solar rays which ripens the fruits of the earth; the currents of wind, so conducive to the fertility of the seasons; the cool and refreshing showers; and the universal harmony and wise uniformity of arrangement which governs all these things: lastly, the everlasting order of the planets, which return to the self-same place at their appointed times: are not all these (as well as the perfect ministry of the stars, obedient to a divine law) evident proofs of the ordinance of God? Again, do the mountain heights, the deep and hollow vallies, the level and extensive plains (useful as they are, as well as pleasing to the eye), appear to exist independently of the will of God? Or do not the proportion and alternate succession of land and water (serviceable, the one for husbandry, the other for the transport of foreign produce) afford a clear demonstration of His exact and perfect providential care? For instance, the mountains contain a store of water, which the level ground receives, and after imbibing sufficient for the renovation of the soil, passes the residue onward to the ocean. And still we dare to say that all these things happen by chance, and evince no design; unable though we be to shew by what shape or form this chance is represented; a thing which has neither intellectual nor sensible existence; which rings in our ears as the mere sound of an unsubstantial name!

CHAPTER VII

IN REGARD TO THINGS ABOVE OUR COMPREHENSION, WE SHOULD GLORIFY THE CREATOR'S WISDOM, AND ATTRIBUTE THEIR CAUSES TO HIM ALONE, AND NOT TO CHANCE

IN fact, this word "chance" is the expression of men who think vaguely and at random; who are unable to understand the causes of these things, and who, owing to the feebleness of their own apprehensions, conceive that those things for which they cannot assign a reason, are ordered without reason or design. There are, unquestionably, some things which possess wonderful natural properties, and the full understanding and explanation of which is very obscure: for example, the nature of hot springs. For no one can easily explain the cause of so powerful a fire; and it is indeed surprising that though surrounded on all sides by a body of cold water, it loses none of its native heat. These phenomena appear to be of rare occurrence throughout the world, being intended, I am persuaded, to afford to mankind convincing evidence of the power of that Providence which ordains that two directly opposite natures, heat and cold, should thus proceed from the self-same source. Many indeed, yea, numberless are the gifts which God has bestowed for the comfort and enjoyment of man; and of these the fruit of the olive tree and the vine deserve especial notice; the one for its power of renovating and cheering the spirit, the other because it not only ministers to our enjoyment, but is adapted for the cure of bodily disease. Marvellous, too, is the course of rivers, flowing night and day with unceasing motion, and presenting a type of everlasting life: and equally wonderful is the alternate succession of day and night.

CHAPTER VIII

THAT GOD BESTOWS AN ABUNDANT SUPPLY OF WHATEVER IS SUITED TO THE WANTS OF MAN, AND MINISTERS BUT SPARINGLY TO HIS PLEASURES; IN BOTH CASES WITH A VIEW TO HIS ADVANTAGE

LET what has been said suffice to prove that nothing exists without reason and design, and that reason itself and providence are of God. It is He who has also distributed the metals, as gold, silver, copper, and the rest, in due proportion;

ordaining an abundant supply of those which would be most needed and generally employed, while He dispensed those which serve the purposes merely of pleasure and luxury with a liberal and yet a sparing hand, holding a mean between parsimony and profusion. For the searchers for metals, were those which are employed for ornament procured in equal abundance with the rest, would be impelled by avarice to despise and neglect those which are serviceable for husbandry, or building, or the construction of ships; and would care for those only which conduce to luxury and a superfluous excess of wealth. Hence it is, as they say, that the search for gold and silver is far more difficult and laborious than that for any other metals, the severity of the toil thus acting as a counterpoise to the urgency of the desire. And how many instances might still further be enumerated of the workings of that Divine Providence which, in all the gifts which it has so unsparingly conferred upon us, plainly invites us to the practice of self-control and all other virtues, and warns us against that covetous spirit which so ill becomes us? To trace the secret reasons of all these things is indeed a task which exceeds the power of human faculties. For how can the intellect of a frail and perishable being arrive at the knowledge of perfect truth, or apprehend in its purity the counsel of God from the beginning?

CHAPTER IX

OF THE PHILOSOPHERS, WHO WERE LED INTO ERRORS OF JUDGMENT, AND SOME OF THEM INTO DANGER, BY THEIR DESIRE OF UNIVERSAL KNOWLEDGE—ALSO OF THE DOCTRINES OF PLATO

WE ought, therefore, to aim at objects which are within our power, and exceed not the capacities of our nature. For the persuasive influence of argument has a tendency to draw most of us away from the simplicity of truth, which has happened to many philosophers, who have employed them selves in reasoning, and searching into the secrets of nature, and who, as often as the magnitude of the subject surpasses their powers of investigation, adopt various devices for obscuring the truth. Hence their diversities of judgment, and contentious opposition to each others' doctrines, and this notwithstanding their pretensions to wisdom. Hence, too, popular commotions have arisen, and severe sentences, passed by those in power, apprehensive of the overthrow of hereditary institutions, have proved destructive to many of the disputants themselves. Socrates, for example, elated by his skill in argumentation, indulging his power of overcoming the stronger by the weaker reason, and playing continually with the subtleties of controversy, fell a victim to the jealousy of his own countrymen and fellow-citizens. Pythagoras, too, who laid special claim to the virtues of silence and self-control, was convicted of falsehood. For he declared to the Italians that the doctrines which he had received during his travels in Egypt, and which had long before been divulged by the priests of that nation, were a personal revelation to himself from God. Lastly, Plato himself, the gentlest and most refined of all, who first essayed to draw men's thoughts from sensible to intellectual and eternal objects, and taught them to aspire to sublimer speculations, in the first place declared (and indeed with truth), that God is exalted above every essence. To Him he added a second, distinguishing them numerically as two, though both possessing one perfection, and the being of the second Deity proceeding from the first. For He is the author and controller of the universe, and therefore supreme: while the second, as the obedient agent of His commands, refers the origin of all creation to Him as the cause. In accordance, therefore, with the soundest reason, we may say that there is one Being whose care and providence are over all things, even God the Word, who has ordered all things; and the Word Himself, who is God, is also the Son of God. For by what name can we designate Him except by this title of the Son, without falling into the most grievous error? Thus far, then, Plato's sentiments were sound; but in what follows he appears to have wandered from the truth, in that he introduces a plurality of gods, to each of whom he assigns specific forms. And this has given occasion to still greater error among the unthinking portion of mankind, who pay no regard to the providence of the Supreme God, but worship images of their own devising, made in the likeness of men or other animals. Hence it appears that the transcendent intellect and admirable learning of this philosopher, tinged as they were with such errors as these, were by no means free from impurity and defilement. And yet he seems to me to retract, and correct his own words, when he plainly declares that a rational soul is the breath of God, and divides all things into two classes, intellectual, and sensible: the one simple, the other consisting of bodily structure; the one comprehended by the intellect alone, the other estimated by the judgment and the senses. The former class, therefore, which partakes of the divine spirit, and is uncompounded and immaterial, is eternal, and inherits everlasting life; in which the latter, being entirely resolved into the elements of which it is composed, has no share. He further teaches the admirable doctrine, that those who have passed a life of virtue, that is, the spirits of good and holy men, are enshrined, after their separation from the body, in the fairest mansions of heaven. A doctrine not merely to be admired, but profitable too. For who can believe in such a statement, and aspire to such a happy lot, without desiring to practise righteousness and virtue, and to turn aside from vice? Consistently with this doctrine he represents the spirits of the wicked as tossed on the streams of Acheron and Pyriphlegethon, and borne like the fragments of shattered vessels on their waves.

CHAPTER X

OF THOSE WHO REJECT THE DOCTRINES OF PHILOSOPHERS, AS WELL AS THOSE OF SCRIPTURE: AND THAT WE OUGHT TO YIELD OUR ASSENT TO THE POETS IN ALL THINGS, OR NOT AT ALL

THERE are, however, some persons so infatuated, that neither their attention nor their fears are excited when they meet with such sentiments as these: nay, they even treat them with contempt and scorn, as if they listened to the inventions of fable; applauding, perhaps, the beauty and eloquence of the style, but abhorring the severity of the precepts therein conveyed. And yet they give credence to the fictions of the poets, and fill both civilized and barbarous countries with legends of vanity and falsehood. For the poets assert that the judgment of souls after death is committed to men whose parentage they ascribe to the gods, and extol the severe and impartial sentence of those whom they represent as arbiters of the conduct of the dead. The same poets describe the conflicts and usages of war as existing amongst the gods, and speak of them as subject to the power of fate. Some of these deities they picture to us as cruel and relentless, others as strangers to all care for the human race, and others again as morose and stern in their character. They introduce them also as mourning the slaughter of their own children, thus implying their inability to succour, not strangers only, but those most dear to them, in the hour of peril. They describe them, too, as subject to human passions, and sing of their battles and wounds, their joys and sorrows. And in all this they appear worthy of belief. For if we suppose them to be moved by a divine impulse to attempt the poetic art, we are bound to give our full assent to what they utter under this inspiration. They speak, then, of the calamities to which their divinities are subject; calamities which truly are probable enough. But it will be objected that it is the privilege of poets to lie, since the peculiar province of poetry is to charm the spirits of the hearers, while truth is confined to the strict relation of mere matters of fact. Let us grant that it is a characteristic of poetry occasionally to conceal the truth. But they who speak falsehood do it not without an object; being influenced either by a desire of personal advantage, or possibly, being conscious of some evil conduct, they are induced to disguise the truth by dread of the threatening vengeance of the laws. But surely it were possible for them (in my judgment), by adhering faithfully to truth at least while treating of the nature of the Supreme Being, to avoid the guilt at once of falsehood and impiety.

CHAPTER XI

ON THE COMING OF OUR LORD IN THE FLESH; ITS NATURE, AND CAUSE

WHOEVER, then, has pursued a course unworthy of a life of virtue, and is conscious of having spent his days in trespass and disorder, let him repent, and turn with enlightened spiritual vision to God; and let him abandon his past career of wickedness, content if he attain to wisdom even in his declining years. We, however, have received no aid from human instruction; nay, whatever graces of character are esteemed of good report by those who have understanding, are entirely the gift of God. And I am able to oppose no feeble buckler against the deadly weapons of Satan's armoury; I mean the knowledge I possess of those things which are pleasing to Him: and of these I will select such as are appropriate to my present design, while I proceed to sing the praises of the Father of all. But do Thou, Anointed Saviour of mankind, be present to aid me in my hallowed task! Instruct me worthily to sound Thy praises, and Thyself direct the words which celebrate Thy virtues! And now, let no one expect to listen to the artificial graces of studied language: for well I know that the nerveless eloquence of those who speak to charm the ear, and whose aim is rather to secure applause than to preserve chaste propriety of style, is distasteful to hearers of sound judgment. It is asserted, then, by some profane and senseless persons, that Christ, whom we worship, was justly condemned to death, and that He who is the Author of life to all, was Himself deprived of life. That such an assertion should be made by those who have once dared to enter the paths of impiety, who have cast aside all fear, and all thought of concealing their own depravity, is not surprising. But it is beyond the bounds of folly itself that they should be able, as it seems, really to persuade themselves that the incorruptible God yielded to the violence of men, and not rather to that love alone which He bore to the human race: that they should fail to perceive that Divine dignity and forbearance is changed by no insult, is moved from its intrinsic steadfastness by no revilings; but is ever the same, breaking down and repelling, by the spirit of wisdom and true greatness, the savage fierceness of those who assail it. The gracious kindness of God had determined to abolish iniquity, and to exalt modesty and justice. Accordingly He gathered a company of the wisest among men, and ordained that most noble and useful form of doctrine, which is calculated to lead the good and blessed of mankind to an imitation of His own providential care. And what higher blessing can we speak of than this, that God should prescribe the way of righteousness, and make those who are counted worthy of His instruction like Himself; that goodness might be communicated to all classes of mankind, and eternal felicity be the result? This is the glorious victory: this the true power: this the mighty work, worthy of its Author, the reclaiming of all people to the path of virtue: and the glory of this triumph we joyfully ascribe to Thee, thou Saviour of all! But thou, vile and wretched Blasphemy, whose glory is in the rumours of calumny and falsehood; thy power is to deceive and prevail with the inexperience of youth, and with men who still retain the folly of youth. These thou seducest from the service of the true God, and settest up false idols as the objects of their worship and their prayers; and thus the reward of their folly awaits thy deluded victims: for Christ, who is God, and the Son of God, the Author of every blessing, is outraged by their slanderous invectives. Is not the worship of the best and wisest of the nations of this world worthily directed to that God, who, while possessing boundless power, remains immoveably true to His own purpose, and retains undiminished His characteristic kindness and love to man? Away, then, ye impious (for still ye may while vengeance on your transgressions is yet withheld); begone to your sacrifices, your feasts, your scenes of revelry and riot, wherein, under the semblance of religion, your hearts are devoted to profligate enjoyment, and yourselves are the willing slaves of your own pleasures. No knowledge have ye of any good, nor even of the first commandment of the mighty God, who both declares His will to man, and gives commission to His Son to direct the course of human life, that they who have passed a career of virtue and self-control may obtain (according to the judgment of that Son) a second, yea, a blessed and happy existence. I have now declared the decree of God respecting the life which He prescribes to man, neither ignorantly, as many have done, nor resting on the ground of opinion or conjecture. But it may be that some will ask, Whence this title of Son? Whence this generation of which we speak, if God be indeed only One, and incapable of union with another? We are, however, to consider generation as of two kinds; one in the way of natural birth, which is known to all; the other, that which is the effect of an eternal cause, the mode of which is seen by the prescience of God, and by those among men whom He loves. For he who is wise will recognize the cause which regulates the harmony of creation. Since, then, nothing exists without a cause, of necessity the cause of existing substances preceded their existence. But since the world and all things that it contains exist, and are preserved, their preserver must have had a prior existence: so that Christ is the cause of all things that exist, and their preservation the effect of their existence: even as the Father is the cause of the Son, and the Son the effect of that cause. Enough, then, has been said to prove His priority of existence. But how do we explain His descent to this earth, His condescension to the society of men? The motive of His advent (as the prophets had foretold), originated in His watchful care for the interests of all: for it needs must be that the Creator should care for His own works. But when the time came for Him to assume a terrestrial body, and to sojourn on this earth, He devised for Himself a new mode of birth. Conception was there, yet apart from marriage: childbirth, yet pure virginity: and a maiden became the mother of God! An eternal nature received a beginning of temporal existence: a sensible form of a spiritual essence, a material manifestation of incorporeal brightness, appeared. Alike wondrous were the circumstances which attended this great event. A radiant dove (like that which flew from the ark of Noah) alighted on the Virgin's bosom: and accordant with this impalpable union, purer than chastity, more guileless than innocence itself, were the results which followed. From infancy possessing the wisdom of God; received with reverential awe by the Jordan, in whose waters He was baptized; gifted with that royal unction, the spirit of universal intelligence; with knowledge and power to perform wondrous works, and to heal diseases beyond the reach of human art; He yielded a swift and unhindered assent to the prayers of men, to whose welfare, indeed, His whole life was devoted without reserve. His doctrines instilled, not prudence only, but real wisdom: His hearers were instructed, not in the mere social virtues, but in the ways which conduct to the spiritual world; and devoted themselves to the contemplation of immutable and eternal things, and the knowledge of the Supreme Father. The benefits which He bestowed were no common blessings: for blindness, the gift of sight; for helpless weakness, the vigour of health; in the place of death, restored and renovated life. I dwell not on that lavish provision in the wilderness, whereby a scanty measure of food became a complete and enduring supply for the wants of a mighty multitude. Thus do we render thanks to Thee according to our feeble power, our God and Saviour, Christ; supreme Providence of the mighty Father, who both savest us from evil, and impartest to us Thy most blessed doctrine: thus we essay, not indeed to celebrate Thy praise, but to speak the language of thanksgiving. For what mortal is he who shall worthily declare Thy praise, of whom we learn that Thou didst from nothing call creation into being, and illumine it with Thy light; that Thou didst regulate the confusion of the elements by the laws of harmony and order? But chiefly we mark Thy loving-kindness, in that Thou hast caused those whose hearts inclined to Thee to desire earnestly a divine and blessed life, and hast provided that, like merchants of true blessings, they might impart to many others the wisdom and happiness they had received; themselves, meanwhile, reaping the everlasting fruit of virtue. Freed from the trammels of vice, and imbued with the love of their fellow-men, they keep mercy ever before their eyes, and realize in hope the promises of faith; devoted to modesty, and all those virtues which the past career of human life had thrown aside, but which were now restored by Him whose providence is over all. No other power could be found to devise a remedy for such evils, and for that spirit of injustice which had heretofore asserted its dominion over the race of men. The provident care of Christ, however, could reach the circumstances even here, and with ease restored whatever had been disordered by violence and the licentiousness of human passion. And this restoring power He exercised without concealment or reserve. For He knew that, though there were some whose thoughts were able to recognize and understand His power, others there were whose brutish and senseless nature led them to rely exclusively on the testimony of their own senses. In open day, therefore, that no one, whether good or evil, might find room for doubt, He manifested His blessed and wondrous healing power; restoring the dead a second time to life, and renewing with a word the powers of those who had been bereft of bodily sense. Can we, in short, suppose, that to render the sea firm as the solid ground, to still the raging of the storm, and finally to ascend to heaven, after turning the unbelief of men to steadfast faith by the performance of these wondrous acts, demanded less than almighty power, was less than the work of God? Nor was the time of His passion unaccompanied by like wonders: when the sun was darkened, and the shades of night obscured the light of day. Then terror every where seized the hearts of men, and the thought that the end of all things was already come, and that chaos, such as had been ere the order of creation began, would once more prevail. Then, too, the cause was sought of so terrible an evil, and in what respect the trespasses of men had provoked the wrath of Heaven; until God Himself, who surveyed with dignity and calm contempt the arrogance of the ungodly, renewed the face of heaven, and adorned it with the host of stars; the gloomy sadness of nature disappeared, and her pristine beauty was again restored.

CHAPTER XII

OF THOSE WHO ARE IGNORANT OF THIS MYSTERY; AND THAT THEIR LGNORANCE IS VOLUNTARY. THE BLESSINGS WHICH AWAIT THOSE WHO KNOW IT, ESPECIALLY SUCH AS DIE IN THE CONFESSION OF THE FAITH

BUT it will be said by some, to whom the language of impiety is a familiar thing, that it was in the power of God to ameliorate and soften the natural will of man. What better way, I ask, what more effectual method could be devised for reclaiming evil man, than converse with God Himself? Was not He visibly present to teach them the principles of virtuous conduct? And if the personal instructions of God were without effect, how much more, had He continued silent and unseen? What, then, had power to hinder this most blessed doctrine? The perverse folly of man. For the clearness of our perceptions is at once obscured, as often as we receive with angry impatience those precepts which are given for our blessing and advantage. In truth, it was the very choice of men to disregard these precepts, and to turn from the commandments delivered to them; though had they listened, they would have gained a reward well worthy such attention, and that not for the present only, but the future life, which is indeed the only real existence. For the reward of obedience to God is imperishable and everlasting life, to which they may aspire who know Him, and frame their course of life so as to afford a pattern to others, and as it were a perpetual standard for the imitation of those who desire to excel in virtue. Therefore was the doctrine committed to men of understanding, that the truths which they communicated might be kept with care and a pure conscience by the members of their households, and that thus a truthful and steadfast observance of God's commands might be secured, the fruit of which is that boldness in the prospect of death which springs from pure faith and genuine holiness before God. He who is thus armed can withstand the tempest of the world, and is sustained even to martyrdom by the invincible power of God, whereby he boldly overcomes the greatest terrors, and is accounted worthy of a crown of glory by Him to whom he has thus nobly testified. Nor does he himself assume the praise, knowing full well that it is God who gives the power both to endure, and to fulfil with ready zeal the Divine commands. And well may such a course as this receive the meed of never-failing remembrance and everlasting honour. For as the martyr's life is one of sobriety and obedience to the will of God, so is his death an example of true greatness and generous fortitude of soul. Hence it is followed by hymns and psalms, and songs of praise to the all-seeing God: and a sacrifice of thanksgiving is offered in memory of such men, a bloodless, a harmless sacrifice, wherein is no need of the fragrant frankincense, no need of life; but only enough of pure light to suffice the assembled worshippers. Many, too, there are whose charitable spirit leads them to prepare a temperate banquet for the comfort of the needy, and the relief of those who had been driven from their homes: a custom which can only be deemed burdensome or useless by those whose thoughts are not accordant with the divine and sacred doctrine.

CHAPTER XIII

THAT THERE IS A NECESSARY DIFFERENCE BETWEEN CREATED THINGS. THAT THE PROPENSITY TO GOOD AND EVIL DEPENDS ON THE WILL OF MAN: AND THAT, CONSEQUENTLY, JUDGMENT IS A NECESSARY AND REASONABLE THING

THERE are, indeed, some who venture with rash presumption to find fault with God, and ask why it is that He has not created one and the same natural disposition for all, but rather has ordained the existence of many things different, nay, contrary in their nature, whence arises the dissimilarity of our moral conduct and character. Would it not (say they) have been better, both as regards obedience to the commands of God, and a just apprehension of Himself, and for the confirmation of individual faith, that all mankind should be of the same moral character? It is indeed ridiculous to expect that this could be the case, and to forget that the constitution of the world is different from that of the things that are in the world; that physical and moral objects are not identical in their nature, nor the affections of the body the same as those of the soul. For the immortal soul far exceeds the material world in dignity, and is more blessed than the perishable and terrestrial creation, in proportion as it is noble and more allied to God. Nor is the human race excluded from participation in the divine goodness: though this is not the lot of all indiscriminately, but of those only who search deeply into the Divine nature, and propose the knowledge of sacred things as the leading object of their lives.

CHAPTER XIV

THAT CREATED NATURE DIFFERS INFINITELY FROM UNCREATED BEING; TO WHICH MAN MAKES THE NEAREST APPROACH BY A LIFE OF VIRTUE

SURELY it must be the very height of folly to compare created with eternal things, which latter have neither beginning nor end, while the former, having been originated and called into being, and having received a commencement of their existence at some definite time, must consequently, of necessity have an end. How then can things which have thus been made, bear comparison with Him who has ordained their being? Were this the case, the power to command their existence could not rightly be attributed to Him. Nor can celestial things be compared to Him, any more than the material with the intellectual world, or copies with the models from which they are formed. Nay, is it not absurd thus to confound all things, and to obscure the honour of God by comparing Him with men, or even with beasts? And is it not characteristic of madmen, utterly estranged from a life of sobriety and virtue, to affect a power equivalent to that of God? If indeed we in any sense aspire to blessedness like that of God, our duty is to lead a life according to His commandments: so shall we, having finished a course consistent with the laws which He has prescribed, dwell for ever, superior to the power of fate, in eternal mansions. For the only power in man which can be elevated to a comparison with that of God, is sincere and guileless service and devotion of heart to Himself, with the contemplation and study of whatever pleases Him, the raising our affections above the things of earth, and directing our thoughts, as far as we may, to high and heavenly objects: for from such endeavours a victory accrues to us more valuable than many blessings. The cause, then, of that difference which subsists, as regards the inequality both of dignity and power in created beings, is such as I have described. In this the wise acquiesce with abundant thankfulness and joy: while those who are dissatisfied, display their own folly, and their arrogance will reap its due reward.

CHAPTER XV

OF THE SAVIOUR'S DOCTRINES AND MIRACLES; AND THE BENEFITS HE CONFERS ON THOSE WHO OWN SUBJECTION TO HIM

THE Son of God invites all men to the practice of virtue, and presents Himself to all who have understanding hearts, as the teacher of His saving precepts. Unless, indeed, we will deceive ourselves, and remain in wretched ignorance of the fact, that for our advantage, that is, to secure the blessing of the human race, He performed His course on earth; and, having called around Him the best men of their age, committed to them instructions full of profit, and of power to preserve them in the path of a virtuous life; teaching them the faith and righteousness which are the true remedy against the adverse power of that malignant spirit whose delight it is to ensnare and delude the ignorant and unwary. Accordingly He visited the sick, relieved the feeble from the sorrows which encompassed them, and consoled those who felt the extremity of penury and want. He commended also sound and rational sobriety of character, enjoining His followers to endure with dignity and patience every kind of injury and contempt: teaching them to regard such as visitations permitted by their Father, and that victory is ever theirs who nobly bear the evils which befall them. For He assured them that the highest strength of all consisted in this steadfastness of soul, combined with that philosophy which is nothing else than the knowledge of truth and goodness, producing in men the generous habit of imparting to their poorer brethren those riches which they have themselves acquired by honourable means. At the same time He utterly forbade all proud oppression, declaring that, as He had come to associate with the lowly, so those who despised the lowly would be excluded from His favour. Such and so great was the test whereby He proved the faith of those who owned allegiance to His authority, and thus He not only prepared them for the contempt of danger and terror, but taught them at the same time the most genuine confidence in Himself. Once, too, His rebuke was uttered to restrain the zeal of one of His companions, who yielded too easily to the impulse of passion, when he assaulted with the sword, and, eager to protect his Saviour's life, exposed his own. Then it was that He bade him desist, and return his sword to its sheath, reproving him for his distrust of refuge and safety in Himself, and declaring solemnly that all who should essay to retaliate an injury by like aggression, or use the sword, should perish by a violent death. This is indeed heavenly wisdom, to choose rather to endure than to inflict injury, and to be ready, should necessity so require, to suffer, but not to do, wrong. For since injurious conduct is in itself a most serious evil, it is not the injured party, but the injuring, on whom the heaviest punishment must fall. It is indeed possible for one who is subject to the will of God to avoid the evil both of committing and of suffering injury, provided his confidence be firm in the protection of that God whose aid is ever present to shield His servants from harm. For how should that man who trusts in God attempt to seek for resources in himself? In such a case he must abide the conflict with uncertainty of victory: and no man of understanding could prefer a doubtful to a certain issue. Again, how is that man likely to harbour distrust of God, who has had experience of manifold dangers, and has at all times been easily delivered, by His power and will alone, from all his troubles: who has passed (as it were) through the sea which was levelled by the Saviour's word, and afforded a solid road for the passage of the people? This is, I believe, the sure basis of faith, the true foundation of confidence, that we find such miracles as these performed and perfected at the command of the God of Providence. Hence it is that even in the midst of trial we find no cause to repent of our faith, but retain an unshaken hope in God; and when this habit of confidence is established in the soul, God Himself dwells in the inmost thoughts. But He is of invincible power: the soul, therefore, which has within it Him who is thus invincible, will not be overcome by the perils which may surround it. Besides, we learn this truth from the victory of God Himself, who, while intent on providing for the blessing of mankind, though grievously insulted by the malice of the ungodly, yet passed unharmed through the sufferings of His passion, and gained a mighty conquest, an everlasting crown of triumph, over all iniquity; thus accomplishing the purpose of His own providence and love as regards the just, and trampling on the cruelty of the impious and unjust.

CHAPTER XVI

THE COMING OF CHRIST WAS PREDICTED BY THE PROPHETS; AND WAS ORDAINED TO BE THE OVERTHROW OF IDOLS AND IDOLATROUS CITIES

LONG since had His passion, as well as His advent in the flesh, been predicted by the prophets. The time, too, of His incarnation had been foretold, and the manner in which the fruits of iniquity and profligacy, so ruinous to the works and ways of righteousness, should be destroyed, and the whole world partake of the virtues of wisdom and sound discretion, through the almost universal prevalence of those principles of conduct which the Saviour should promulge, over the minds of men; whereby the worship of God should be confirmed, and the rites of superstition utterly abolished. By these not the slaughter of animals alone, but the sacrifice of human victims, and the pollutions of an accursed worship, had been devised: as, for example, by the laws of Assyria and Egypt, the lives of innocent men were offered up in images of brass or earth. Therefore have these nations received a recompense worthy so foul a worship. Memphis and Babylon (it was declared) shall be wasted, and left desolate with their fathers' gods. Now these things I speak not from the report of others, but having myself been present, and an actual witness of the wretched fate which has befallen these cities. Memphis lies desolate; that city which was the pride of the once mighty Pharaoh, whose power Moses crushed at the Divine command, and destroyed his army (which had proved victorious over numerous and mighty nations, an army strong in defences and in arms), not by the flight of arrows or the hurling of hostile weapons, but by holy prayer alone, and quiet supplication.

CHAPTER XVII

OF THE WISDOM OF MOSES, WHICH WAS AN OBJECT OF IMITATION TO THE WISE AMONG HEATHEN NATIONS. ALSO CONCERNING DANIEL, AND THE THREE CHILDREN

NO nation has ever been more highly blessed than that which Moses led: none would have continued to enjoy higher blessings, had they not willingly withdrawn themselves from the guidance of the Holy Spirit. But who can worthily describe the praises of Moses himself; who, after reducing to order an unruly nation, and disciplining their minds to habits of obedience and respect, out of captivity restored them to a state of freedom, turned their mourning into gladness, and so far elevated their hopes, that, through the excess of contrast with their former circumstances, and the abundance of their prosperity, the spirit of the people was elated with haughtiness and pride? So far did he surpass in wisdom those who had lived before him, that even the wise men and philosophers who are extolled by heathen nations aspired to imitate his wisdom. Of these Pythagoras was one, the fame of whose virtuous character was so widely spread, that Plato, himself a model of discretion, proposed his self-control as the standard of his own conduct. Again, how great and terrible the cruelty of that ancient Syrian king, over whom Daniel triumphed, the prophet who unfolded the secrets of futurity, whose actions evinced transcendent greatness of soul, and the lustre of whose character and life shone conspicuous above all? The name of this tyrant was Nebuchadnezzar, whose race afterward became extinct, and his vast and mighty power was transferred to Persian hands. The wealth of this tyrant was then, and is even now, celebrated far and wide, as well as his ill-timed devotion to the service of his false deities, his idol statues, lifting their heads to heaven, and formed of various metals, and the terrible and savage laws ordained to uphold this worship. These terrors Daniel, sustained by genuine piety towards the true God, utterly despised, and predicted that the tyrant's unseasonable zeal would be productive of fearful evil to himself. He failed, however, to convince the tyrant (for excessive wealth is an effectual barrier to true soundness of judgment), and at length the monarch displayed the savage cruelty of his character, by commanding that the righteous prophet should be exposed to the fury of wild beasts. Noble, too, indeed was the united spirit of testimony exhibited by those brethren (whose example others have since followed, and have won I surpassing glory by their faith in the Saviour's name), those I mean, who stood unharmed in the fiery furnace, and the terrors appointed to devour them, repelling by the holy touch of their bodies the name by which they were surrounded. On the overthrow of the

Assyrian Empire, which was destroyed by the lightning vengeance of Heaven, the providence of God conducted Daniel to the court of Cambyses the Persian king. Yet envy followed him even here; nor envy only, but the deadly plots of the magians against his life, with a succession of many and urgent dangers, from all which he was easily delivered by the providential care of Christ, and shone conspicuous in the practice of every virtue. Three times in the day did he present his prayers to God, and memorable were the proofs of supernatural power which he displayed: and hence the magians, filled with envy at the very efficacy of his petitions, represented the possession of such power to the king as fraught with danger, and prevailed on him to adjudge this distinguished benefactor of the Persian people to be devoured by savage lions. Daniel, therefore, thus condemned, was consigned to the lions' den (not indeed to suffer death, but to win unfading glory); and though surrounded by these ferocious beasts of prey, he found them more gentle than the men who had enclosed him there. Supported by the power of calm and modest prayer, he was enabled to subdue the natural ferocity of all these animals, furious as they were. Cambyses, on learning the event (for so mighty a proof of Divine power could not possibly be concealed), amazed at the marvellous story, and repenting the too easy credence he had given to the slanderous charges of the magians, resolved, notwithstanding, to be himself a witness of the spectacle. But when he saw the prophet with uplifted hands rendering praises to Christ, and the lions crouching, and as it were worshipping, at his feet; immediately he adjudged the magians, to whose persuasions he had listened, to perish by the self-same sentence. The beasts, erewhile so gentle, rushed at once upon their victims, and with all the fierceness of their nature tore and destroyed them all.

CHAPTER XVIII

OF THE ERYTHRÆAN SIBYL, WHO POINTED IN A PROPHETIC ACROSTIC AT OUR LORD AND HIS PASSION. THE ACROSTIC IS "JESUS CHRIST, SON OF GOD, SAVIOUR, CROSS"

MY desire, however, is to derive even from foreign sources a testimony to the Divine nature of Christ. For on such testimony it is evident that even those who blaspheme His name must acknowledge that He is God, and the Son of God, if indeed they will accredit the words of those whose sentiments coincided with their own. The Erythræan Sibyl, then, who herself assures us that she lived in the sixth generation after the flood, was a priestess of Apollo, who wore the sacred fillet in imitation of the God she served, who guarded also the tripod encompassed with the serpent's folds, and returned prophetic answers to those who approached her shrine; having been devoted by the folly of her parents to this service, a service productive of nothing good or noble, but only of indecent fury, such as we find recorded in the case of Daphne. On one occasion, however, having rushed into the sanctuary of her vain superstition, she became really filled with inspiration from above, and declared in prophetic verses the future purposes of God; plainly indicating the advent of Jesus by the initial letters of these verses, forming an acrostic in these words: JESUS CHRIST, SON OF GOD, SAVIOUR, CROSS. The verses themselves are as follows:—

Judgment! Earth's oozing pores shall mark the day;
Earth's heavenly king His glories shall display:
Sovereign of all, exalted on His throne,
Unnumbered multitudes their God shall own;
Shall see their Judge, with mingled joy and fear,
Crowned with His saints, in human form appear.
How vain, while desolate earth's glories lie,
Riches, and pomp, and man's idolatry!
In that dread hour, when Nature's fiery doom
Startles the slumb'ring tenants of the tomb,
Trembling all flesh shall stand; each secret wile,
Sins long forgotten, thoughts of guilt and guile,
Open beneath God's searching light shall lie:
No refuge then, but hopeless agony.
O'er heaven's expanse shall gathering shades of night
From earth, sun, stars, and moon, withdraw their light;
God's arm shall crush each mountain's towering pride;
On ocean's plain no more shall navies ride.
Dried at the source, no river's rushing sound
Shall soothe, no fountain slake the parched ground.
Around, afar, shall roll the trumpet's blast,
Voice of wrath long delayed, revealed at last.
In speechless awe, while earth's foundations groan,
On judgment's seat earth's kings their God shall own.
Uplifted then, in majesty divine,
Radiant with light, behold Salvation's Sign!
Cross of that Lord, who, once for sinners given,
Reviled by man, now owned by earth and heaven,
O'er every land extends His iron sway.

Such is the name these mystic lines display;
Saviour, eternal king, who bears our sins away.

It is evident that the virgin uttered these verses under the influence of Divine inspiration. And I cannot but esteem her blessed, whom the Saviour thus selected to unfold His gracious purpose towards us.

CHAPTER XIX

THAT THIS PROPHECY RESPECTING OUR SAVIOUR WAS NOT THE FICTION OF ANY MEMBER OF THE CHRISTIAN CHURCH, BUT THE TESTIMONY OF THE ERYTHRÆAN SIBYL, WHOSE BOOKS WERE TRANSLATED INTO LATIN BY CICERO BEFORE THE COMING OF CHRIST. ALSO THAT VIRGIL MAKES MENTION OF THE SAME, AND OF THE BIRTH OF THE VIRGIN'S CHILD: THOUGH HE SPOKE OBSCURELY, FROM FEAR OF THE RULING POWERS

MANY, however, who admit that the Erythræan Sibyl was really a prophetess, yet refuse to credit this prediction, and imagine that some one professing our faith, and not unacquainted with the poetic art, was the composer of these verses. They hold, in short, that they are a forgery, and alleged to be the prophecies of the Sibyl on the ground of their containing useful moral sentiments, tending to restrain licentiousness, and to lead man to a life of sobriety and decorum. Truth, however, in this case is evident, since the diligence of our countrymen has made a careful computation of the times; so that there is no room to suspect that this poem was composed after the advent and condemnation of Christ, or that the general report is false, that the verses were a prediction of the Sibyl in an early age. For it is allowed that Cicero was acquainted with this poem, which he translated into the Latin tongue, and incorporated with his own works. This writer was put to death during the ascendancy of Antony, who in his turn was conquered by Augustus, whose reign lasted fifty-six years. Tiberius succeeded, in whose age it was that the Saviour's advent enlightened the world, the mystery of our most holy religion began to prevail, and as it were a new race of men commenced: of which (I suppose) the prince of Latin poets thus speaks:

Behold, a new, a heaven-born race appears.

And again, in another passage of the Bucolics:

Sicilian Muses, sound a loftier strain.

What can be clearer than this? For he adds,

The voice of Cuma's oracle is heard again.

Evidently referring to the Cumæan Sibyl. Nor was even this enough: the poet goes further, as if irresistibly impelled to bear his testimony. What then does he say?

Behold! the circling years new blessings bring:
The virgin comes, with her the long-desired king.

Who, then, is the virgin who was to come? Is it not she who was filled with, and with child of, the Holy Spirit? And why is it impossible that she who was with child of the Holy Spirit should be and ever continue to be a virgin? This king, too, will return, and by his coming lighten the sorrows of the world. The poet adds,

Thou, chaste Lucina, greet the new-born child,
Beneath whose reign the iron offspring ends,
A golden progeny from heaven descends;
His kingdom banished virtue shall restore,
And crime shall threat the guilty world no more.

We perceive that these words are spoken plainly and at the same time darkly, by way of allegory. Those who search deeply for the import of the words, are able to discern the Divinity of Christ. But lest any of the powerful in the imperial city might be able to accuse the poet of writing anything contrary to the laws of the country, and subverting the religious sentiments which had prevailed from ancient times, he intentionally obscures the truth. For he was acquainted, as I believe, with that blessed mystery which gave to our Lord the name of Saviour: but, that he might avoid the severity of cruel men, he drew the thoughts of his hearers to objects with which they were familiar, saying that altars must be erected, temples raised, and sacrifices offered, to the new-born child. His concluding words also are adapted to the sentiments of those who were accustomed to such a creed; for he says:—

CHAPTER XX

A FURTHER QUOTATION FROM VIRGIL RESPECTING CHRIST, WITH ITS INTERPRETATION, SHEWING THAT THE MYSTERY WAS INDICATED THEREIN DARKLY, AS MIGHT BE EXPECTED FROM A POET

A life immortal he shall lead, and be
By heroes seen, himself shall heroes see;

evidently meaning the righteous.

The jarring nations he in peace shall bind,
And with paternal virtues rule mankind.

Unbidden earth her earliest fruits shall bring,
And fragrant herbs, to greet her infant king.

Well indeed was this admirably wise and accomplished man acquainted with the cruel character of the times. He proceeds:

The goats, uncalled, full udders home shall bear;
The lowing herds no more fierce lions fear.

Truly said: for faith will not stand in awe of the mighty in the imperial palace.

His cradle shall with rising flowers be crown'd:
The serpent's brood shall die; the sacred ground
Shall weeds and poisonous plants refuse to bear;
Each common bush th' Assyrian rose shall wear.

Nothing could be said more true or more consistent with the Saviour's excellency than this. For the power of the Divine Spirit presents the very cradle of God, like fragrant flowers, to the new-born race. The serpent, too, and the venom of that serpent, perishes, who originally beguiled our first parents, and drew their thoughts from their native innocence to the enjoyment of forbidden pleasures, that they might experience that ruin which threatened them in case of disobedience. For before the Saviour's advent, the serpent's power was shewn in subverting the souls of those who were sustained by no well grounded hope, and ignorant of that immortality which awaits the righteous. But after that He had suffered, and was separated for a season from the body which He had assumed, the power of the resurrection was revealed to man through the communication of the Holy Spirit: and whatever stain of human guilt might yet remain was removed by the washing of the sacred laver.

Then indeed could the Saviour bid His followers rejoice, and, remembering His adorable and glorious resurrection, expect the like for themselves. Truly, then, the poisonous race may be said to be extinct. Death himself is extinct, and the truth of the resurrection sealed. Again, the Assyrian race is gone, which first led the way to faith in God. But when he speaks of the growth of amomum every where, he alludes to the multitude of the true worshippers of God. For it is as though a multitude of branches, crowned with fragrant flowers, and fitly watered, sprung from the self-same root. Most justly said, Maro, thou wisest of poets! and with this all that follows is consistent.

But when heroic worth his youth shall hear,
And learn his father's virtues to revere,

By the praises of heroes, he indicates the works of righteous men: by the virtues of His Father he speaks of the creation and everlasting structure of the world; and, it may be, of those laws by which God's beloved Church is guided, and ordered in a course of righteousness and virtue. Admirable, again, is the advance to higher things of that state of life which is intermediate, as it were, between good and evil, and which seldom admits a sudden and rapid change:

Unlaboured harvests shall the fields adorn,

That is, the fruit of the Divine law springs up for the service of men.

And clustered grapes shall blush on every thorn.

Far otherwise has it been during the corrupt and lawless period of human life.

The knotted oaks shall showers of honey weep,
And through the matted grass the liquid gold shall creep.

He here describes the folly and obduracy of the men of that age: and perhaps he also intimates that they who suffer hardships in the cause of God, shall reap sweet fruits of their own endurance.

Yet, of old fraud some footsteps shall remain;
The merchant still shall plough the deep for gain:
Great cities shall with walls be compassed round,
And sharpened shares shall vex the fruitful ground:
Another Tiphys shall new seas explore;
Another Argo land the chiefs upon the Iberian shore;
Another Helen other wars create,
And great Achilles urge the Trojan fate.

Well said, wisest of bards! Thou hast carried the license of a poet precisely to the proper point. For it was not thy purpose to assume the functions of a prophet, to which thou hadst no claim. I suppose also he was restrained by a sense of the danger which threatened one who should assail the credit of ancient religious practice. Cautiously, therefore, and securely, as far as possible, he presents the truth to those who have faculties to understand it; and while he denounces the munitions and conflicts of war (which indeed are still to be found in the course of human life), he describes our Saviour as proceeding to the war against Troy, understanding by Troy the world itself. And surely He did maintain the struggle against the opposing powers of evil, sent on that mission both by the designs of His own providence and the commandment of His Almighty Father. How, then, does the poet proceed?

But when to ripen'd manhood he shall grow,

that is, when, having arrived at the age of manhood, He shall utterly remove the evils which encompass the path of human life, and tranquillize the world by the blessings of peace:—

The greedy sailor shall the seas forego;
No keel shall cut the waves for foreign ware,

For every soil shall every product bear.
The labouring hind his oxen shall disjoin;
No plough shall hurt the glebe, no pruning-hook the vine;
Nor wool shall in dissembled colours shine:
But the luxurious father of the fold,
With native purple, and unborrow'd gold,
Beneath his pompous fleece shall proudly sweat;
And under Tyrian robes the lamb shall bleat.
Mature in years, to ready honours move,
O of celestial seed, O foster son of Jove!
See, labouring nature calls thee to sustain
The nodding frame of heaven, and earth, and main!
See to their base restored, earth, seas, and air;
And joyful ages, from behind, in crowding ranks appear.
To sing thy praise, would heaven my breath prolong,
Infusing spirits worthy such a song,
Not Thracian Orpheus should transcend my lays,
Nor Linus, crown'd with never-fading bays;
Though each his heavenly parent should inspire;
The Muse instruct the voice, and Phœbus tune the lyre.
Should Pan contend in verse, and thou my theme,
Arcadian judges should their God condemn.

Behold (says he) how the mighty world and the elements together manifest their joy.

CHAPTER XXI

THAT THESE THINGS CANNOT HAVE BEEN SPOKEN OF A MERE MAN: AND THAT UNBELIEVERS, OWING TO THEIR IGNORANCE OF RELIGION, KNOW NOT EVEN THE ORIGIN OF THEIR OWN EXISTENCE

IT may be some will foolishly suppose that these words were spoken of the birth of a mere ordinary mortal. But if this were all, what reason could there be that the earth should need neither seed nor plough, that the vine should require no pruning-hook, or other means of culture? How can we suppose these things to be spoken of a mere mortal's birth? For nature is the minister of the Divine will, not an instrument obedient to the command of man. Indeed, the very joy of the elements indicates the advent of God, not the conception of a human being. The prayer, too, of the poet that his life might be prolonged is a proof of the Divinity of Him whom he invoked: for we desire life and preservation from God, and not from man. Indeed, the Erythræan Sibyl thus appeals to God: "Why, O Lord, dost Thou compel me still to foretell the future, and not rather remove me from this earth to await the blessed day of Thy coming?" And Virgil adds to what he had said before:

Begin, sweet boy! with smiles thy mother know,
Who ten long months did with thy burden go.
No mortal parents smiled upon thy birth:
No nuptial joy thou know'st, no feast of earth.

How could His parents have smiled on Him? For His Father is God, who is a Power without sensible quality, existing, not in any definite shape, but as comprehending other beings, and not, therefore, in a human body. And who knows not that the Holy Spirit has no participation in the nuptial union? For what desire can exist in the disposition of that good which all things else desire? What fellowship, in short, can wisdom hold with pleasure? But let these arguments be left to those who ascribe to Him a human origin, and who care not to purify themselves from all evil in word as well as deed. On thee, Piety, I call to aid my words, on thee who art the very law of purity, most desirable of all blessings, teacher of holiest hope, assured promise of immortality! Thee, Piety, and thee, Clemency, I adore. We who have obtained thine aid owe thee everlasting gratitude for thy healing power. But the multitudes whom their innate hatred of thyself deprives of thy succour, are equally estranged from God Himself, and know not that the very cause of their existence, and that of all the ungodly, is connected with the rightful worship of Him who is Lord of all: for the world itself is His, and all that it contains.

CHAPTER XXII

THE EMPEROR THANKFULLY ASCRIBES HIS VICTORIES AND ALL OTHER BLESSINGS TO CHRIST; AND CONDEMNS THE CONDUCT OF THE TYRANT MAXIMIN, THE VIOLENCE OF WHOSE PERSECUTION HAD ENHANCED THE GLORY OF THE CHRISTIAN RELIGION

TO thee, Piety, I ascribe the cause of my own prosperity, and of all that I now possess. To this truth the happy issue of all my endeavours bears testimony: my battles, my victories, and triumphs over conquered foes. This truth the great city itself allows with joy and praise. The people, too, of that much-loved city accord in the same sentiment, though once, deceived by ill-grounded hopes, they chose a ruler unworthy of themselves, a ruler who speedily received the chastisement which his audacious deeds deserved. But be it far from me now to recall the memory of these events, while holding converse with thee, Piety, and essaying with earnest endeavour to address thee with holy and gentle words. Yet will I say one thing, which haply will not offend. A furious, a cruel, and implacable war was maintained by the tyrants against thee, Piety, and thy holy churches: nor were there wanting some in Rome itself who exulted at a calamity so grievous to the public weal. Nay, the battlefield was prepared; when thou didst stand forth, and present thyself a voluntary victim, supported by faith in God. Then indeed it was that the cruelty of ungodly men, which raged incessantly like a devouring fire, wrought for thee a wondrous and ever memorable glory. Astonishment seized the spectators themselves, when they beheld the very executioners who tortured the bodies of their holy victims wearied out, and at a loss to invent fresh cruelties; the bonds loosened, the engines of torture powerless, the flames extinguished, while the sufferers preserved their constancy unshaken even for a moment. What, then, hast thou gained by these atrocious deeds, most impious of men? And what was the cause of thy insane fury? Thou wilt say, doubtless, these acts of thine were done in honour of the gods. What gods are these? or what worthy conception hast thou of the Divine nature? Thinkest thou the gods are subject to angry passions as thou art? Were it so indeed, it had been better for thee to wonder at their strange determination than obey their harsh command, when they urged thee to the unrighteous slaughter of innocent men. Thou wilt allege, perhaps, the customs of thy ancestors, and the opinion of mankind in general, as the cause of this conduct. I grant the fact: for those customs are very like the acts themselves, and proceed from the self-same source of folly. Thou thoughtest, it may be, that some special power resided in images formed and fashioned by human art; and hence thy reverence, and diligent care lest they should be defiled: those mighty and highly exalted gods, thus dependent on the care of men!

CHAPTER XXIII

OF CHRISTIAN CONDUCT. THAT GOD IS PLEASED WITH THOSE WHO LEAD A LIFE OF VIRTUE: AND THAT WE MUST EXTECT A JUDGMENT AND FUTURE RETRIBUTION

COMPARE our religion with your own. Is there not with us genuine concord, and unwearied love of others? If we reprove a fault, is not our object to admonish, not to destroy; our correction, for safety, not for cruelty? Do we not exercise, not only sincere faith towards God, but fidelity in the relations of social life? Do we not pity the unfortunate? Is not ours a life of simplicity, which disdains to cover evil beneath the mask of fraud and hypocrisy? Do we not acknowledge the true God, and His undivided sovereignty? This is real godliness: this is religion sincere and truly undefiled: this is the life of wisdom; and they who have it are travellers (as it were) on a noble road which leads to eternal life. For he who has entered on such a course, and keeps his soul pure from the pollutions of the body, does not wholly die: rather may he be said to complete the service appointed him by God, than to die. Again, he who confesses allegiance to God is not easily overborne by insolence or rage, but nobly stands under the pressure of necessity; and the trial of his constancy is as it were a passport to the favour of God. For we cannot doubt that the Deity is pleased with excellence in human conduct. For it would be absurd indeed if the powerful and the humble alike acknowledge gratitude to those from whose services they receive benefit, and repay them by services in return, and yet that He who is supreme and sovereign of all, nay, who is Good itself, should be negligent in this respect. Rather does He follow us throughout the course of our lives, is near us in every act of goodness, accepts, and at once rewards our virtue and obedience; though He defers the full recompense to that future period, when the actions of our lives shall pass under His review, and when those who are clear in that account shall receive the reward of everlasting life, while the wicked shall be visited with the penalties due to their crimes.

CHAPTER XXIV

OF DECIUS, VALERIAN, AND AURELIAN, WHO EXPERIENCED A MISERABLE END IN CONSEQUENCE OF THEIR PERSECUTION OF THE CHURCH

TO thee, Decius, I now appeal, who hast trampled with insult on the labours of the righteous: to thee, the hater of the Church, the punisher of those who lived a holy life: what is now thy condition after death? How hard and wretched thy present circumstances! Nay, the interval before thy death gave proof enough of thy miserable fate, when, overthrown with all thine army on the plains of Scythia, thou didst expose the vaunted power of Rome to the contempt of the Goths. Thou, too, Valerian, who didst manifest the same spirit of cruelty towards the servants of God, hast afforded an example of righteous judgment. A captive in the enemies' hands, led in chains while yet arrayed in the purple and imperial attire, and at last thy skin stripped from thee, and preserved by command of Sapor the Persian king, thou hast left a perpetual trophy of thy calamity. And thou, Aurelian, fierce perpetrator of every wrong, how signal was thy fall, when, in the midst of thy wild career in Thrace, thou wast slain on the public highway, and didst fill the furrows of the road with thine impious blood!

CHAPTER XXV

OF DIOCLETIAN, WHO IGNOBLY ABDICATED THE IMPERIAL THRONE, AND WAS TERRIFIED BY THE DREAD OF LIGHTNING FOR HIS PERSECUTION OF THE CHURCH

DIOCLETIAN, however, after the display of relentless cruelty as a persecutor, evinced a consciousness of his own guilt, and, owing to the affliction of a disordered mind, endured the confinement of a mean and separate dwelling. What, then, did he gain by his active hostility against our God? Simply this, I believe, that he passed the residue of his life in continual dread of the lightning's stroke. Nicomedia attests the fact; eyewitnesses, of whom I myself am one, declare it. The palace, and the emperor's private chamber were destroyed, consumed by lightning, devoured by the fire of heaven. Men of understanding hearts had indeed predicted the issue of such conduct; for they could not keep silence, nor conceal their grief at such unworthy deeds; but boldly and openly expressed their feelings, saying one to another: "What madness is this? and what an insolent abuse of power, that man should dare to fight against God; should deliberately insult the most holy and just of all religions; and plan, without the slightest provocation, the destruction of so great a multitude of righteous persons? O rare example of moderation to his subjects! Worthy instructor of his army in the care and protection due to their fellow-citizens! Men who had never seen the backs of a retreating army plunged their swords into the breasts of their own countrymen!" At length, indeed, the providence of God took vengeance on these unhallowed deeds; but not without severe damage to the state, and an effusion of blood, which, if shed in battle with barbarian enemies, had been sufficient to purchase a perpetual peace. For the entire army of the emperor of whom I have just spoken, becoming subject to the authority of a worthless person, who had violently usurped the supreme authority at Rome (the providence of God intending to restore freedom to that great city), was destroyed in several successive battles. And when we remember the cries with which those who were oppressed, and who ardently longed for their native liberty, implored the help of God; and their praise and thanksgiving to Him on the removal of the evils under which they had groaned, when that liberty was regained, and free and equitable intercourse restored; do not these things every way afford convincing proofs of the providence of God, and His affectionate regard for the interests of mankind?

CHAPTER XXVI

THE EMPEROR ASCRIBES HIS PERSONAL PIETY TO GOD; AND SHEWS THAT WE ARE BOUND TO SEEK SUCCESS FROM GOD, AND ATTRIBUTE IT TO HIM; BUT TO CONSIDER FAILURE AS THE RESULT OF OUR OWN NEGLIGENCE

WHEN men commend my services, which owe their origin to the inspiration of Heaven, do they not clearly establish the truth that God is the cause of the exploits I have performed? Assuredly they do: for it belongs to God to do whatever is best, and to man, to perform the commands of God. I believe, indeed, the best and noblest course of action is, when, before an attempt is made, we provide as far as possible for a secure result: and surely all men know that the holy service in which these hands have been employed has originated in pure and genuine faith towards God; that whatever has been done for the common welfare has been effected by active exertion combined with supplication and prayer; the consequence of which has been as great an amount of individual and public benefit as each could, venture to hope for himself and those he holds most dear. They have witnessed battles, and have been spectators of a war in which the providence of God has granted victory to this people: they have seen how He has favoured and seconded our prayers. For righteous prayer is a thing invincible; and no one fails to attain his object who addresses holy supplication to God: nor is a refusal possible, except in the case of wavering faith; for God is ever favourable, ever ready to approve of human virtue. While, therefore, we allow that occasional error is common to man, we cannot arraign God as the cause of human error. Hence it becomes all pious persons to render thanks to the Preserver of all, first for our own individual security, and then for the happy posture of public affairs: at the same time intreating the favour of Christ with holy prayers and constant supplications, that He would continue to us our present blessings. For He is the invincible friend and protector of the righteous: He is the supreme arbiter of all things, the prince of immortality, the awarder of everlasting life.

THE ORATION OF EUSEBIUS PAMPHILUS, IN PRAISE OF THE EMPEROR CONSTANTINE, PRONOUNCED ON THE THIRTIETH ANNIVERSARY OF HIS REIGN

PROLOGUE TO THE ORATION

I COME not forward prepared with a fictitious narrative, nor with elegance of language to captivate the ear, desiring to charm my hearers as it were with a syren's voice; nor shall I present the draught of pleasure in cups of gold decorated with lovely flowers (I mean the graces of style), to those who are pleased with such things. Rather would I follow the precepts of the wise, and admonish all to avoid and turn aside from the beaten road, and keep themselves from contact with the vulgar crowd. I come, then, prepared to celebrate our emperor's praises in a newer strain; and, though the number be infinite of those who desire to be my companions in my present task, I am resolved to shun the common track of men, and to pursue that untrodden path which it is unlawful to enter on with unwashed feet. Let those who admire a vulgar style, abounding in puerile subtleties, and who court a pleasing and popular muse, essay (since pleasure is the object they have in view) to charm the ears of men by a narrative of merely human merits. Those, however, whose minds have embraced a wider compass of wisdom, who are acquainted with Divine as well as human knowledge, and are able to appreciate the choice of a nobler subject, will prefer those virtues of the emperor which Heaven itself approves, and his pious actions, to his merely human accomplishments; and will leave to inferior encomiasts the task of celebrating his inferior merits. For since our emperor is gifted as well with that sacred wisdom which has immediate reference to God, as with the knowledge which concerns the interests of men; let those who are competent to such a task describe his secular acquirements, great and transcendent as they are, and fraught with advantage to mankind (for all that characterizes the emperor is great and noble), yet still inferior to his diviner qualities, to those who stand without the sacred precincts. Let those, however, who are within the sanctuary, and have access to its inmost and untrodden recesses, close the doors against every profane ear, and unfold as it were the secret mysteries of our emperor's character to the initiated alone. And let those who have purified their ears in the streams of piety, and raised their thoughts on the soaring wing of the mind itself, join the solemn quire around the Sovereign Lord of all, and learn in silence the divine mysteries. Meanwhile let the sacred oracles, given, not by the spirit of divination (or rather let me say of madness and folly), but by the inspiration of Divine truth, be our instructors in these mysteries; speaking to us of sovereignty, generally: of Him who is the Supreme Sovereign of all, and the heavenly array which surrounds His throne: of that exemplar of imperial power which is before us, contrasted with that which is false and spurious in its character: and, lastly, of the consequences which result from both. With these oracles, then, to initiate us in the knowledge of the sacred mysteries, let us essay, as follows, the commencement of our divine subject.

CHAPTER I

THE ORATION

WE celebrate this day the solemn festival of our great emperor: and we his servants rejoice therein, feeling the inspiration of our sacred theme. He who presides over our solemnity is the Great Sovereign Himself; He, I mean, who is truly great; of whom I affirm (nor will the sovereign who hears me be offended, but will rather approve of this ascription of praise to God), that HE is above and beyond all created things, the Highest, the Greatest, the most Mighty One; whose throne is the arch of heaven, and the earth the footstool of his feet. His being none can worthily comprehend; and the ineffable splendour of the glory which surrounds Him repels the gaze of every eye from His Divine majesty. His ministers are the heavenly hosts; His armies the supernal powers, who own allegiance to Him as their Master, Lord, and King. The countless multitudes of angels, the companies of archangels, the quires of holy spirits, draw from and reflect His radiance as from the fountains of everlasting light. Yea, every light, and specially those divine and incorporeal intelligences whose place is beyond the heavenly sphere, celebrate this august Sovereign with lofty and sacred strains of praise. The vast expanse of heaven, like an azure veil, is interposed between those without, and those who inhabit His royal mansions: while round this expanse the sun and moon, with the rest of the heavenly luminaries (like torch-bearers around the entrance of the imperial palace), perform, in honour of their Sovereign, their appointed courses; holding forth, at the word of His command, an ever-burning light to those whose lot is cast in the darker regions without the pale of heaven. And surely when I remember that our own victorious emperor renders praises to this Mighty Sovereign, I do well to follow him, knowing as I do that to Him alone we owe that imperial power under which we live. The pious Cæsars, instructed by their father's wisdom, acknowledge Him as the source of every blessing: the soldiery, the entire body of the people, both in the country and in the cities of the empire, with the governors of the several provinces, assembling together in accordance with the precept of their great Saviour and Teacher, worship Him. In short, the whole family of mankind, of every nation, tribe, and tongue, both collectively and severally, however diverse their opinions on other subjects, are unanimous in this one confession; and, in obedience to the reason implanted in them, and the spontaneous and uninstructed impulse of their own minds, unite in calling on the One and only God. Nay, does not the universal frame of earth acknowledge Him her Lord, and declare, by the vegetable and animal life which she produces, her subjection to the will of a superior Power? The rivers, flowing with abundant stream, and the perennial fountains, springing from hidden and exhaustless depths, ascribe to Him the cause of their marvellous source. The mighty waters of the sea, enclosed in chambers of unfathomable depth, and the swelling surges, which lift themselves on high, and menace as it were the earth itself, shrink back when they approach the shore, checked by the power of His Divine law. The duly measured fall of winter's rain, the rolling thunder, the lightning's flash, the eddying currents of the winds, and the airy courses of the clouds, all reveal His presence to those to whom His Person is invisible. The all-radiant sun, who holds his constant career through the lapse of ages, owns Him Lord alone, and, obedient to His will, dares not depart from his appointed path. The inferior splendour of the moon, alternately diminished and increased at stated periods, is subject to His Divine command. The beauteous mechanism of the heavens, glittering with the hosts of stars, moving in harmonious order, and preserving the measure of each several orbit, proclaims Him the giver of all light: yea, all the heavenly luminaries, maintaining at His will and word a grand and perfect unity of motion, pursue the track of their ethereal career, and complete in the lapse of revolving ages their distant course. The alternate recurrence of day and night, the changing seasons, the order and proportion of the universe, all declare the manifold wisdom of His boundless power. To Him the unseen agencies which hold their course throughout the expanse of space, render the due tribute of praise. To Him this terrestrial globe itself, to Him the heavens above, and the quires beyond the vault of heaven, give honour as to their mighty Sovereign: the angelic hosts greet Him with ineffable songs of praise; and the spirits which draw their being from incorporeal light, adore Him as their Creator and their God. The everlasting ages which were before this heaven and earth, with other periods beside them, infinite, and antecedent to all visible creation, acknowledge Him the sole and supreme Sovereign and Lord. Lastly, He who is in all, before, and after all, His only begotten Son and pre-existent Word, the great High Priest of the mighty God, elder than all time and every age, devoted to His Father's glory, first and alone makes intercession with Him for the salvation of mankind. Supreme and pre-eminent Ruler of the universe, He shares the glory of His Father's kingdom: for He is that Light, which, transcendent above the universe, encircles the Father's Person, interposing and dividing between the eternal and uncreated Essence and all derived existence: that Light which, streaming from on high, proceeds from that Deity who knows not origin or end, and illumines the super-celestial regions, and all that heaven itself contains, with the radiance of wisdom bright beyond the splendour of the sun. This is He who holds a supreme and universal dominion over this world, who is over and in all things, and pervades all things visible and invisible; the Word of God. From whom and by whom our divinely-favoured emperor, receiving as it were a transcript of the Divine sovereignty, directs, in imitation of God Himself, the administration of this world's affairs.

CHAPTER II

THIS only begotten Word of God reigns, from ages which had no beginning, to infinite and endless ages, the partner of His Father's kingdom. And our emperor, ever beloved by Him, who derives the source of imperial authority from above, and is strong in the power of his sacred title, has controlled the empire of the world for a long period of years. Again, that Preserver of the universe orders these heavens and earth, and the celestial kingdom, consistently with His Father's will. Even so our emperor whom He loves, by bringing those whom he rules on earth to the only begotten Word and Saviour, renders them fit subjects of His kingdom. And as He who is the common Preserver of mankind, by His invisible and Divine power as the good shepherd, drives far away from His flock, like savage beasts, those apostate spirits which once flew through the airy tracts above this earth, and fastened on the souls of men; so this His friend, graced by His heavenly favour with victory over all his foes, subdues and chastens the open adversaries of the truth in accordance with the usages of war. He who is the pre-existent Word, the Preserver of all things, imparts to His disciples the seeds of true wisdom and salvation, and at once enlightens and gives them understanding in the knowledge of His Father's kingdom. Our emperor, His friend, acting as interpreter to the Word of God, aims at recalling the human race to the knowledge of God; proclaiming clearly in the ears of all, and declaring with powerful voice the laws of truth and godliness to all who dwell on the earth. Once more, the universal Saviour expands the heavenly gates of His Father's kingdom to those whose course is thitherward from this world. Our emperor, emulous of His divine example, having purged his earthly dominion from every stain of impious error, invites each holy and pious worshipper within his imperial mansions, earnestly desiring to save with all its crew that mighty vessel of which he is the appointed pilot. And he alone of all who have wielded the imperial power of Rome being honoured by the Supreme Sovereign with a reign of three decennial periods, now celebrates this festival, not, as his ancestors might have done, in honour of infernal demons, or the apparitions of seducing spirits, or of the fraud and deceitful arts of impious men; but as an act of thanksgiving to Him by whom he has thus been honoured, and in acknowledgment of the blessings he has received at His hands. He does not, in imitation of ancient usage, defile his imperial mansions with blood and gore, nor propitiate the infernal deities with fire, and smoke, and sacrificial offerings; but dedicates to the universal Sovereign a pleasant and acceptable sacrifice, even his own imperial soul, and a mind truly fitted for the service of God. For this sacrifice alone is grateful to Him: and this sacrifice our emperor has learned, with purified mind and thoughts, to present as an offering without the intervention of fire and blood, while, his own piety strengthened by the truthful doctrines with which his soul is stored, he sets forth in magnificent language the praises of God, and imitates His divine philanthropy by his own imperial acts. Wholly devoted to Him, he dedicates himself as a noble offering, a first-fruit of that world the government of which is intrusted to his charge. This first and greatest sacrifice our emperor first dedicates to God; and then, as a faithful shepherd, he offers, not "famous hecatombs of firstling lambs," but the souls of that flock which is the object of his care, those rational beings whom he leads to the knowledge and pious worship of God.

CHAPTER III

AND gladly does He accept and welcome this sacrifice, and commend the presenter of so august and noble an offering, by protracting his reign to a lengthened period of years, giving larger proofs of His beneficence in proportion to the emperor's holy services to Himself. Accordingly He permits him to celebrate each successive festival during great and general prosperity throughout the empire, advancing one of his sons, at the recurrence of each decennial period, to a share of his own imperial power. The eldest, who bears his father's name, he received as his partner in the empire about the close of the first decade of his reign: the second, next in point of age, at the second; and the third in like manner at the third decennial period, the occasion of this our present festival. And now that the fourth period has commenced, and the time of his reign is still further prolonged, he desires to extend his imperial authority by calling still more of his kindred to partake his power; and, by the appointment of the Cæsars, fulfils the predictions of the holy prophets, according to what they uttered ages before: "And the saints of the Most High shall take the kingdom." And thus the Almighty Sovereign Himself accords an increase both of years and of children to our most pious emperor, and renders his sway over the nations of the world still fresh and flourishing, as though it were even now springing up in its earliest vigour. He it is who appoints him this present festival, in that He has made him victorious over every enemy that disturbed his peace: He it is who displays him as an example of true godliness to the human race. And thus our emperor, like the radiant sun, illuminates the most distant subjects of his empire through the presence of the Cæsars, as with the far piercing rays of his own brightness. To us who occupy the eastern regions he has given a son worthy of himself; a second and a third respectively to other departments of his empire, to be as it were brilliant reflectors of the light which proceeds from himself. Once more, having harnessed, as it were, under the selfsame yoke the four most noble Cæsars as horses in the imperial chariot, he sits on high and directs their course by the reins of holy harmony and concord; and, himself every where present, and observant of every event, thus traverses every region of the world. Lastly, invested as he is with a semblance of heavenly sovereignty, he directs his gaze above, and frames his earthly government according to the pattern of that Divine original, feeling strength in its conformity to the monarchy of God. And this conformity is granted by the universal Sovereign to man alone of the creatures of this earth: for He only is the author of sovereign power, who decrees that all should be subject to the rule of one. And surely monarchy far transcends every other constitution and form of government: for that democratic equality of power which is its opposite, may rather be described as anarchy and disorder. Hence there is one God, and not two, or three, or more: for to assert a plurality of gods is plainly to deny the being of God at all. There is one Sovereign; and His Word and royal Law is one: a Law not expressed in syllables and words, not written or engraved on tablets, and therefore subject to the ravages of time; but the living and self-subsisting Word, who Himself is God, and who administers His Father's kingdom on behalf of all who are after Him and subject to His power. His attendants are the heavenly hosts; the myriads of God's angelic ministers; the super-terrestrial armies, of unnumbered multitude; and those unseen spirits within heaven itself, whose agency is employed in regulating the order of this world. Ruler and chief of all these is the royal Word, acting as Regent of the Supreme Sovereign. To Him the names of Captain, and great High Priest, Prophet of the Father, Angel of mighty counsel, Brightness of the Father's light, Only begotten Son, with a thousand other titles, are ascribed in the oracles of the sacred writers. And the Father, having constituted Him the living Word, and Law, and Wisdom, the fulness of all blessing, has presented this best and greatest gift to all who are the subjects of His sovereignty. And He Himself, who pervades all things, and is every where present, unfolding His Father's bounties to all with unsparing hand, has accorded a specimen of His sovereign power even to His rational creatures of this earth, in that He has provided the mind of man, who is formed after His own image, with divine faculties, whence it is capable of other virtues also, which flow from the same heavenly source. For He only is wise, who is the only God: He only is essentially good: He only is of mighty power, the Parent of justice, the Father of reason and wisdom, the Fountain of light and life, the Dispenser of truth and virtue: in a word, the Author of empire itself, and of all dominion and power.

CHAPTER IV

BUT whence has man this knowledge, and who has ministered these truths to mortal ears? Or whence has a tongue of flesh the power to speak of things so utterly distinct from fleshly or material substance? Who has gazed on the invisible King, and beheld these perfections in Him? The bodily sense may comprehend elements and their combinations, of a nature kindred to its own: but no one yet has boasted to have scanned with corporeal eye, that unseen kingdom which governs all things; nor has mortal nature yet discerned the beauty of perfect wisdom. Who has beheld the face of justice through the medium of earthly faculties? And whence came the idea of legitimate sovereignty and royal power to man? Whence the thought of absolute dominion to a being composed of flesh and blood? Who declared those forms which are invisible and undefined, and that incorporeal essence which has no external form, to the mortals of this earth? Surely there was but one interpreter of these things; the all-pervading Word of God. For He is the author of that rational and intelligent being which exists in man; and, being Himself one with His Father's Divine nature, He sheds upon His offspring the out-flowings of His Father's bounty. Hence the natural and untaught powers of thought, which all men, Greeks or Barbarians, alike possess: hence the perception of reason and wisdom, the seeds of integrity and justice, the understanding of the arts of life, the knowledge of virtue, the precious name of wisdom, and the noble love of philosophic learning. Hence the knowledge of all that is great and good: hence apprehension of God Himself, and a life worthy of His worship: hence the royal authority of man, and his invincible lordship over the creatures of this world. And when that Word, who is the Parent of rational beings, had impressed a character on the mind of man according to the image and likeness of God, and had made him a royal creature, in that He gave him alone of all earthly creatures capacity to rule and to obey (as well as forethought and foreknowledge even here, concerning the promised hope of His heavenly kingdom, because of which He Himself came, and, as the Parent of His children, disdained not to hold converse with mortal men); He continued to cherish the seeds which Himself had sown, and renewed His gracious favours from above; holding forth to all the promise of sharing His heavenly kingdom. Accordingly He called men, and exhorted them to be ready for their heavenward journey, and to provide themselves with the garment which became their calling. And by an indescribable power He filled the world in every part with His doctrine, expressing by the similitude of an earthly kingdom that heavenly one to which He earnestly invites all mankind, and presents it to them as a worthy object of their hope.

CHAPTER V

AND in this hope our divinely-favoured Emperor partakes even in this present life, gifted as he is by God with native virtues, and having received into his soul the outflowings of His favour. His reason he derives from the great Source of all reason: he is wise, and good, and just, as having fellowship with perfect Wisdom, Goodness, and Justice: virtuous, as following the pattern of perfect virtue: valiant, as partaking of heavenly strength. And truly may he deserve the imperial title, who has formed his soul to royal virtues, according to the standard of that celestial kingdom. But he who is a stranger to these blessings, who denies the Sovereign of the universe, and owns no allegiance to the heavenly Father of spirits; who invests not himself with the virtues which become an emperor, but overlays his soul with moral deformity and baseness; who for royal clemency substitutes the fury of a savage beast; for a generous temper, the incurable venom of malicious wickedness; for prudence, folly: for reason and wisdom, that recklessness which is the most odious of all vices (for from it, as from a spring of bitterness, proceed the most pernicious fruits; such as profligacy of life, covetousness, murder, impiety and defiance of God); surely one abandoned to such vices as these, however he may be deemed powerful through despotic violence, has no true title to the name of Emperor. For how should he whose soul is impressed with a thousand absurd ideas of false deities, be able to exhibit a counterpart of the true and heavenly sovereignty? Or how can he be absolute lord of others, who has subjected himself to the dominion of a thousand cruel masters? a slave of low delights and ungoverned lust, a slave of wrongfully-extorted wealth, of rage and passion, as well as of cowardice and terror; a slave of ruthless demons, and soul-destroying spirits? Let, then, our emperor, on the testimony of truth itself, be declared alone worthy of the title; who is dear to the Supreme Sovereign Himself; who alone is free, nay, who is truly lord: above the thirst of wealth, superior to the love of women; victorious even over natural pleasures; controlling, not controlled by, anger and passion. He is indeed an emperor, and bears a title corresponding to his deeds; a VICTOR in truth, who has gained the victory over those passions which overmaster the rest of men: whose character is formed after the Divine original of the Supreme Sovereign, and whose mind reflects, as in a mirror, the radiance of his virtues. Hence is our emperor perfect in discretion, in goodness, in justice, in courage, in piety, in devotion to God: he truly and only is a philosopher, since he knows himself, and is fully aware that supplies of every blessing are showered on him from a source quite external to himself, even from heaven itself. Declaring the august title of supreme authority by the splendour of his vesture, he alone worthily wears that imperial purple which so well becomes him. He is indeed an emperor, who calls on and implores in prayer the favour of his heavenly Father night and day, and whose ardent desires are fixed on His celestial kingdom. For he knows that present things, subject as they are to decay and death, flowing on and disappearing like a river's stream, are not worthy to be compared with Him who is sovereign of all; and therefore it is that he longs for the incorruptible and spiritual kingdom of God. And this kingdom he trusts he shall obtain, elevating his mind as he does in sublimity of thought above the vault of heaven, and filled with inexpressible longing for the glories which shine there, in comparison with which he deems the precious things of this present world but darkness. For he sees earthly sovereignty to be but a petty and fleeting dominion over a mortal and temporary life, and rates it not much higher than the goatherd's, or shepherd's, or herdsman's power: nay, as more burdensome than theirs, and exercised over more stubborn subjects. The acclamations of the people, and the voice of flattery, he reckons rather troublesome than pleasing, because of the steady constancy of his character, and thorough discipline of his mind. Again, when he beholds the military service of his subjects, the vast array of his armies, the multitudes of horse and foot, entirely devoted to his command, he feels no astonishment, no pride at the possession of such mighty power; but turns his thoughts inward on himself, and recognizes the same common nature there. He smiles at his vesture, embroidered with gold and flowers, and at the imperial purple and diadem itself, when he sees the multitude gaze in wonder (like children at a bugbear) on the splendid spectacle. Himself superior to such feelings, he clothes his soul with the knowledge of God, that vesture, the broidery of which is temperance, justice, piety, and all other virtues; a vesture such as truly becomes a sovereign.

The wealth which others so much desire, as gold, silver, or precious gems, he regards, as they really are, as in themselves mere stones and worthless matter, of no avail to preserve or defend from evil. For what power have these things to free from disease, or repel the approach of death? And knowing as he does this truth by personal experience in the use of these things, he regards the splendid attire of his subjects with calm indifference, and smiles at the weakness of those to whom they prove attractive. Lastly, he abstains from all excess in food and wine, and leaves superfluous dainties to gluttons, judging that such indulgences, however suitable to others, are not so to him, and deeply convinced of their pernicious tendency, and their effect in darkening the intellectual powers of the soul. For all these reasons, our divinely-taught and noble-minded emperor, aspiring to higher objects than this life affords, calls upon his heavenly Father as one who longs for His kingdom; exhibits a pious spirit in each action of his life; and finally, as a wise and good instructor, imparts to his subjects the knowledge of Him who is the Sovereign Lord of all.

CHAPTER VI

AND God Himself, as an earnest of future reward, assigns to him now as it were tricennial crowns composed of prosperous periods of time; and now, after the revolution of three circles of ten years, He grants permission to all mankind to celebrate this general, nay rather, this universal festival. And while those on earth thus rejoice, crowned as it were with the flowers of divine knowledge, surely we may not unduly suppose that the heavenly quires, attracted by a natural sympathy, unite their joy with the joy of those on earth: nay, that the Supreme Sovereign Himself, as a gracious Father, delights in the worship of duteous children, and for this reason is pleased to honour the author and cause of their obedience with a lengthened period of time; and, far from limiting his reign to three decennial circles of years, He extends it to the remotest period, even to far distant eternity. Now eternity in its whole extent is beyond the power of decline or death: its beginning and extent alike incapable of being scanned by mortal thoughts. Nor will it suffer its central point to be perceived, nor that which is termed its present duration to be grasped by the inquiring mind. Far less, then, the future, or the past: for the one is not, but is already gone; while the future has not yet arrived, and therefore is not. As regards what is termed the present time, it vanishes even as we think or speak, more swiftly than the word itself is uttered. Nor is it possible in any sense to apprehend this time as present; for we must either expect the future, or contemplate the past; the present slips from us, and is gone, even in the act of thought. Eternity, then, in its whole extent, resists and refuses subjection to mortal reason, while it acknowledges its own Sovereign and Lord, and bears Him as it were mounted on itself, rejoicing in the fair trappings which He bestows. And He Himself, not binding it (as the poet imagined) with a golden chain, but as it were controlling its movements by the reins of ineffable wisdom, has adjusted its months and seasons, its times and years, and the alternations of day and night, with perfect harmony, and has thus attached to it limits and measures of various kinds. For eternity, being in its nature direct, and stretching onward into infinity, and receiving its name, eternity, as having an everlasting existence; and being similar in all its parts, or rather having no division or distance; progresses only in a line of direct extension. But God, who has distributed it by intermediate sections, and has divided it, like a far extended line, in many points, has included in it a vast number of portions; and though it is in its nature one, and resembles unity itself, He has attached to it a multiplicity of numbers, and has given it, though formless in itself, an endless variety of forms. For first of all He framed in it formless matter, as a substance capable of receiving all forms. He next, by the power of the number two, imparted quality to matter, and gave beauty to that which before was void of all grace. Again, by means of the number three, He framed a body compounded of matter and form, and presenting the three dimensions of breadth, and length, and depth. Then, from the doubling of the number two, He devised the quaternion of the elements, earth, water, air, and fire, and ordained them to be everlasting sources for the supply of this universe. Again, the number four produces the number ten. For the aggregate of one, and two, and three, and four, is ten. And three multiplied with ten discovers the period of a month: and twelve successive months complete the course of the sun. Hence the revolutions of years, and changes of the seasons, which give grace, as it were by a tissue of many-coloured flowers, to that eternity which before was formless and devoid of beauty, for the refreshment and delight of those whose lot it is to traverse therein the course of life. For as the ground is denned by stated distances for those who run in hope of obtaining the prize; and as the road of those who travel on a distant journey is marked by resting-places and measured intervals, that the traveller's courage may not fail at the interminable prospect; even so the Sovereign of the universe, controlling eternity itself within the restraining power of His own wisdom, directs and turns its course as He judges best. The same God, I say, who thus clothes the once undefined eternity as with fair colours and blooming flowers, gladdens the day with the solar rays; and, while He overspreads the night with a covering of darkness, yet causes the glittering stars, as golden spangles, to shine therein. It is He who lights up the brilliancy of the morning star, the changing splendour of the moon, and the glorious companies of the starry host, and has arrayed the expanse of heaven, like some vast mantle, in colours of varied beauty. Again, having created the lofty and profound expanse of air, and caused the world in its length and breadth to feel its cooling influence, He decreed that the air itself should be graced with birds of every kind, and left open this vast ocean of space to be traversed by every creature, visible or invisible, whose course is through the tracts of heaven. In the midst of this atmosphere He poised the earth, as it were its centre, and encompassed it with the ocean as with a beautiful azure vesture: and having ordained this earth to be at once the home, the nurse, and the mother of all the creatures it contains, and watered it both with rain and water-springs, He caused it to abound in plants and flowers of every species, for the enjoyment of life. And when He had formed man in His own likeness, the noblest of earthly creatures, and dearest to Himself, a creature gifted with intellect and knowledge, the child of reason and wisdom; He gave him dominion over all other animals which move and live upon the earth. For man was in truth of all earthly creatures the dearest to God: man, I say, to whom, as an indulgent Father. He has subjected the brute creation; for whom He has made the ocean navigable, and crowned the earth with a profusion of plants of every kind; to whom He has granted reasoning faculties for acquiring all science; under whose control He has placed even the creatures of the deep, and the winged inhabitants of the air; to whom He has permitted the contemplation of celestial objects, and revealed the course and changes of the sun and moon, and the periods of the planets and fixed stars. In short, to man alone of earthly beings has He given commandment to acknowledge Him as his heavenly Father, and to celebrate His praises as the Supreme Sovereign of eternity itself, the unchangeable course of which the Creator has limited by the four seasons of the year, terminating the winter by the approach of spring, and regulating as with an equal balance that season which commences the annual period. Having thus graced the eternal course of time with the varied productions of spring, He added the summer's heat; and then granted as it were a relief of toil by the interval of autumn: and lastly, refreshing and cleansing the season by the showers of winter, He brings it, rendered sleek and glossy (like a noble steed), by these abundant rains, once more to the gates of spring. As soon, then, as the Supreme Sovereign had thus connected His own eternity by these cords of wisdom with the annual circle, He committed it to the guidance of a mighty Governor, even His only-begotten Word, to whom, as the Preserver of all creation, He yielded the reins of universal power. And He, receiving this inheritance as from a beneficent Father, and uniting all things both above and beneath the circumference of heaven in one harmonious whole, directs their uniform course; providing with perfect justice whatever is expedient for His rational creatures on the earth, appointing its allotted limits to human life, and granting to all alike permission to anticipate even here the commencement of a future existence. For He has taught them that beyond this present world there is a divine and blessed state of being, reserved for those who have been supported here by the hope of heavenly blessings; and that those who have lived a virtuous and godly life will remove hence to a far better habitation; while He adjudges to those who have been guilty and wicked here a place of punishment according to their crimes. Again (as in the distribution of prizes at the public games), He proclaims various crowns to the victors, and invests each with the rewards of different virtues: but for our good emperor, who is clothed in the very robe of piety, He declares that a higher recompense of his toils is prepared; and, as a prelude to this recompense, permits us now to assemble at this festival, which is composed of perfect numbers, of decades thrice, and triads ten times repeated; the last of which, the triad, is the offspring of the unit, while the unit is the mother of number itself, and presides over all months, and seasons, and years, and every period of time. It may indeed be justly termed the origin, foundation, and principle of all number, and derives its name from its abiding character. For, while every other number is diminished or increased according to the subtraction or addition of others, the unit alone continues fixed and steadfast, abstracted from all multitude and the numbers which are formed from it, and resembling that indivisible essence which is distinct from all things beside, but by virtue of participation in which the nature of all things else subsists. For the unit is the originator of every number, since all multitude is made up by the composition and addition of units; nor is it possible without the unit to conceive the existence of number at all. But the unit itself is independent of multitude, apart from and superior to all number; forming, indeed, and making all, but receiving no increase from any. Kindred to this is the triad; equally indivisible and perfect, the first of those sums which are formed of even and uneven numbers. For the perfect number two, receiving the addition of the unit, forms the triad, the first perfect compound number. And the triad, by explaining what equality is, first taught men justice, having itself an equal beginning, and middle, and end. And it is also an image of the mysterious, most holy, and royal Trinity, which, though itself without beginning or origin, yet contains the germs, the reasons, and causes of the existence of all created things: and thus the power of the triad may justly be regarded as the first cause of all things. Again, the number ten, which contains the end of all numbers, and terminates them in itself, may truly be called a full and perfect number, as comprehending every species and every measure of numbers, proportions, concords, and harmonies. For example, the units by addition form and are terminated by the number ten; and having this number as their parent, and as it were the limit of their course, they round this as the goal of their career, and then perform a second circuit, and again a third, and a fourth, until the tenth, and thus by ten decades they complete the hundredth number. Returning thence to the first starting point, they again proceed to the number ten, and, having ten times completed the hundredth number, again they recede, and perform round the same barriers their protracted course, proceeding from themselves back to themselves again, with revolving motion. For the unit is the tenth of ten, and ten units make up a decade, which is itself the limit, the settled goal and boundary of units: it is that which terminates the infinity of number; the term and end of units. Again, the triad combined with the decade, and performing a threefold circuit of tens, produces that most natural number, thirty. For as the triad is in respect to units, so is the number thirty in respect to tens; and it is also the constant limit to the course of that luminary which is second to the sun in brightness. For the course of the moon from one conjunction with the sun to the next, completes the period of a month; after which, receiving as it were a second birth, it recommences a new light, and other days, being adorned and honoured with thirty units, three decades, and ten triads. In the same manner is the universal reign of our victorious emperor distinguished by the Giver of all good, and now enters on a new sphere of blessing, accomplishing, at present, this tricennalian festival, but reaching forward beyond this to far more distant intervals of time, and cherishing the hope of future blessings in the celestial kingdom; where, not a single sun, but infinite hosts of light surround the Almighty Sovereign, each surpassing the splendour of the sun, glorious and resplendent with rays derived from the everlasting source of light. There the soul enjoys its existence, surrounded by fair and unfading blessings; there is a life beyond the reach of sorrow; there the enjoyment of pure and holy pleasures, and a time of unmeasured and endless duration, extending into illimitable space; not defined by intervals of days and months, the revolutions of years, or the recurrence of times and seasons, but commensurate with a life which knows no end. And this life needs not the light of the sun, nor the lustre of the moon or the starry host, since it has the great Luminary Himself, even God the Word, the only begotten Son of the Almighty Sovereign; and hence it is that the mystic and sacred oracles reveal Him to be the Sun of righteousness, and the Light which far transcends all light. We believe that He illumines also the thrice-blessed powers of heaven with the rays of righteousness, and the brightness of wisdom, and that He receives truly pious souls, not within the sphere of heaven alone, but into His own bosom, and confirms indeed the assurances which He Himself has given. No mortal eye has seen, nor ear heard, nor can the mind in its vesture of flesh understand what things are prepared for those who have been here adorned with the graces of godliness; blessings which await thee too, most pious emperor, to whom alone since the world began has the Almighty Sovereign of the universe granted power to purify the course of human life: to whom also He has revealed His own symbol of salvation, whereby He overcame the power of death, and triumphed over every enemy. And this victorious trophy, the scourge of evil spirits, thou hast arrayed against the errors of idol worship, and hast obtained the victory not only over all thy impious and savage foes, but over equally barbarous adversaries, the evil spirits themselves.

CHAPTER VII

FOR whereas we are composed of two distinct natures, I mean of body and spirit, of which the one is visible to all, the other invisible, against both these natures two kinds of barbarous and savage enemies, the one invisibly, the other openly, are constantly arrayed. The one oppose our bodies with bodily force: the other with incorporeal assaults besiege the naked soul itself. Again, the visible barbarians (like the wild nomad tribes), no better than savage beasts, assail the nations of civilized men, ravage their country, and enslave their cities, rushing on those who inhabit them like ruthless wolves of the desert, and destroying all who fall under their power. But those unseen foes, more cruel far than barbarians, I mean the soul-destroying demons whose course is through the regions of the air, had succeeded, through the snares of vile polytheism, in enslaving the entire human race, insomuch that they no longer recognized the true God, but wandered in the mazes of atheistic error. For they procured (I know not whence) gods who never any where existed, and set Him aside who is the only and the true God, as though He were not. Accordingly the generation of bodies was esteemed by them a deity, and so the opposite principle to this, their dissolution and destruction, was also deified. The first, as the author of generative power, was honoured with rites under the name of Venus: the second, as rich, and mighty in dominion over the human race, received the names of Pluto, and Death. For men in those ages, knowing no other than naturally-generated life, declared the cause and origin of that life to be divine: and again, believing in no existence after death, they proclaimed Death himself a universal conqueror and a mighty god. Hence, unconscious of responsibility, as destined to be annihilated by death, they lived a life unworthy of the name, in the practice of actions deserving a thousand deaths. No thought of God could enter their minds, no expectation of Divine judgment, no recollection of, no reflection on, their spiritual existence: acknowledging one dread superior, Death, and persuaded that the dissolution of their bodies by his power was final annihilation, they bestowed on Death the title of a mighty, a wealthy god, and hence the name of Pluto. Thus, then, Death became to them a god; nor only so, but whatever else they accounted precious in comparison with death, whatever contributed to the pleasures and luxuries of life. Hence animal pleasure became to them a god; nutrition, and its production, a god; the fruit of trees, a god; drunken riot, a god; carnal desire and pleasure, a god. Hence the mysteries of Ceres and Proserpine, the rape of the latter, and her subsequent restoration, by Pluto: hence the orgies of Bacchus, and Hercules overcome by drunkenness as by a mightier god: hence the adulterous rites of Cupid and of Venus: hence Jupiter himself infatuated with the love of women, and of Ganymede: hence the licentious legends of deities abandoned to effeminacy and pleasure. Such were the weapons of superstition whereby these cruel barbarians and enemies of the Supreme God afflicted, and indeed entirely subdued, the human race; erecting every where the monuments of impiety, and rearing in every corner the shrines and temples of their false religion. Nay, so far were the ruling powers of those times enslaved by the force of error, as to appease their gods with the blood of their own countrymen and kindred; to whet their swords against those who stood forward to defend the truth; to maintain a ruthless war and raise unholy hands, not against foreign or barbarian foes, but against men bound to them by the ties of family and affection, against brethren, and kinsmen, and dearest friends, who had resolved, in the practice of virtue and true piety, to honour and worship God. Such was the spirit of madness with which these princes sacrificed to their demon deities men consecrated to the service of the King of kings. On the other hand their victims, as noble martyrs in the cause of true godliness, resolved to welcome a glorious death in preference to life itself, and utterly despised these cruelties. Strengthened, as soldiers of God, with patient fortitude, they mocked at death in all its forms; at fire, and sword, and the torment of crucifixion; at exposure to savage beasts, and drowning in the depths of the sea; at the cutting off and scaring of limbs, the digging out of eyes, the mutilation of the whole body; lastly, at famine, the labour of the mines, and captivity: nay, all these sufferings they counted better than any earthly good or pleasure, for the love they bore their heavenly King. In like manner women also evinced a spirit of constancy and courage not inferior to that of men. Some endured the same conflicts with them, and obtained a like reward of their virtue: others, forcibly carried off to be the victims of violence and pollution, welcomed death rather than dishonour; while many, very many more, endured not even to hear the same threats wherewith they were assailed by the provincial governors, but boldly sustained every variety of torture, and sentence of death in every form. Thus did these valiant soldiers of the Almighty Sovereign maintain the conflict with steadfast fortitude of soul against the hostile forces of polytheism: and thus did these enemies of God and adversaries of man's salvation, more cruel far than the ferocious savage, delight in libations of human blood: thus did their ministers drain as it were the cup of unrighteous slaughter in honour of the demons whom they served, and prepare for them this dread and impious banquet, to the ruin of the human race. In these sad circumstances, what course should the God and King of these afflicted ones pursue? Could He be careless of the safety of His dearest friends, or abandon His servants in this great extremity? Surely none could deem him a wary pilot, who, without an effort to save his fellow-mariners, should suffer his vessel to sink with all her crew: surely no general could be found so reckless as to yield his own allies, without resistance, to the mercy of the foe: nor can a faithful shepherd regard with unconcern the straying of a single sheep from his flock, but will rather leave the rest in safety, and dare all things for the wanderer's sake, even, if need be, to contend with savage beasts. The zeal, however, of the great Sovereign of all was for no unconscious sheep: His care was exercised for His own faithful host, for those who sustained the battle for His sake: whose conflicts in the cause of godliness He Himself approved, and honoured those who had returned to His presence with the prize of victory which He only can bestow, uniting them to the angelic quires. Others He still preserved on earth, to communicate the living seeds of piety to future generations; to be at once eyewitnesses of His vengeance on the ungodly, and narrators of the events which they themselves had seen. After this He outstretched His arm in judgment on the adversaries, and utterly destroyed them with the stroke of Divine wrath, compelling them, how reluctant soever, to confess with their own lips and recant their wickedness, but raising from the ground and exalting gloriously those who had long been oppressed and disallowed by all. Such were the dealings of the Supreme Sovereign, who ordained an invincible champion to be the minister of His heaven-sent vengeance (for our emperor's surpassing piety delights in the title of Servant of God), and him He has proved victorious over all that opposed him, having raised him up, an individual against many foes. For they were indeed numberless, being the friends of many evil spirits (though in reality they were nothing, and hence are now no more); but our emperor is one, appointed by, and the representative of, the one Almighty Sovereign. And they, in the very spirit of impiety, destroyed the righteous with cruel slaughter: but he, in imitation of his Saviour, and knowing only how to save men's lives, has spared and instructed in godliness the impious themselves. And so, as truly worthy the name of VICTOR, he has subdued the twofold race of barbarians; soothing the savage tribes of men by prudent embassies, compelling them to know and acknowledge their superiors, and reclaiming them from a lawless and brutal life to the governance of reason and humanity; at the same time that he proved by the facts themselves that the fierce and ruthless race of unseen spirits had long ago been vanquished by a higher power. For He who is the preserver of the universe had punished these invisible spirits by an invisible judgment: and our emperor, as the delegate of the Supreme Sovereign, has followed up the victory, bearing away the spoils of those who have long since died and mouldered into dust, and distributing the plunder with lavish hand among the soldiers of his victorious Lord.

CHAPTER VIII

FOR as soon as he understood that the ignorant multitudes were inspired with a vain and childish dread of these bugbears of error, wrought in gold and silver, he judged it right to remove these also, like stumbling stones thrown in the path of men walking in the dark, and henceforward to open a plain and unobstructed road to all. Having formed this resolution, he considered that no military force was needed for the repression of the evil: a few of his own friends sufficed for this service, and these he sent by a simple expression of his will to visit each several province. Accordingly, sustained by confidence in the emperor's piety and their own personal devotion to God, they passed through the midst of numberless tribes and nations, abolishing this ancient system of error in every city and country. They ordered the priests themselves, in the midst of general laughter and scorn, to bring their gods from their dark recesses to the light of day. They then stripped them of their ornaments, and exhibited to the gaze of all the unsightly reality which had been hidden beneath a painted exterior: and lastly, whatever part of the material appeared to be of value they scraped off and melted in the fire to prove its worth, after which they secured and set apart whatever they judged needful for their purposes, leaving to the superstitious worshippers what was altogether useless, as a memorial of their shame. Meanwhile our admirable prince was himself engaged in a work similar to that we have described. For at the same time that these costly images of the dead were stripped, as we have said, of their precious materials, he also attacked those composed of brass; causing those to be dragged from their places with ropes, and, as it were, carried away captive, whom the dotage of antiquity had esteemed as gods. The next care of our august emperor was to kindle, as it were, a brilliant torch, by the light of which he directed his imperial gaze around, to see if any hidden vestiges of error might yet exist. And as the keen-sighted eagle in its heavenward flight is able to descry from its lofty height the most distant objects on the earth: so did he, whilst residing in the imperial palace of his own fair city, discover, as from a watchtower, a hidden and fatal snare of souls in the province of Phœnicia. This was a grove and temple, not situated in the midst of any city, or in any public place (as mostly is the case with a view to splendour of effect), but apart from the beaten and frequented road, on part of the summit of mount Libanus, and dedicated to the foul demon known by the name of Venus. It was a school of wickedness for all the abandoned votaries of sensuality and impurity. Here men undeserving the name forgot the dignity of their sex, and propitiated the demon by their effeminate conduct: here too unlawful commerce of women, and adulterous intercourse, with other horrible and infamous practices, were perpetrated in this temple as in a place beyond the scope and restraint of law.

Meantime these evils remained unchecked by the presence of any observer, since no one of fair character ventured to visit such scenes. These proceedings, however, could not escape the vigilance of our august emperor, who, having himself inspected them with characteristic forethought, and judging that such a temple was unfit for the light of heaven, gave orders that the building with its offerings should be utterly destroyed. Accordingly, in obedience to the imperial edict, these engines of an abandoned superstition were immediately abolished, and the hand of military force was made instrumental in purging the impurities of the place. And now those who had heretofore lived without restraint, found, in the imperial threat of punishment, an inducement to sobriety of conduct. Thus did our emperor tear the mask from this system of delusive wickedness, and expose it to the public gaze, at the same time proclaiming openly his Saviour's name to all. No advocate appeared; neither god nor demon, prophet nor diviner, could lend his aid to the detected authors of the imposture. For the thick darkness was dispelled which had enveloped the minds of men: enlightened by the rays of true godliness, they condemned the ignorance and pitied the blindness of their forefathers, rejoicing at the same time in their own deliverance from such fatal error. Thus speedily, according to the counsel of the mighty God, and through our emperor's agency, was every enemy, whether visible or unseen, utterly removed: and henceforward peace, the happy nurse of youth, extended her reign throughout the world. Wars were no more, for the gods were not: no more did external or domestic strife, no more did the effusion of human blood, distress mankind, as heretofore, when demon-worship and the madness of idolatry prevailed.

CHAPTER IX

AND now we may well compare the present with former things, and review these happy changes in contrast with the evils that are past, and mark the elaborate care with which in ancient times porches and sacred precincts, groves and temples, were prepared in every city for these false deities, and how their shrines were enriched with abundant offerings. The sovereign rulers of those days had indeed a high regard for the worship of the gods. The nations also and people subject to their power honoured them with images both in the country and in every city, nay, even in their houses and secret chambers, according to the religious practice of their fathers. The fruit, however, of this devotion (far different from the peaceful concord which now meets our view), appeared in war, in battles, and seditions, which harassed them throughout their lives, and deluged their countries with blood and civil slaughter. Again, the objects of their worship could hold out to these sovereigns with artful flattery the promise of prophecies, and oracles, and the knowledge of futurity: yet could they not predict their own destruction, nor forewarn themselves of the coming ruin: and surely this was the greatest and most convincing proof of their imposture. Not one of those whose words once were heard with awe and wonder, had announced the glorious advent of the Saviour of mankind, or that new revelation of divine knowledge which He came to give. Not Pythius himself, nor any of those mighty gods, could apprehend the prospect of their approaching desolation; nor could their oracles point at Him who was to be their conqueror and destroyer. What prophet or diviner could foretell that their rites would vanish at the presence of a new Deity in the world, and that the knowledge and worship of the Almighty Sovereign should be freely given to all mankind? Which of them foreknew the august and pious reign of our victorious emperor, or his triumphant conquests every where over the false demons, or the overthrow of their high places? Which of the heroes has announced the melting down and conversion of the lifeless statues from their useless forms to the necessary uses of men? Which of the gods have yet had power to speak of their own images thus melted and contemptuously reduced to fragments? Where were the protecting powers, that they should not interpose to save their sacred memorials, thus destroyed by man? Where, I ask, are those who once maintained the strife of war, yet now behold their conquerors abiding securely in the profoundest peace? And where are they who upheld themselves in a blind and foolish confidence, and trusted in these vanities as gods; but who, in the very height of their superstitious error, and while maintaining an implacable war with the champions of the truth, perished by a fate proportioned to their crimes? Where is the giant race whose arms were turned against heaven itself; the hissings of those serpents whose tongues were pointed with impious words against the Almighty King? These adversaries of the Lord of all, confident in the aid of a multitude of gods, advanced to the attack with a powerful array of military force, preceded by certain images of the dead, and lifeless statues, as their defence. On the other side our emperor, secure in the armour of godliness, opposed to the numbers of the enemy the salutary and life-giving Sign, as at the same time a terror to the foe, and a protection against every harm; and returned victorious at once over the enemy and the demons whom they served. And then, with thanksgiving and praise (the tokens of a grateful spirit) to the Author of his victory, he proclaimed this triumphant Sign, by monuments as well as words, to all mankind, erecting it as a mighty trophy against every enemy in the midst of the imperial city, and expressly enjoining on all to acknowledge this imperishable symbol of salvation as the safeguard of the power of Rome and of the empire of the world. Such were the instructions which he gave to his subjects generally; but especially to his soldiers, whom he admonished to repose their confidence, not in their weapons, or armour, or bodily strength, but to acknowledge the Supreme God as the giver of every good, and of victory itself. Thus did the emperor (strange and incredible as the fact may seem) himself become the instructor of his army in their religious exercises, and teach them to offer pious prayers in accordance with the divine ordinances, uplifting their hands towards heaven, and raising their mental vision higher still to the King of heaven, on whom they should call as the Author of victory, their preserver, guardian, and helper. He commanded too, that one day should be regarded as a special occasion for religious worship; I mean that which is truly the first and chief of all, the day of our Lord and Saviour; that day the name of which is connected with light, and life, and immortality, and every good. Prescribing the same pious conduct to himself, he honoured his Saviour in the chambers of his palace, performing his devotions according to the Divine commands, and storing his mind with instruction through the hearing of the sacred word. The entire care of his household was intrusted to ministers devoted to the service of God, and distinguished by gravity of life and every other virtue; while his trusty body guards, strong in affection and fidelity to his person, found in their emperor an instructor in the practice of a godly life. Again, the honour with which he regards the victorious Sign is founded on his actual experience of its divine efficacy.

Before this the hosts of his enemies have disappeared: by this the powers of the unseen spirits have been turned to flight: through this the proud boastings of God's adversaries have come to nought, and the tongues of the profane and blasphemous been put to silence. By this Sign the Barbarian tribes were vanquished: through this the rites of superstitious fraud received a just rebuke: by this our emperor, discharging as it were a sacred debt, has performed the crowning good of all, by erecting triumphant memorials of its value in all parts of the world, raising temples and churches on a scale of royal costliness, and commanding all to unite in constructing the sacred houses of prayer. Accordingly these signal proofs of our emperor's magnificence forthwith appeared in the provinces and cities of the empire, and soon shone conspicuously in every country; convincing memorials of the rebuke and overthrow of those impious tyrants who but a little while before had madly dared to fight against God, and, raging like savage dogs, had vented on unconscious buildings that fury which they were unable to level against Him; had thrown to the ground and upturned the very foundations of the houses of prayer, causing them to present the appearance of a city captured and abandoned to the enemy. Such was the exhibition of that wicked spirit whereby they sought as it were to assail God Himself, but soon experienced the result of their own madness and folly. But a little time elapsed, when a single blast of the storm of Heaven's displeasure swept them utterly away, leaving neither kindred, nor offspring, nor memorial of their existence among men: for all, numerous as they were, disappeared as in a moment beneath the stroke of Divine vengeance. Such, then, was the fate which awaited these furious adversaries of God: but he who, armed with the salutary Trophy, had alone opposed them (nay rather, not alone, but aided by the presence and the power of Him who is the only Sovereign), has replaced the ruined edifices on a greater scale, and made the second far superior to the first. For example, besides erecting various churches to the honour of God in the city which bears his name, and adorning the Bithynian capital with another on the greatest and most splendid scale, he has distinguished the principal cities of the other provinces by structures of a similar kind. Above all, he has selected two places in the eastern division of the empire, the one in Palestine (since from thence the life-giving stream has flowed as from a fountain for the blessing of all nations), the other in that metropolis of the East which derives its name from that of Antiochus; in which, as the head of that portion of the empire, he has consecrated to the service of God a church of unparalleled size and beauty. The entire building is encompassed by an enclosure of great extent, within which the church itself rises to a vast elevation, of an octagonal form, surrounded by many chambers and courts on every side, and decorated with ornaments of the richest kind. Again, in the province of Palestine, in that city which was once the seat of Hebrew sovereignty, on the very site of the Lord's sepulchre, he has raised a church of noble dimensions, and adorned a temple sacred to the salutary Cross with rich and lavish magnificence, honouring that everlasting monument, and the trophies of the Saviour's victory over the power of death, with a splendour which no language can describe. In the same country he discovered three places venerable as the localities of three sacred caves: and these also he adorned with costly structures, paying a fitting tribute of reverence to the scene of the first manifestation of the Saviour's presence; while at the second cavern he hallowed the remembrance of His final ascension from the mountain top; and celebrated His mighty conflict, and the victory which crowned it, at the third. All these places our emperor thus adorned in the hope of proclaiming the symbol of redemption to all mankind; that Cross which has indeed repaid his pious zeal; through which his house and throne alike have prospered, his reign has been confirmed for a lengthened series of years, and the rewards of virtue bestowed on his noble sons, his kindred, and their descendants. And surely it is a mighty evidence of the power of that God whom he serves, that He has held the balances of justice with an equal hand, and has apportioned to each party their due reward. With regard to the destroyers of the houses of prayer, the penalty of their impious conduct followed hard upon them: forthwith were they swept away, and left neither race, nor house, nor family behind. On the other hand, he whose pious devotion to his Lord is conspicuous in his every act, who raises royal temples to His honour, and proclaims His name to his subjects by sacred offerings throughout the world, he, I say, has deservedly experienced Him to be the preserver and defender of his imperial house and race. Thus clearly have the dealings of God been manifested, and this through the sacred efficacy of redemption's salutary Sign.

CHAPTER X

MUCH might indeed be said of this salutary Sign, by those who are skilled in the mysteries of our Divine religion. For it is in very truth the symbol of salvation, wondrous to speak of, more wondrous still to conceive; the appearance of which on earth has thrown the fictions of all false religion from the beginning into the deepest shade, has buried superstitious error in darkness and oblivion, and has revealed to all that spiritual light which enlightens the souls of men, even the knowledge of the only true God. Hence the happy and universal change, which leads men to spurn their lifeless idols, to trample under foot the lawless rites of their demon deities, and laugh to scorn the time-honoured follies of their fathers. Hence, too, the establishment in every place of those schools of sacred learning, wherein men are taught the precepts of saving truth, and dread no more those objects of creation which are seen by the natural eye, nor direct a gaze of wonder at the sun, the moon, or stars; but acknowledge Him who is above all these, that invisible Being who is the Creator of them all, and learn to worship Him alone. Such are the blessings resulting to mankind from this great and wondrous Sign, by virtue of which the evils which once existed are now no more, and virtues heretofore unknown shine every where resplendent with the light of true godliness. Discourses, and precepts, and exhortations to a virtuous and holy life, are proclaimed in the ears of all nations. Nay, the emperor himself proclaims them: and it is indeed a marvel that this mighty prince, raising his voice in the hearing of all the world, like an interpreter of the Almighty Sovereign's will, invites his subjects in every country to the knowledge of the true God. No more, as in former times, is the babbling of impious men heard in the imperial palace; but priests and pious worshippers of God together celebrate His majesty with royal hymns of praise. The name of the one Supreme Ruler of the universe is proclaimed to all: the gospel of glad tidings connects the human race with its Almighty King, declaring the grace and love of the heavenly Father to His children on the earth. His praise is every where sung in triumphant strains: the voice of mortal man is blended with the harmony of the angelic quires in heaven; and the reasoning soul employs the body which invests it as an instrument for sounding forth a fitting tribute of praise and adoration to His name. The nations of the East and West are instructed at the same moment in His precepts: the people of the Northern and Southern regions unite with one accord, under the influence of the same principles and laws, in the pursuit of a godly life, in praising the one Supreme God, in acknowledging His only begotten Son their Saviour as the source of every blessing, and our emperor as the one ruler on the earth, together with his pious sons. He himself, as a skilful pilot, sits on high at the helm of state, and directs the vessel with unerring course, conducting his people as it were with favouring breeze to a secure and tranquil haven. Meanwhile the Almighty Sovereign extends the right hand of His power from above for his protection, giving him victory over every foe, and establishing his empire by a lengthened period of years: and He will bestow on him yet higher blessings, and confirm in very deed the truth of His own promises. But on these we may not at present dwell; but must await the change to a better world: for it is not given to mortal eyes or ears of flesh, fully to apprehend the gifts of God.

CHAPTER XI

AND now, victorious and mighty Constantine, in this discourse, whose noble argument is the glory of the Almighty King, let me lay before thee some of the mysteries of His sacred truth: not as presuming to instruct thee, who art thyself taught of God; nor to disclose to thee those secret wonders which He Himself (not through the agency or word of man, but through our common Saviour, and the frequent light of His Divine presence) has long since revealed and unfolded to thy view: but in the hope of leading the unlearned to the light of truth, and displaying before those who know them not the causes and motives of thy pious deeds. True it is that thy noble efforts for the daily worship and honour of the Supreme God throughout the habitable world, are the theme of universal praise. But those records of gratitude to thy Saviour and Preserver which thou hast dedicated in our own province of Palestine, and in that city from which as from a fountain-head the word of salvation has issued forth to all mankind; and again, the hallowed edifices and consecrated temples which thou hast raised as trophies of His victory over death; and those lofty and noble structures, imperial monuments of an imperial spirit, which thou hast erected in honour of the everlasting memory of the Saviour's tomb; the cause, I say, of these things is not equally obvious to all. Those, indeed, who are enlightened in heavenly knowledge by the power of the Divine Spirit, well understand the cause, and justly admire and bless thee for that counsel and resolution which Heaven itself inspired. On the other hand the ignorant and spiritually-blind regard these designs with open mockery and scorn, and deem it a strange and unworthy thing indeed that so mighty a prince should waste his zeal on the graves and monuments of the dead. "Were it not better (such a one might say) to cherish those rites which are hallowed by ancient usage; to seek the favour of those gods and heroes whose worship is observed in every province; instead of rejecting and disclaiming them, because subject to the calamities incident to man? Surely they may claim equal honours with Him who Himself lias suffered: or, if they are to be rejected, as not exempt from the sorrows of humanity, the same award would justly be pronounced respecting Him." Thus, with important and contracted brow, might he give utterance in pompous language to his self-imagined wisdom. Filled with compassion for this ignorance, the gracious Word of our most beneficent Father freely invites, not such a one alone, but all who are in the path of error, to receive instruction in Divine knowledge; and has ordained the means of such instruction throughout the world, in every country and village, in cultivated and desert lands alike, and in every city: and, as a gracious Saviour and Physician of the soul, calls on the Greek and the Barbarian, the wise and the unlearned, the rich and the poor, the servant and his master, the subject and his lord, the ungodly, the profane, the ignorant, the evil-doer, the blasphemer, alike to draw near, and hasten to receive His heavenly cure. And thus in time past had He clearly announced to all the pardon of former transgressions, saying, "Come unto me, all ye that labour and are heavy laden, and I will give you rest." And again, "I am not come to call the righteous, but sinners, to repentance." And He adds the reason, saying, "For they that are whole need not a physician, but they that are sick." And again, "I desire not the death of a sinner, but rather that he should repent." Hence it is only for those who are themselves imbued with the principles of Divine faith, and understand the motives of that zeal of which these works are the result, to appreciate the more than human impulse by which our emperor was guided, to admire his piety toward God, and to believe his care for the memorial of our Saviour's resurrection to be a desire imparted from above, and truly inspired by that Sovereign, to be whose faithful servant and minister for good is his proudest boast. In full persuasion, then, of thy approval, most mighty emperor, I desire at this present time to proclaim to all the reasons and motives of thy pious works. I desire to stand as the interpreter of thy designs, to explain the counsels of a soul devoted to the love of God. I propose to teach all men (what all should know who care to understand the principles on which our Saviour God employs His power), the reasons for which He who was the pre-existent Controller of all things at length descended to us from heaven: the reasons for which He assumed our nature, and submitted even to the power of death. I shall declare the causes of that immortal life which followed, and of His resurrection from the dead. Once more, I shall adduce convincing proofs and arguments, for the sake of those who yet need such testimony: and now let me commence my appointed task.

Those who transfer the worship due to that God who formed and rules the world to the works of His hand; who hold the sun and moon, or other parts of this material system, nay, the elements themselves, earth, water, air, and fire, in equal honour with the Creator of them all; who give the name of gods to things which never would have had existence, or even name, except as obedient to that Word of God who made the world: such persons in my judgment resemble those who overlook the master hand which gives its magnificence to a royal palace; and, while lost in wonder at its roofs and walls, the paintings of varied beauty and colouring which adorn them, and its gilded ceilings and sculptures, ascribe to them the praise of that skill which belongs to the artist whose work they are: whereas they should assign the cause of their wonder, not to these visible objects, but to the architect himself, and confess that the proofs of skill are indeed manifest, but that he alone is the possessor of that skill who has made them what they are. Again, well might we liken those to children, who should admire the seven-stringed lyre, and disregard him who invented or has power to use it: or those who forget the valiant warrior, and adorn his spear and shield with the chaplet of victory: or, lastly, those who hold the squares and streets, the public buildings, temples, and gymnasia of a great and royal city in equal honour with its founder; forgetting that their admiration is due, not to lifeless stones, but to him whose wisdom planned and executed these mighty works. Not less absurd is it for those who regard this universe with the natural eye to ascribe its origin to the sun, or moon, or any other heavenly body. Rather let them confess that these are themselves the works of a higher wisdom, remember the Maker and Framer of them all, and render to Him the praise and honour which are due to no created objects. Nay rather, inspired by the sight of these very objects, let them address themselves with full purpose of heart to glorify and worship Him who is now invisible to mortal eye, but perceived by the clear and unclouded vision of the soul, the supremely sovereign Word of God. To take the instance of the human body: no one has yet conferred the attribute of wisdom on the eyes, or head, the hands, or feet, or other members, far less on the outward clothing, of a wise and learned man: no one terms the philosopher's household furniture and utensils, wise: but every rational person admires that invisible and secret power, the mind of the man himself. How much more, then, is our admiration due, not to the visible mechanism of the universe, material as it is, and formed of the self-same elements; but to that invisible Word who has moulded and arranged it all, who is the only-begotten Son of God, and whom the Maker of all things, who far transcends all being, has begotten of Himself, and appointed Lord and Governor of this universe? For since it was impossible that perishable bodies, or the rational spirits which He had created, should approach the Supreme God, by reason of their immeasurable distance from His perfections (for He is unbegotten, above and beyond all creation, ineffable, inaccessible, unapproachable, dwelling, as His holy word assures us, in the light which none can enter; but they were created from nothing, and are infinitely far removed from His unbegotten Essence); well has the all-gracious and Almighty God interposed as it were an intermediate Power between Himself and them, even the Divine omnipotence of His only-begotten Word. And this Power, which is in perfect nearness and intimacy of union with the Father, which abides in Him, and shares His secret counsels, has yet condescended, in fulness of grace, as it were to conform itself to those who are so far removed from the supreme majesty of God. How else, consistently with His own holiness, could He who is far above and beyond all things unite Himself to corruptible and corporeal matter? Accordingly the Divine Word, thus connecting Himself with this universe, and receiving into His hands the reins, as it were, of the world, turns and directs it as a skilful charioteer according to His own will and pleasure. The proof of these assertions is evident. For supposing that those component parts of the world which we call elements, as earth, water, air, and fire, the nature of which is manifestly without intelligence, are self-existent; and if they have one common essence, which they who are skilled in natural science call the great receptacle, mother, and nurse of all things; and if this itself be utterly devoid of shape and figure, of life and reason; whence shall we say it has obtained its present form and beauty? To what shall we ascribe the distinction of the elements, or the union of things contrary in their very nature? Who has commanded the liquid water to sustain the heavy element of earth? Who has turned back the waters from their downward course, and carried them aloft in clouds? Who has bound the force of fire, and caused it to lie latent in wood, and to combine with substances most contrary to itself? Who has mingled the cold air with heat, and thus reconciled the enmity of opposing principles? Who has devised the continuous succession of the human race, and given it as it were an endless term of duration? Who has moulded the male and female form, adapted their mutual relations with perfect harmony, and given one common principle of production to every living creature? Who changes the character of the fluid and corruptible seed, which in itself is void of sense, and gives it its prolific power? Who is at this moment working these and ten thousand effects more wonderful than these, nay, surpassing all wonder, and with invisible influence is daily and hourly perpetuating the production of them all? Surely the wonder-working and truly omnipotent Word of God may well be deemed the efficient cause of all these things: that Word who, diffusing Himself through all creation, pervading height and depth with incorporeal energy; and embracing the length and breadth of the universe within His mighty grasp, has compacted and reduced to order this entire system, from whose inert and formless matter He has framed for Himself an instrument of perfect harmony, the nicely balanced chords and notes of which He touches with all-wise and unerring skill. He it is who governs the sun, and moon, and the other luminaries of heaven by inexplicable laws, and directs their motions for the service of the universal whole. None other is it than this Word of God who has stooped to the earth on which we live, and created the manifold species of animals, and the fair varieties of the vegetable world. None less than He has penetrated the recesses of the deep, has given their being to the finny race, and produced the countless forms of life which there exist. It is He who fashions the burden of the womb, and informs it in nature's laboratory with the principle of life. By Him the fluid and heavy moisture is raised on high, and then, sweetened by a purifying change, descends in measured quantities to the earth, and at stated seasons in more profuse supply. Like a skilful husbandman, He fully irrigates the land, tempers the moist and dry in just proportion, diversifying the whole with brilliant flowers, with aspects of varied beauty, with pleasant fragrance, with successive fruits, and countless gratifications for the taste of men. But why do I dare essay a hopeless task, to recount the mighty works of the Word of God, and describe an energy which surpasses mortal thought? By some, indeed, He has been termed the Nature of the universe, by others, the Soul of the world, by others, Destiny. Others again have declared Him to be the most High God Himself, strangely confounding things most widely different; bringing down to this earth, uniting to a corruptible and material body, and assigning an intermediate place between rational and irrational, mortal and immortal beings, to that supreme and unbegotten Power who is Lord of all.

CHAPTER XII

ON the other hand, the sacred doctrine teaches that He who is the supreme Source of good, and Cause of all things, is beyond all comprehension, and therefore inexpressible by word, or speech, or name; surpassing the power, not of language only, but of thought itself. Uncircumscribed by place, or body; neither in heaven, nor in ethereal space, nor in any other part of the universe; but entirely independent of all things else, He pervades the depths of unexplored and secret wisdom. The sacred oracles teach us to acknowledge Him as the only true God, apart from all corporeal essence, distinct from all subordinate ministration. Hence it is said that all things are from Him, but not by Him. And He Himself dwelling as Sovereign in secret and undiscovered regions of unapproachable light, ordains and disposes all things by the single power of His own will. At His will whatever is, exists; without that will, it cannot be. And His will is in every case for good, since He is essentially Goodness itself. But He by whom are all things, even God the Word, proceeding in an ineffable manner from the Father above, as from an everlasting and exhaustless fountain, flows onward like a river with a full and abundant stream of power for the preservation of the universal whole. And now let us select an illustration from our own experience. The invisible and undiscovered mind within us (the essential nature of which no one has ever known), sits as a monarch in the seclusion of his secret chambers, and alone resolves on our course of action. From this mind the faculty of speech proceeds, as an only child from its father's bosom, begotten in a manner and by a power inexplicable to us; and is the first messenger of its father's thoughts, declares his secret counsels, and, conveying itself to the ears of others, accomplishes his designs. And thus the advantage of this faculty is enjoyed by all: yet no one has ever yet beheld that invisible and hidden mind, which is the parent of speech itself. In the same manner (or rather in a manner which far surpasses all comparison), the perfect Word of the Supreme God, as the only-begotten Son of the Father (not consisting in the power of utterance, nor comprehended in syllables and parts of speech, nor conveyed by a voice which vibrates on the air; but being Himself the living and effectual Word of the most High, and subsisting personally as the rower and Wisdom of God), proceeds from His Father's Deity and kingdom. Thus, being the perfect Offspring of a perfect Father, and the common Preserver of all things, He diffuses Himself with living power throughout creation, and pours from His own fulness abundant supplies of reason, wisdom, light, and every other blessing, not only on objects nearest to Himself, but on those most remote, whether in earth, or sea, or any other sphere of being. To all these He appoints with perfect equity their limits, places, laws, and inheritance, allotting to each their suited portion according to His sovereign will. To some He assigns the super-terrestrial regions, to others heaven itself as their habitation: others He places in ethereal space, others in air, and others still on earth. He it is who transfers mankind from hence to another sphere, impartially reviews their conduct here, and bestows a recompense according to the life and habits of each. By Him provision is made for the life and food, not of rational creatures only, but also of the brute creation, for the service of men; and while to the latter He grants the enjoyment of a perishable and fleeting term of existence, the former He invites to a share in the possession of immortal life. Thus universal is the agency of the Word of God: every where present, and pervading all things by the power of His intelligence, He looks upward to His Father, and governs this lower creation (inferior to and consequent upon Himself), in accordance with His will, as the common Preserver of all things. Intermediate, as it were, and attracting the created to the uncreated Essence, this Word of God exists as an unbroken bond between the two, uniting things most widely different by an inseparable tie. He is the Providence which rules the universe; the guardian and director of the whole: He is the Power and Wisdom of God, the only-begotten Word, God begotten of God Himself. For "In the beginning was the Word, and the Word was with God, and the Word was God. All things were made by Him; and without Him was not anything made that was made:" as we learn from the words of the sacred writer. Through His vivifying power all nature grows and flourishes, refreshed by His continual showers, and invested with a vigour and beauty ever new. Guiding the reins of the universe, He holds its onward course in conformity to the Father's will; and moves, as it were, the helm of this mighty ship. This glorious Agent, the only-begotten Son of the Supreme God, begotten by the Father as His perfect Offspring, the Father has given to this world as the highest of all goods; infusing His word (as spirit into a lifeless body) into unconscious nature; imparting light and energy to that which in itself was a rude, inanimate, and formless mass, through the Divine power. Him therefore it is ours to acknowledge and regard as every where present, and giving life to matter and the elements of nature: in Him we see Light, even the spiritual offspring of inexpressible Light: One indeed in essence, as being the Son of one Father; but possessing in Himself many and varied powers. The world is indeed divided into many parts; yet let us not therefore suppose that there are many independent Agents: nor, though creation's works be manifold, let us thence assume the existence of many gods. How grievous the error of those childish and infatuated advocates of polytheistic worship, who deify the constituent parts of the universe, and divide into many that system which is only one! Such conduct resembles theirs who should abstract the eyes of an individual man, and term them the man himself, and the ears, another man, and so the head: or again, by an effort of thought should separate the neck, the breast and shoulders, the feet and hands, or other members, nay, the very powers of sense, and thus pronounce an individual to be a multitude of men. Such folly must surely be rewarded with contempt by men of sense. Yet such is he who from the component parts of a single world can devise for himself a multitude of gods, or even deem that world which is the work of a Creator, and consists of many parts, to be itself a god: not knowing that the Divine Nature can in no sense be divisible into parts; since, if compounded, it must be so through the agency of another power; and that which is so compounded can never be Divine. How indeed could it be so, if composed of unequal and dissimilar, and hence of worse and better elements? Simple, indivisible, uncompounded, the Divine Nature exists at an infinite elevation above the visible constitution of this world. And hence we are assured by the clear testimony of the sacred Herald, that the Word of God, who is before all things, must be the sole Preserver of all intelligent beings: while God, who is above all, and the Author of the generation of the Word, being Himself the Cause of all things, is rightly called the Father of the Word, as of His only-begotten Son, Himself acknowledging no superior Cause. God, therefore, Himself is One, and from Him proceeds the one only-begotten Word, the omnipresent Preserver of all things. And as the many-stringed lyre is composed of different chords, both sharp and flat, some slightly, others tensely strained, and others intermediate between the two extremes, yet all attuned according to the rules of harmonic art; even so this material world, compounded as it is of many elements, containing opposite and antagonist principles (as moisture and dryness, cold and heat), yet blended into one harmonious whole, may justly be termed a mighty instrument framed by the hand of God: an instrument on which the Divine Word, Himself not composed of parts or opposing principles, but indivisible and uncompounded, performs with perfect skill, and produces a melody at once accordant with the will of His Father the Supreme Lord of all, and glorious to Himself. Again, as there are manifold external and internal parts and members comprised in a single body, yet one invisible soul, one undivided and incorporeal mind pervades the whole; so is it in this creation, which, consisting of many parts, yet is but one: and so the One mighty, yea, Almighty Word of God, pervading all things, and diffusing Himself with undeviating energy throughout this universe, is the Cause of all things that exist therein. Survey the compass of this visible world. Seest thou not how the same heaven contains within itself the countless courses and companies of the stars? Again, the sun is one, and yet eclipses many, nay all other luminaries, by the surpassing glory of his rays. Even so, as the Father Himself is One, His Word is also One, the perfect Son of that perfect Father. Should any one object because they are not more, as well might he complain that there are not many suns, or moons, or worlds, and a thousand things beside; like the madman, who would fain subvert the fair and perfect course of Nature herself As in the visible, so also in the spiritual world: in the one the same sun diffuses his light throughout this material earth; in the other the One Almighty Word of God illumines all things with invisible and secret power. Again, there is in man one spirit, and one faculty of reason, which yet is the active cause of numberless effects. The same mind, instructed in many things, will essay to cultivate the earth, to build and guide a ship, and construct houses: nay, the one mind and reason of man is capable of acquiring knowledge in a thousand forms: the same mind shall understand geometry and astronomy, and discourse on the rules of grammar, and rhetoric, and the healing art. Nor will it excel in science only, but in practice too: and yet no one has ever supposed the existence of many minds in one human form, nor expressed his wonder at a plurality of being in man, because he is thus capable of varied knowledge. Suppose one were to find a shapeless mass of clay, to mould it with his hands, and give it the form of a living creature; the head in one figure, the hands and feet in another, the eyes and cheeks in a third, and so to fashion the ears, the mouth and nose, the breast and shoulders, according to the rules of the plastic art. The result, indeed, is a variety of figure, of parts and members in the one body; yet must we not suppose it the work of many hands, but ascribe it entirely to the skill of a single artist, and yield the tribute of our praise to him who by the energy of a single mind has framed it all. The same is true of the universe itself, which is one, though consisting of many parts: yet surely we need not suppose many creative powers, nor invent a plurality of gods. Our duty is to adore the all-wise and all-perfect agency of Him who is indeed the Power and the Wisdom of God, whose undivided force and energy pervades and penetrates the universe, creating and giving life to all things, and furnishing to all, collectively and severally, those manifold supplies of which He is Himself the source. Even so one and the same impression of the solar rays illumines the air at once, gives light to the eyes, warmth to the touch, fertility to the earth, and growth to plants. The same luminary constitutes the course of time, governs the motions of the stars, performs the circuit of the heavens, imparts beauty to the earth, and displays the power of God to all: and all this he performs by the sole and unaided force of his own nature. In like manner fire lias the property of refining gold, and fusing lead, of dissolving wax, of parching clay, and consuming wood; producing these varied effects by one and the same burning power. So also the Supreme Word of God, pervading all things, every where existent, every where present in heaven and earth, governs and directs the visible and invisible creation, the sun, the heaven, and the universe itself, with an energy inexplicable in its nature, irresistible in its effects. From Him, as from an everlasting fountain, the sun, the moon, and stars receive their light: and He for ever rules that heaven which He has framed as the fitting emblem of His own greatness. The angelic and spiritual powers, the incorporeal and intelligent beings which exist beyond the sphere of heaven and earth, are filled by Him with light and life, with wisdom and virtue, with all that is great and good, from His own peculiar treasures. Once more, with one and the same creative skill, He ceases not to furnish the elements with substance, to regulate the union and combinations, the forms and figures, and the innumerable qualities of organized bodies; preserving the varied distinctions of animal and vegetable life, of the rational and the brute creation; and supplying all things to all with equal power: thus proving Himself the Author, not indeed of the seven-stringed lyre, but of that system of perfect harmony which is the workmanship of the One world-creating Word.

CHAPTER XIII

AND now let us proceed to explain the reasons for which this mighty Word of God descended to dwell with men. Our ignorant and foolish race, incapable of comprehending Him who is Lord of heaven and earth, proceeding from His Father's Deity as from the supreme fountain, ever present throughout the world, and evincing by the clearest proofs His providential care for the interests of man; have ascribed the adorable title of Deity to the sun, and moon, the heaven and the stars of heaven. Nor did they stop here, but deified the earth itself, its products, and the various substances by which animal life is sustained, and devised images of Ceres, of Proserpine, of Bacchus, and many such as these. Nay, they shrank not from giving the name of gods to the very conceptions of their own minds, and the speech by which those conceptions are expressed; calling the mind itself Minerva, and language Mercury, and affixing the names of Mnemosyne and the Muses to those faculties by means of which science is acquired. Nor was even this enough: advancing still more rapidly in the career of impiety and folly, they deified their own evil passions, which it behoved them to regard with aversion, or restrain by the principles of self-control. Their very lusts, and those unruly desires which are ruinous to the health of the soul, the members of the body which tempt to impurity, and even base and licentious pleasure itself, they described under the titles of Cupid, Priapus, Venus, and other kindred terms. Nor did they stop even here. Degrading their thoughts of God to this corporeal and mortal life, they deified their fellow-men, conferring the names of gods and heroes on those who had experienced the common lot of all, and vainly imagining that the Divine and imperishable Essence could frequent the tombs and monuments of the dead. Nay, more than this: they paid divine honours to animals of various species, and to the most noxious reptiles: they felled trees, and excavated rocks, they provided themselves with brass, and iron, and other metals, of which they fashioned resemblances of the male and female human form, of beasts, and creeping things; and these they made the objects of their worship. Nor did this suffice. To the evil spirits themselves which lurked within their statues, or lay concealed in secret and dark recesses, eager to drink their libations, and inhale the odour of their sacrifices, they ascribed the same divine honours. Once more, they endeavoured to secure the familiar aid of these spirits, and the unseen powers which move through the tracts of air, by charms of forbidden magic, and the compulsion of unhallowed songs and incantations. Again, different nations have adopted different persons as objects of their worship. The Greeks have rendered to Bacchus, Hercules, Æsculapius, Apollo, and others who were mortal men, the titles of gods and heroes. The Egyptians have deified Horus and Isis, Osiris, and other mortals such as these. And thus they who boast of the wondrous skill whereby they have discovered geometry, astronomy, and the science of number, know not (wise as they are in their own conceit), nor understand how to estimate the measure of the power of God, or calculate His exceeding greatness above the nature of irrational and mortal beings. Hence they shrank not from applying the name of gods to the most hideous of the brute creation, to venomous reptiles and savage beasts. The Phœnicians deified Melcatharus, Usorus, and others; mere mortals, and with little claim to honour: the Arabians, Dusaris and Obodas: the Getæ, Zamolxis: the Cilicians, Mopsus: and the Thebans, Amphiaraus: in short, each nation has adopted its own peculiar deities, differing in no respect from their fellow-mortals, being simply and truly men. Again, the Egyptians with one consent, the Phœnicians, the Greeks, nay, every nation beneath the sun, have united in worshipping the very parts and elements of the world, and even the produce of the ground itself. And, which is most surprising, though acknowledging the adulterous, unnatural, and licentious crimes of their deities, they have not only filled every city, and village, and district with temples, shrines, and statues in their honour, but have followed their evil example to the ruin of their own souls. We hear of gods and the sons of gods described by them as heroes and good genii, titles entirely opposed to truth, honours utterly at variance with the qualities they are intended to exalt. It is as if one who desired to point out the sun and the luminaries of heaven, instead of directing his gaze thitherward, should grope with his hands on the ground, and search for the celestial powers in the mud and mire. Even so mankind, deceived by their own folly and the craft of evil spirits, have believed that the Divine and spiritual Essence which is far above heaven and earth could be compatible with the birth, the affections, and death, of mortal bodies here below. To such a pitch of madness did they proceed, as to sacrifice the dearest objects of their affection to their gods, regardless of all natural ties, and urged by frenzied feeling to slay their only and best beloved children. For what can be a greater proof of madness, than to offer human sacrifice, to pollute every city, and even their own houses, with kindred blood? Do not the Greeks themselves attest this, and is not all history filled with records of the same impiety? The Phœnirians devoted their best beloved and only children as an annual sacrifice to Saturn. The Rhodians, on the sixth day of the month Metageitnion, offered human victims to the same god. At Salamis, a man was pursued in the temple of Minerva Agraulis and Diomede, compelled to run thrice round the altar, afterwards pierced with a lance by the priest, and consumed as a burnt offering on a blazing pile. In

Egypt, human sacrifice was most abundant. At Heliopolis three victims were daily offered to Juno, for whom king Amoses, impressed with the atrocity of the practice, commanded the substitution of an equal number of waxen figures. In Chios, and again in Tenedos, a man was slain and offered up to Omadian Bacchus. At Sparta they immolated human beings to Mars; in Crete to Saturn. In Laodicea of Syria a virgin was yearly slain in honour of Minerva; for whom a hart is now the substitute. The Libyans and Carthaginians appeased their gods with human victims. The Dumateni of Arabia buried a boy annually beneath the altar. History informs us that the Greeks without exception, the Thracians also, and Scythians, were accustomed to human sacrifice before they marched forth to battle. The Athenians record the immolation of the virgin children of Leus, and the daughter of Erechtheus. Who knows not that at this day a human victim is offered in Rome itself at the festival of Jupiter Latiaris? And these facts are confirmed by the testimony of the most approved philosophers. Diodorus, the epitomiser of libraries, affirms that two hundred of the noblest youths were sacrificed to Saturn by the Libyan people, and that three hundred more were voluntarily offered by their own parents. Dionysius, the compiler of Roman history, expressly says that Jupiter and Apollo demanded human sacrifices of the people termed the Aborigines, in Italy. He relates that on this demand they offered a proportion of all their produce to the gods; but that, because of their refusal to slay human victims, they became involved in manifold calamities, from which they could obtain no release until they had decimated themselves, a sacrifice of life which proved the desolation of their country. Such and so great were the evils which of old afflicted the human race. Nor was this the full extent of their misery: they groaned beneath the pressure of other evils equally numerous and irremediable. All nations, whether civilized or barbarous, throughout the world, as if actuated by a demoniac frenzy, were infected with sedition as with some fierce and terrible disease: insomuch that the human family was irreconcileably divided against itself; the great system of society was distracted and torn asunder; and in every corner of the earth men stood opposed to each other, and strove with fierce contention on questions of law and government. Nay, more than this: with passions aroused to fury, they engaged in mutual conflicts, so frequent that their lives were passed as it were in uninterrupted warfare. None could undertake a journey except as prepared to encounter an enemy: in the very country and villages the rustics girded on the sword, provided themselves with armour rather than with the implements of rural labour, and deemed it a noble exploit to plunder and enslave any who belonged to a neighbouring state. Nay, more than this: from the fables they had themselves devised respecting their own deities, they deduced occasions for a vile and abandoned life, and wrought the ruin of body and soul by licentiousness of every kind. Not content with this, they even overstepped the bounds which nature had defined, and together committed incredible and nameless crimes, "men with men (in the words of the sacred writer) working that which is unseemly, and receiving in themselves that recompense of their error which was meet." Nor did they stop even here; but perverted their natural thoughts of God, and denied that the course of this world was directed by His providential care, ascribing the existence and constitution of all things to the blind operation of chance, or the necessity of fate. Once more: believing that soul and body were alike dissolved by death, they led a brutish life, unworthy of the name: careless of the nature or existence of the soul, they dreaded not the tribunal of Divine justice, expected no reward of virtue, nor thought of chastisement as the penalty of an evil life. Hence it was that whole nations, a prey to wickedness in all its forms, were wasted by the effects of their own brutality: some living in the practice of most vile and lawless incest with mothers, others with sisters, and others again corrupting their own daughters. Some were found who slew their confiding guests; others who fed on human flesh; some strangled, and then feasted on, their aged men; others threw them alive to dogs. The time would fail me were I to attempt to describe the multifarious symptoms of the inveterate malady which had asserted its dominion over the whole human race. Such, and numberless others like these, were the prevailing evils, on account of which the gracious Word of God, full of compassion for His human flock, had long since, by the ministry of His prophets, and earlier still (and later also), by that of men distinguished by pious devotion to God, invited those thus desperately afflicted to their own cure; and had, by means of laws, exhortations, and doctrines of every kind, proclaimed to man the principles and elements of true godliness. But when mankind, distracted and torn as I have said (not indeed by wolves and savage beasts, but by ruthless and soul-destroying spirits of evil), no longer needed merely human agency, but a help superior to that of man; then it was that the Word of God, obedient to His all-gracious Father's will, at length Himself appeared, and most willingly made His abode amongst us. The causes of His advent I have already described, induced by which He condescended to the society of man; not in His wonted form and manner (for He is incorporeal, and present every where throughout the world, proving by His agency both in heaven and earth the greatness of His almighty power), but in a character new and hitherto unknown. Assuming a mortal body, He deigned to associate and converse with men; desiring, through the medium of their own likeness, to save our mortal race.

CHAPTER XIV

AND now let us explain the cause for which the incorporeal Word of God assumed this mortal body as a medium of intercourse with man. How, indeed, else than in human form, could that Divine and impalpable, that immaterial and invisible Essence manifest itself to those who sought for God in created and earthly objects, unable or unwilling otherwise to discern the Author and Maker of all things? As a fitting means, therefore, of communication with mankind, He assumed a mortal body, as that with which they were themselves familiar; for like (it is proverbially said) loves its like. To those, then, whose affections were engaged by visible objects, who looked for gods in statues and lifeless images, who imagined the Deity to consist in material and corporeal substance, nay, who conferred on men the title of divinity, the Word of God presented Himself in this form. Hence He procured for Himself this body as a thrice hallowed temple, a sensible habitation of an intellectual power; a noble and most holy form, of far higher worth than any lifeless statue. The material and senseless image, fashioned by base mechanic hands, of brass or iron, of gold or ivory, wood or stone, may be a fitting abode for evil spirits: but that Divine form, wrought by the power of heavenly wisdom, was possessed of life and spiritual being; a form animated by every excellence, the dwelling-place of the Word of God, a holy temple of the holy God. Thus the embodied Word conversed with and was known to men, as kindred with themselves; yet yielded not to passions such as theirs, nor owned, as the natural soul, subjection to the body. He parted not with aught of His intrinsic greatness, nor changed His proper Deity. For as the all-pervading radiance of the sun receives no stain from contact with dead and impure bodies; much less can the incorporeal power of the Word of God be injured in its essential purity, or part with any of its greatness, from spiritual contact with a human body. Thus, I say, did our common Saviour prove Himself the benefactor and preserver of all, displaying His wisdom through the instrumentality of His human nature, even as a musician uses the lyre to evince his skill. The Grecian fable tells us that Orpheus had power to charm ferocious beasts, and tame their savage spirit, by striking the chords of his instrument with a master hand: and this story is celebrated by the Greeks, and generally believed, that an unconscious instrument could subdue the untamed brute, and draw the trees of the forest from their places, in obedience to its melodious power. But He who is the author of perfect harmony, the all-wise Word of God, desiring to apply every remedy to the manifold diseases of the souls of men, employed that human nature which is the workmanship of His own wisdom, as an instrument by the melodious strains of which He soothed, not indeed the brute creation, but savages endued with reason; healing each furious temper, each fierce and angry passion of the soul, both in civilized and barbarous nations, by the remedial power of His Divine doctrine. Like a physician of perfect skill, he met the diseases of their souls who sought for God in nature and in bodies, by a fitting and kindred remedy, and shewed them God in human form. And then, with no less care for the body than the soul, He presented before the eyes of men wonders and signs, as proofs of His Divine power, at the same time instilling into their ears of flesh the doctrines which He Himself uttered with a corporeal tongue. In short, He performed all His works through the medium of that body which He had assumed for the sake of those who else were incapable of apprehending His Divine nature. In all this He was the servant of His Father's will, Himself remaining still the same as when with the Father; unchanged in essence, unimpaired in nature, unfettered by the trammels of mortal flesh, nor hindered by His abode in a human body from being elsewhere present. Nay, at the very time of His intercourse with men, He was pervading all things, was with and in the Father, and even then was caring for all things both in heaven and earth. Nor was He precluded, as we are, from being present every where, or from the continued exercise of His Divine power. He gave of His own to man, but received nothing in return: He imparted of His Divine power to mortality, but derived no accession from mortality itself. Hence His human birth to Him brought no defilement; nor could His impassible Essence suffer at the dissolution of His mortal body. For let us suppose a lyre to receive an accidental injury, or its chords to be broken; it does not follow that the performer on it suffers: nor, if a wise man's body undergo punishment, can we fairly assert that his wisdom, or the soul within him, are maimed or burned. Far less can we affirm that the inherent power of the Word sustained any detriment from His bodily passion, any more than, as in the instance we have already used, the solar rays which are shot from heaven to earth contract defilement, though in contact with mire and pollution of every kind. We may, indeed, assert that these things partake of the radiance of the light, but not that the light is contaminated, or the sun defiled, by this contact with other bodies, which indeed are themselves not contrary to nature. But the Saviour, the incorporeal Word of God, being Life and spiritual Light itself, whatever He touches with Divine and incorporeal power must of necessity become endued with the intelligence of light and life. Thus, if He touch a body, it becomes enlightened and sanctified, is at once delivered from all disease, infirmity, and suffering, and that which before was lacking is supplied by a portion of His fulness. And such was the tenor of His life on earth; now proving the sympathies of His human nature with our own, and now revealing Himself as the Word of God: wondrous and mighty in His works as God; foretelling the events of the far distant future; declaring in every act, by signs, and wonders, and supernatural powers, that Word whose presence was so little known; and finally, by His Divine teaching, inviting the souls of men to prepare for those mansions which are above the heavens.

CHAPTER XV

WHAT now remains, but to account for those which are the crowning facts of all; I mean His death, so far and widely known, the manner of His passion, and the mighty miracle of His resurrection after death: and then to establish the truth of these events by the clearest testimonies? For the reasons detailed above He used the instrumentality of a mortal body, as a figure becoming His Divine majesty, and like a mighty sovereign employed it as His interpreter in His intercourse with men, performing all things consistently with His own Divine power. Supposing, then, at the end of His sojourn among men, He had by any other means suddenly withdrawn Himself from their sight, and, secretly removing that interpreter of Himself, the form which He had assumed, had hastened to flee from death, and afterwards by His own act had consigned His mortal body to corruption and dissolution: doubtless in such a case He would have been deemed a mere phantom by all. Nor would He have acted in a manner worthy of Himself, had He who is Life, the Word, and the Power of God, abandoned this interpreter of Himself to corruption and death. Nor, again, would His warfare with the spirits of evil have received its consummation by conflict with the power of death. The place of His retirement must have remained unknown; nor would His existence have been believed by those who had not seen Him for themselves. No proof would have been given that He was superior to death; nor would He have delivered mortality from the law of its natural infirmity. His name had never been heard throughout the world; nor could He have inspired His disciples with contempt of death, or encouraged those who embraced His doctrine to hope for the enjoyment of a future life with God. Nor would He have fulfilled the assurances of His own promise, nor have accomplished the predictions of the prophets concerning Himself. Nor would He have undergone the last conflict of all; for this was to be the struggle with the power of death. For all these reasons, then, and inasmuch as it was necessary that the mortal body which had rendered such service to the Divine Word should meet with an end worthy its sacred occupant, the manner of His death was ordained accordingly. For since but two alternatives remained: either to consign His body entirely to corruption (and so to bring the scene of life to a dishonoured close), or else to prove Himself victorious over death, and render mortality immortal by an act of Divine power; the former of these alternatives would have contravened His own promise. For as it is not the property of fire to cool, nor of light to darken, no more is it compatible with life, to deprive of life, or with Divine intelligence, to act in a manner contrary to reason. For how could it be consistent with reason, that He who had promised life to others, should permit His own body, the form which He had chosen, to perish beneath the power of corruption? That He who had inspired His disciples with hopes of immortality, should yield this exponent of His Divine counsels to be destroyed by death? The second alternative was therefore needful: I mean, that He should assert His dominion over the power of death. But how? should this be a furtive and secret act, or openly performed, and in the sight of all? So mighty an achievement, had it remained unknown and unrevealed, must have failed of its effect as regards the interests of men; whereas the same event, if openly declared and understood, would, from its wondrous character, redound to the common benefit of all. With reason, therefore, since it was needful to prove His body victorious over death, and that not secretly, but before the eyes of men, He shrank not from the trial (this indeed would have argued fear, and a sense of inferiority to the power of death), but maintained that conflict with the enemy which has rendered mortality immortal; a conflict undertaken for the life, the immortality, the salvation of mankind. Suppose one desired to shew us that a vessel could resist the force of fire; how could he better prove the fact, than by casting it into the furnace and thence withdrawing it entire and unconsumed? Even thus the Word of God, who is the source of life to all, desiring to prove the triumph of that body over death which He had assumed for man's salvation, and to make this body partake His own life and immortality, pursued a course consistent with this object. Leaving His body for a little while, and delivering it up to death in proof of its mortal nature, He soon redeemed it from death, in vindication of that Divine power whereby He has manifested the immortality which He has promised to be utterly beyond the sphere of death. The reason of this is clear. It was needful that His disciples should receive ocular proof of the certainty of that resurrection on which He had taught them to rest their hopes as a motive for rising superior to the fear of death. It was indeed most needful that they who purposed to pursue a life of godliness should receive a clear impression of this essential truth: more needful still for those who were destined to declare His name in all the world, and to communicate to mankind that knowledge of God which He had before ordained for all nations. For such the strongest conviction of a future life was necessary, that they might be able with fearless and unshrinking zeal to maintain the conflict with Gentile and polytheistic error: a conflict the dangers of which they would never have been prepared to meet, except as habituated to the contempt of death. Accordingly, in arming His disciples against the power of this last enemy, He delivered not His doctrines in mere verbal precepts, nor attempted to prove the soul's immortality by persuasive and probable arguments; but displayed to them in His own person a real victory over death. Such was the first and greatest reason of our Saviour's conflict with the power of death, whereby He proved to His disciples the impotence of that which is the terror of all mankind, and afforded a visible evidence of the reality of that life which He had promised; presenting as it were a first-fruit of our common hope, of future life and immortality in the presence of God. The second cause of His resurrection was, that the Divine power might be manifested which dwelt in His mortal body. Mankind had heretofore conferred divine honours on men who had yielded to the power of death, and had given the titles of gods and heroes to mortals like themselves. For this reason, therefore, the Word of God evinced His gracious character, and proved to man His own superiority over death, recalling His mortal body to a second life, displaying an immortal triumph over death in the eyes of all, and teaching them to acknowledge the Author of such a victory to be the only true God, even in death itself. I may allege yet a third cause of the Saviour's death, He was the victim offered to the Supreme Sovereign of the universe for the whole human race: a victim, too, consecrated not merely for the necessities of man, but for the overthrow of the errors of demon worship. For as soon as the one holy and mighty sacrifice, the sacred body of our Saviour, had been slain for man, to be as a ransom for all nations, heretofore involved in the guilt of impious superstition, thenceforward the power of impure and unholy spirits was utterly abolished, and every earth-born and delusive error was at once weakened and destroyed. Thus, then, this salutary victim taken from among themselves, I mean the mortal body of the Word, was offered on behalf of the common race of men. This was that sacrifice delivered up to death, of which the sacred oracles speak: "Behold the Lamb of God, which taketh away the sin of the world." And again, as follows: "He was led as a sheep to the slaughter, and as a lamb before the shearer is dumb." They declare also the cause, saying: "He bears our sins, and is pained for us: yet we accounted Him to be in trouble, and in suffering, and in affliction. But He was wounded on account of our sins, and bruised because of our iniquities: the chastisement of our peace was upon Him; and by His bruises we were healed. All we as sheep have gone astray; every one has gone astray in his way; and the Lord gave him up for our sins."

Such were the causes which led to the offering of the human body of the Word of God. But forasmuch as He was the great high priest, consecrated to the Supreme Lord and King, and therefore more than a victim, the Word, the Power, and the Wisdom of God; He soon recalled His body from the grasp of death, presented it to His Father as the first-fruit of our common salvation, and raised this trophy, a proof at once of His victory over death and Satan, and of the abolition of human sacrifices, for the blessing of all mankind.

CHAPTER XVI

AND now the time is come for us to proceed to the demonstration of these things; if indeed such truths require demonstration, and if the aid of testimony be needful to confirm the certainty of palpable facts. Such testimony, however, shall here be given; and let it be received with an attentive and gracious ear. Of old the nations of the earth, the entire human race, were variously distributed into provincial, national, and local governments, subject to kingdoms and principalities of many kinds. The consequences of this variety were war and strife, depopulation and captivity, which raged, both locally and generally, with unceasing fury. Hence, too, the countless subjects of history; adulteries, and rapes of women; hence the woes of Troy, and the ancient tragedies, so well and widely known; the origin of which may justly be ascribed to the delusion of polytheistic error. But when that instrument of our redemption, the thrice holy body of Christ (which proved itself superior to all Satanic fraud, and free from evil both in word and deed), was raised, at once for the abolition of ancient evils, and in token of His victory over the powers of darkness; the energy of these evil spirits was at once destroyed. The manifold forms of government, the tyrannies and republics, the siege of cities, and devastation of countries caused thereby, were now no more: One God was proclaimed to all mankind; and at the same time one universal power, the Roman empire, arose and flourished. The enduring and implacable hatred of nation against nation was now removed: and as the knowledge of One God, and one way of religion and salvation, even the doctrine of Christ, was made known to all mankind; so at the self-same period, the entire dominion of the Roman empire being vested in a single sovereign, profound peace reigned throughout the world. And thus, by the express appointment of the same God, two roots of blessing, the Roman empire, and the doctrine of Christian piety, sprang up together for the benefit of men. For before this time the various countries of the world, as Syria, Asia,

Macedonia, Egypt, and Arabia, had been severally subject to different rulers. The Jewish people, again, had established their dominion in the land of Palestine. And these nations, in every village, city, and district, actuated by a truly insane and devilish spirit, were engaged in incessant and murderous war and conflict. But two mighty powers, coincident in the time of their origin, I mean the Roman empire, which henceforth was swayed by a single sovereign, and the Christian religion, subdued and reconciled these contending elements. Our Saviour's mighty power destroyed at once the many governments and the many gods of the powers of darkness, and proclaimed to all men, both rude and civilized, to the extremities of the earth, the sole sovereignty of God Himself. Meantime the Roman empire, the causes of multiplied governments being thus removed, effected an easy conquest of those which yet remained; its object being to unite all nations in one harmonious whole; an object in great measure already secured, and destined to be still more perfectly attained, even to the final conquest of the ends of the habitable world, by means of the salutary doctrine, and through the aid of that Divine power which facilitates and smooths its way. And surely this must appear a wondrous fact to those who will examine the question in the love of truth, and desire not to cavil at these blessings. The falsehood of demon superstition was convicted: the inveterate strife and mutual hatred of the nations was removed: at the same time One God, and the knowledge of that God, were proclaimed to all: one universal empire prevailed; and the whole human race, subdued by the controlling power of peace and concord, received one another as brethren, and responded to the feelings of their common nature. Hence, as children of one God and Father, and owning true religion as their common mother, they saluted and welcomed each other with words of peace. Thus the whole world appeared like one well-ordered and united family: each one might journey unhindered as far as and whithersoever he pleased: men might securely travel from West to East, and from East to West, as to their own native country: in short, the ancient oracles and predictions of the prophets were fulfilled, more numerous than we can at present cite, and those especially which speak as follows concerning the saving Word of God. "He shall have dominion from sea to sea, and from the river to the ends of the earth." And again, "In His days shall righteousness spring up; and abundance of peace." "And they shall beat their swords into plough-shares, and their spears into sickles: and nation shall not take up sword against nation, neither shall they learn to war any more." These words, predicted ages before in the Hebrew tongue, have received in our own day a visible fulfilment, by which the testimonies of the ancient oracles are clearly confirmed. And now, if thou still desire more ample proof, receive it, not in words, but from the facts themselves. Open the eyes of thine understanding; expand the gates of thought; pause awhile, and consider; inquire of thyself as though thou wert another, and thus diligently examine the nature of the case. What king or prince in any age of the world, what philosopher, legislator, or prophet, in civilised or barbarous lands, has attained so great a height of excellence (I say not after death, but while living still, and full of mighty power), as to fill the ears and tongues of all mankind with the praises of his name? Surely none save our only Saviour has done this, when, after His victory over death, He spoke the word to His followers, and fulfilled it by the event, saying to them, "Go ye, and make disciples of all nations in my name." He it was who gave the distinct assurance, that His gospel must be preached in all the world for a testimony to all nations, and immediately verified His word: for within a little time the world itself was filled with His doctrine. How, then, will those who cavilled at the commencement of my speech be able to reply to this? For surely the force of ocular testimony is superior to any verbal argument. Who else than He, with an invisible and yet potent hand, has driven from human society like savage beasts that ever noxious and destructive tribe of evil spirits who of old had made all nations their prey, and by the motions of their images had practised many a delusion among men? Who else, beside our Saviour, by the invocation of His name, and by unfeigned prayer addressed through Him to the Supreme God, has given power to banish from the world the remnant of those wicked spirits to those who with genuine and sincere obedience pursue the course of life and conduct which He has Himself prescribed? Who else but He has taught His followers to offer those bloodless and reasonable sacrifices which are performed by prayer and the secret worship of God? Hence is it that throughout the habitable world altars are erected, and churches dedicated, wherein these spiritual and rational sacrifices are offered as a sacred service by every nation to the One Supreme God. Once more, who but He, with invisible and secret power, has suppressed and utterly abolished those bloody sacrifices which were offered with fire and smoke, as well as the cruel and senseless immolation of human victims; a fact which is attested by the heathen historians themselves? For it was not till after the publication of the Saviour's Divine doctrine, about the time of Hadrian's reign, that the practice of human sacrifice was universally abandoned. Such and so manifest are the proofs of our Saviour's power and energy after death. Who then can be found of spirit so obdurate as to withhold his assent to the truth, and refuse to acknowledge His life to be Divine? Such deeds as I have described are done by the living, not the dead; and visible acts are to us as evidence of those which we cannot see. It is as it were an event of yesterday that an impious and godless crew disturbed and confounded the peace of human society, and withal possessed mighty power. But these, as soon as life departed, lay prostrate on the earth, worthless as dung, breathless, motionless, bereft of speech, and have left neither fame nor memorial behind. For such is the condition of the dead; and he who no longer lives is nothing: and how can he who is nothing be capable of any act? But how shall His existence be called in question, whose active power and energy are greater than in those who are still alive? And though He be invisible to the natural eye, yet the discerning faculty is not in outward sense. We do not comprehend the rules of art, or the theories of science, by bodily sensation; nor has any eye yet discerned the mind of man. Far less, then, the power of God: and in such cases our judgment is formed from apparent results. Even thus are we bound to judge of our Saviour's invisible power, and decide by its manifest effects whether we shall acknowledge the mighty operations which He is even now carrying on to be the works of a living agent; or whether they shall be ascribed to one who has no existence; or, lastly, whether the inquiry be not absurd and inconsistent in itself. For with what reason can we assert the existence of one who is not? Since all allow that that which has no existence is devoid of that power, and energy, and action, which are the characteristics of the living, the contrary those of the dead.

CHAPTER XVII

AND now the time is come for us to consider the works of our Saviour in our own age, and to contemplate the living operations of the living God. For how shall we describe these mighty works save as living proofs of the power of a living agent, who truly enjoys the life of God? If any one inquire the nature of these works, let him now attend. But recently a class of persons, impelled by furious zeal, and backed by equal power and military force, evinced their enmity against God, by destroying His churches, and overthrowing from their foundations the buildings dedicated to His worship. In short, in every way they directed their attacks against the unseen God, and assailed Him with a thousand shafts of impious words. But He who is invisible avenged Himself with an invisible hand. By the single fiat of His will His enemies were utterly destroyed. But a little while, and they were flourishing in great prosperity, exalted by their fellow men as worthy of divine honour, and blessed with a continued period of power and glory, so long as they had maintained peace and amity with Him whom they afterwards opposed. As soon, however, as they dared openly to resist His will, and to set their gods in array against Him whom we adore; immediately, according to the will and power of that God against whom their arms were raised, they all received the judgment due to their audacious deeds. Constrained to yield and flee before His power, together they acknowledged His Divine nature, and hastened to reverse the measures which they had before essayed. Our Saviour, therefore, without delay erected trophies of this victory, and once more adorned the world with holy temples and consecrated houses of prayer; in every city and village, nay, throughout all countries, and even in barbaric wilds, ordaining the erection of churches and sacred buildings to the honour of the Supreme God and Lord of all. Hence it is that these hallowed edifices are deemed worthy to bear His name, and receive not their appellation from men, but from the Lord Himself, from which circumstance they are called churches, or houses of the Lord. And now let him who will stand forth and tell us who, after so complete a desolation, has re-erected and restored these sacred buildings? Who, when all hope appeared extinct, has caused them to rise on a nobler scale than heretofore? And well may it claim our wonder, that this renovation was not subsequent to the death of those adversaries of God, but whilst the destroyers of these edifices were still alive; so that the recantation of their evil deeds came in their own words and edicts. And this they did, not in the sunshine of prosperity and ease (for then we might suppose that benevolence or clemency might be the cause), but at the very time that they were suffering under the stroke of Divine vengeance. Who, again, has been able to retain in obedience to His heavenly precepts, after so many successive storms of persecution, nay, in the very crisis of danger, so many persons throughout the world devoted to the pursuit of sacred philosophy, and those holy quires of virgins who had dedicated themselves to a life of perpetual chastity and purity? Who taught them cheerfully to persevere in the exercise of protracted fasting, and to embrace a life of severe and consistent self-denial? Who has persuaded multitudes of either sex to devote themselves to the study of sacred things, and prefer to bodily nutriment that intellectual food which is suited to the wants of a rational soul? Who has instructed barbarians and peasants, yea, feeble women, slaves, and children, in short, unnumbered multitudes of all nations, to live in the contempt of death; persuaded of the immortality of their souls, conscious that human actions are observed by the unerring eye of justice, expecting God's award to the righteous and the wicked, and therefore true to the practice of a just and virtuous life? For they needed to be actuated by these motives, in order to patient perseverance in the course of godliness. Surely these are the acts which our Saviour, and He alone, even now performs. And now let us pass from these topics, and endeavour by inquiries such as these that follow to convince the objector's obdurate understanding. Come forward, then, whoever thou art, and speak the words of reason: utter, not the thoughts of a senseless heart, but those of an intelligent and enlightened mind: speak, I say, after deep and solemn converse with thyself. Who of the sages whose names have yet been known to fame, has ever been foreknown and proclaimed from the remotest ages, as our Saviour was by the prophetic oracles to the once divinely-favoured Hebrew nation? But His very birth-place, the period of His advent, the manner of His life, His miracles, and words, and mighty acts, were anticipated and recorded in the sacred volumes of these prophets. Again, who so present an avenger of crimes against Himself; so that, as the immediate consequence of their impiety, the entire Jewish people were scattered by an unseen power, their royal seat utterly removed, and their very temple with its holy things levelled with the ground? Who, like our Saviour, has uttered predictions at once concerning that impious nation and the establishment of His Church throughout the world, and has equally verified both by the event? Respecting the temple of these wicked men, He said: "Your house is left unto you desolate:" and, "There shall not be left one stone upon another in this place, that shall not be thrown down." And again, of His Church He says; "I will build my church upon a rock, and the gates of hell shall not prevail against it." How wondrous, too, must that power be deemed which summoned obscure and unlettered men from their fisher's trade, and made them the legislators and instructors of the human race! And how clear a demonstration of His Deity do we find in the promise so well performed, that He would make them fishers of men: in the power and energy which He bestowed, so that they composed and published writings of such authority that they were translated into every civilized and barbarous language, were read and pondered by all nations, and the doctrines contained in them accredited as the oracles of God! How marvellous His predictions of the future, and the testimony whereby His disciples were forewarned that they should be brought before kings and rulers, and should endure the severest punishments, not indeed as criminals, but simply for their confession of His name! Or who shall adequately describe the power with which He prepared them thus to suffer with a willing mind, and enabled them, strong in the armour of godliness, to maintain a constancy of spirit indomitable in the midst of conflict? Or how shall we enough admire that steadfast firmness of soul which strengthened, not merely His immediate followers, but their successors also, even to our present age, in the joyful endurance of every infliction, and every form of torture, in proof of their devotion to the Supreme God? Again, what monarch has prolonged his government through so vast a series of ages? Who else has power to make war after death, to triumph over every enemy, to subjugate each barbarous and civilized nation and city, and to subdue his adversaries with an invisible and secret hand? Lastly, and chief of all, what slanderous lip shall dare to question that universal peace (to which we have already referred), established by His power throughout the world? For thus the mutual concord and harmony of all nations coincided in point of time with the extension of our Saviour's doctrine and preaching in all the world: a concurrence of events predicted in long ages past by the prophets of God. The day itself would fail me, gracious emperor, should I attempt to exhibit in a single view those cogent proofs of our Saviour's Divine power which even now are visible in their effects; a power which no human being, in civilized or barbarous nations, has ever yet attained. But why do I speak of men, since of the beings whom all nations have deemed divine, none has appeared on earth with power like to His? If it be so, let the fact now be proved. Come forward, ye philosophers, and tell us what god or hero has yet been known to fame, who has delivered the doctrines of eternal life and a heavenly kingdom as He has done who is our Saviour? Who, like Him, has persuaded multitudes throughout the world to pursue the principles of Divine wisdom, to fix their hope on heaven itself, and look forward to the mansions there reserved for them that love God? What god or hero in human form has ever held his course from East to West, a course co-extensive as it were with the solar light, and irradiated mankind with the bright and glorious beams of his doctrine, causing each nation of the earth to render united worship to the One true God? What god or hero yet, as He has done, has set aside each object of false worship among barbarous and polished nations; has ordained that divine honours should be withheld from all, and claimed obedience to that command: and then, though singly conflicting with the power of all, has utterly destroyed the opposing hosts; victorious over the gods and heroes of every age, and causing Himself alone, in every region of the habitable world, to be acknowledged by all people as the Son of God? Who else has commanded the nations inhabiting the continents and islands of this mighty globe to assemble weekly on the Lord's day, and to observe it as a festival, not indeed for the pampering of the body, but for the comfort and invigoration of the soul by instruction in Divine truth? What god or hero, exposed, as our Saviour was, to so sore a conflict, has raised the trophy of victory over every foe? For they indeed, from first to last, unceasingly assailed His doctrine and His people: but He who is invisible, by the exercise of a secret power, has raised His servants and the sacred houses of their worship to the height of glory.

But why should we still vainly aim at detailing those Divine proofs of our Saviour's power which no language can worthily express; which need indeed no words of ours, but themselves appeal in loudest tones to those whose mental ears are open to the truth? Surely it is a strange, a wondrous fact, unparalleled in the annals of human life; that the blessings we have described should be accorded to our mortal race, and that He who is in truth the only, the eternal Son of God, should thus be visible on earth.

CHAPTER XVIII

THESE words of ours, however, gracious Sovereign, may well appear superfluous in your ears, convinced as you are, by frequent and personal experience, of our Saviour's Deity; yourself also, in actions still more than words, a herald of the truth to all mankind. Yourself, it may be, will vouchsafe at a time of leisure to relate to us the abundant manifestations which your Saviour has accorded you of His presence, and the oft-repeated visions of Himself which have attended you in the hours of sleep. I speak not of those secret suggestions which to us are unrevealed: but of those principles which He has instilled into your own mind, and which are fraught with general interest and benefit to the human race. You will yourself relate in worthy terms the visible protection which your Divine shield and guardian has extended in the hour of battle; the ruin of your open and secret foes; and His ready aid in time of peril. To Him you will ascribe relief in the midst of perplexity; defence in solitude; expedients in extremity; foreknowledge of events yet future; your forethought for the general weal; your power to investigate uncertain questions; your conduct of most important enterprises; your administration of civil affairs; your military arrangements, and correction of abuses in all departments; your ordinances respecting public right; and, lastly, your legislation for the common benefit of all. You will, it may be, also detail to us those particulars of His favour which are secret to us, but to you well known, and treasured in the recesses of your royal memory. Such, doubtless, are the reasons, and such the convincing proofs of your Saviour's power, which caused you to raise that sacred edifice which presents to all, believers and unbelievers alike, a trophy of His victory over death, a holy temple of the holy God: to consecrate those noble and splendid monuments of immortal life and His heavenly kingdom: to offer memorials of our Almighty Saviour's conquest which well become the imperial dignity of him by whom they are bestowed. With such memorials have you adorned that edifice which witnesses of eternal life: thus, as it were in imperial characters, ascribing victory and triumph to the heavenly Word of God: thus proclaiming to all nations, with a voice too clear to be misunderstood, and in deed as well as word, your own devout and holy confession of His name.

Made in the USA
Middletown, DE
11 March 2021

35380064R00156